MW00533441

Only-Child Experience and Adulthood

Also by Bernice Sorensen

COUNSELLING FOR YOUNG PEOPLE (*with Judith Mabey*)

Only-Child Experience and Adulthood

Bernice Sorensen
Psychotherapist

© Bernice Sorensen 2008

All rights reserved. No reproduction, copy or transmission of this publication may be made without written permission.

No paragraph of this publication may be reproduced, copied or transmitted save with written permission or in accordance with the provisions of the Copyright, Designs and Patents Act 1988, or under the terms of any licence permitting limited copying issued by the Copyright Licensing Agency, 90 Tottenham Court Road, London W1T 4LP.

Any person who does any unauthorized act in relation to this publication may be liable to criminal prosecution and civil claims for damages.

The author has asserted her right to be identified as the author of this work in accordance with the Copyright, Designs and Patents Act 1988.

First published 2008 by
PALGRAVE MACMILLAN
Houndmills, Basingstoke, Hampshire RG21 6XS and
175 Fifth Avenue, New York, N.Y. 10010
Companies and representatives throughout the world

PALGRAVE MACMILLAN is the global academic imprint of the Palgrave Macmillan division of St. Martin's Press, LLC and of Palgrave Macmillan Ltd. Macmillan® is a registered trademark in the United States, United Kingdom and other countries. Palgrave is a registered trademark in the European Union and other countries.

ISBN-13: 978–0–230–52101–8 hardback
ISBN-10: 0–230–52101–0 hardback

This book is printed on paper suitable for recycling and made from fully managed and sustained forest sources. Logging, pulping and manufacturing processes are expected to conform to the environmental regulations of the country of origin.

A catalogue record for this book is available from the British Library.

Library of Congress Cataloging-in-Publication Data
Sorensen, Bernice, 1951–
   Only-child experience and adulthood/Bernice Sorensen.
     p. cm.
   Includes bibliographical references and index.
   ISBN 0–230–52101–0 (alk. paper)
   1. Only child—Psychology.   2. Child development.
   3. Adulthood—Case studies.   I. Title.
   HQ777.3.S67 2008
   155.44′2—dc22   2007050067

10 9 8 7 6 5 4 3 2 1
17 16 15 14 13 12 11 10 09 08

Transferred to Digital Printing in 2009

Contents

Acknowledgements   viii

Introduction   ix
    Structure of the book   xii

Part I   Transcending the Stereotypes

1   The Politics of the Only-Child   3
    Psychoanalytic literature   5
    Birth order studies and evolutionary theory   9
    The research focusing on sibling relationships 12
    Quantitative research studies on only-children 14
    Only-children in China   16
    Research critique   19
    Family therapy and family systems therapy   23
    Three types of only-children   25
    Qualitative studies on only-children   26
    Parenting an only-child   29
    Summary   35

2   The Research Framework   37
    A qualitative approach   37
    Witness   39
    Heuristic research and reflexivity   40
    Life-story and narrative inquiry   41
    Voice   44
    Interviews   47
    Analysis   48
    Ethical considerations   49
    Reliability and validity   50

3   Co-Researchers' Stories   52
    Georgina: dependent and independent   52
    Anna: being in the middle   57

Lyn: creating the siblings she missed   60
Amy: her mother's carer   64
Poppy: a claustrophobic childhood   67
Kate: spoiled not spoilt   72
Carol: recapturing childhood specialness   75
Magritte: alone and independent   79

4   **Only-Child Voices and Life-Stages**   **83**
The three voices   83
The intra-personal voice   85
The inter-personal voice   89
The extra-personal voice   93
Only-child life-stages   97

Part II   A Multiplicity of Voices

5   **Research Data and the World Wide Web**   **105**
Using the world wide web   105
Onlychild website   106
'Beinganonly': Internet message board   110
Articles, workshops and the media   113

6   **Stories from China and Taiwan**   **115**
Ivy's story   116
Yukinori's story   122
Reflections   129

7   **Life-Stories and Life-Stages**   **131**
Six only-child life stages   131
Kim: indulged but positive and confident   133
John: actor and self-critic   135
Matt: staying attached to his parents   137
Daisy: a little adult   139
Paul: socially disabled   141
Kay: parenting her parents   143
Sylvia: overprotected   146
Maria: entangled yet neglected   149
James: carried shame   152
Gunnar: the family romance   154
Reflections   155

Part III Implications for Therapy

8 **The Only-Child Archetype: A Folktale** 159
An archetype 160
The handless maiden 161

9 **The Only-Child Matrix** 164
Only-child matrix 164
Lack of connectedness 167
Aloneness and space 170
Commitment: dependency versus independence 172
Specialness, grandiosity and responsibility 173
Self-esteem 174
Triangular relationships 177
Enmeshment 179
Separation and individuation 183
The effect of the only-child stereotype on parent and child 187
Shame 190

10 **Gathering the Threads** 196
Therapists and birth order assumptions 198
Do non-only-children fit the only-child archetype? 201
Only-children of single parents and adopted only-children 202
Final reflections 202

References 205

Further Reading 213

Index 215

Acknowledgements

This book is dedicated to adult only-children. In particular, my co-researchers who have accompanied me on my journey over the past six years to discover and capture the only-child experience, hand in hand with the hundreds of adult only-children who have responded from across the world to my website and offered their own stories.

Thanks also go to Kate MaGuire, Maja O'Brien and Kim Etherington who supported my initial research.

A special thanks to James van Tromp for converting the only-child matrix into a professional diagram.

I am very grateful to Jane Dawson who has followed this process with love and attention, sharing her ideas and experience.

Finally, I want to acknowledge my children, Jens and Elise, who had to live with their mother tied to a computer once again and to Paul, my husband, who I met as a consequence of this research. He has given me invaluable support and as an only-child, he has been someone with whom I could share both intellectually and emotionally and whose ideas have contributed to the book's final form.

Introduction

Writing this book and carrying out the initial research has been one of the most challenging experiences of my life. I think this is a result of the various ways the public in general view having one child. Over the years I have come to realise that most people have a very specific view of what it means to be brought up an only-child. This in turn leads to inevitable comparisons between sibling children and non-sibling children. As an only-child myself, I was clear from the outset that this would not be a comparative study of only-child adults with those who had experienced life with a sibling. The stereotypes surrounding only-children have themselves grown out of this type of comparison. Although aware of the negative stereotype, I did not realise what a large part it would play in my research and how it might influence the way others perceived my work.

Negative stereotypes of only-children permeate the existing research whilst over-population and the growing numbers of only-children worldwide has made it a political issue. I have attempted to address these issues throughout the book. However, my original intention to research the only-child experience was to understand more fully what this experience might be and to see whether growing up without siblings had an impact on the only-child themselves, not just in childhood but later in life. As a psychotherapist I was interested in the meaning adult only-children gave to their experience and also to what extent they saw it as having affected their emotional and social development. Throughout this book I have tried to be as transparent as possible concerning my own views and starting point. My own bias can be seen in my thoughts and reflections that I have included where appropriate. This is based on the belief that we all have bias and that to be open about it acknowledges the subjective nature of the research. As a researcher I have taken a postmodern view that sees all experience as inter-subjective, rather than a positivist modern approach which values the attempt to objectify the researcher and the research. Hence woven through this book are some of my own personal experiences and my own reflexivity which has been both challenging and at times painfully revealing.

My personal interest in researching the experience of growing up an only-child, and how that subsequently shaped the way I see the world, began during a conversation with a colleague some years ago who is also an only-child. Sitting one hot summer's day, in a café, on the beach in Brighton, we spoke about our experiences as children and how we felt they had affected the way we both saw and experienced the world. Our childhood backgrounds were not similar. Jane was brought up by restrictive working-class parents in Manchester; her childhood had been constricted and dominated by her overbearing mother. In comparison, my own parents aspired to the middle classes and had a more laissez faire approach to parenting. I had a very close relationship with my mother but paradoxically felt excluded from my parents' relationship, leaving me feeling both strongly attached to my mother and yet apart and unconnected to the 'family'.

In my earlier years I wondered what it would be like to have a sibling but my parents (both the youngest of four) assured me that I was lucky not to have one. They believed there were many more advantages in being the only one than having siblings, and my mother had no interest in having another child once her teaching career was established. Perhaps my research has been an unconscious quest to see if I was genuinely lucky! Certainly the research itself has been dogged by the idea that being an only-child is either intrinsically bad or good. This was not my starting point. I came from a position that there were both advantages and disadvantages. As a psychotherapist, I am much more interested in looking at the phenomena which make up the experience of growing up an only-child in a sibling-dominated society. As meaning is also essential to my therapeutic approach, it was equally important to explore the meaning each individual gave to their experience of growing up an only-child. I explored this meaning from both an intra-psychic and inter-psychic level. However, early in my research it became evident that the social perspective of an only-child upbringing, in what is still a predominantly sibling society, has a huge impact on that experience. The negative stereotypes of only-children have been challenged, even dismissed, but others have arisen in their place which although considered to be positive are, I believe, equally detrimental. Stereotypes affect social perception which in turn affects the intra- and inter-psychic worlds of the only-child not just in childhood but throughout life.

Questions that have focused my thoughts and clarified my ideas have been important and are the backbone of this book. Specifically, I have been concerned to understand how growing up primarily with adults might cause only-children to feel different. Whilst considering this, further questions arose:

- Where do only-children get the opportunity to develop social and emotional relationships with other children? Is it the same as having siblings?

- If the oedipal triangle is never offset by another child, does this mean the power of the parent is much greater and therefore more likely to have an adverse effect if the child has experienced insecure attachment? Do siblings help to balance negative parental influence?

- Do parents in a sibling society see themselves in a place of deficit in not providing a sibling? If so, do they feel they need to do or give more as parents, to assuage the fear of producing a child that fits the only-child stereotype? Can this pass to the child as shame?

- If aloneness is a central feature of the experience of onlies, can this be both negative and positive? If an only-child's experience is one of secure attachment, enabling a sense of embodied well being, can this lead to greater creativity?

This book explores the experience of being brought up without siblings and uses the term 'only-child' to refer to both children and adults, as the experience of being an only one lasts throughout adult life and is often felt more poignantly in later years when parents die. I also use the plural 'onlies' to denote only-children collectively.

The book is based on my experience of working for 30 years as a therapist, with young people and adults, many of whom have been only-children. It is also based on a doctoral research study which aimed to contribute to our understanding of the subjective experience of the only-child adult and how it affects the way they see the world and inter-relate with others, with the aim of giving insight into the world of the adult only-child to therapists. The original study focused on in-depth interviews of eight female adult only-children over two years. This research ran concurrently with some Internet research that developed as a result of setting up a website: onlychild.org.uk. The latter expanded the research by publishing the stories of the original co-researchers, inviting responses from only-children (and non-onlies) all over the world, men and women alike. The response has been enormous and the website is continually updated with new stories that contain people's reflections about growing up as an only-child and the personal meaning a life without siblings has had. This element of reciprocity is based on a narrative approach and sees us all living storied lives. People resonate with the stories of other people's experience of their only-childness, and this invites a response because stories stimulate memories, reflections and fantasies of anticipated and yearned experiences. For the only-child, this is a continual desire for siblings often lasting throughout life. The heart of this book is made up of stories told to me either through interviews or via email. The stories are an invitation for you to look at the experiences of only-children and decide for yourself whether their experience of growing up without siblings is different although not unique. I also endeavour to develop the themes that emerge to offer a structure or archetypal image of the only-child experience which takes into account the intra-, inter- and extra-psychic dimensions of that experience.

Structure of the book

The book is divided into three parts. Part I is based on my doctoral research and looks at the stereotypes concerning only-children which have impacted on the way society views the only-child; how parents subsequently treat their only-child; and the affect this has on the only-child's psychological development. Part II develops these ideas further using material from interviews and emails from across the world. These demonstrate that there are a set of identifiable only-child experiences which I discuss in Part III as an only-child matrix or archetype and look at implications for therapy when working with adult only-children.

In Part I, Chapter 1 traces the psychological literature to identify the ideas surrounding the development of only-children and traces the diverse and often contradictory views. For example, Adler (1928) encapsulates the thinking about only-children at the turn of the twentieth century. It is largely negative, but does contain many of the elements that belong to the stereotype of the only-child. In Adler's day, only-children were the exception, but to what extent have ideas changed in the twenty-first century with increasing numbers of only-children? Do Adler's observations and that of other psychologists and psychotherapists reflect social norms *or* influence them? These will be some of the questions I will be addressing.

In Chapter 2 I discuss the philosophical and epistemological underpinnings of the research that I undertook over a four-year period. I explain in detail the rationale for the type of research undertaken. This grew out of reading the existing literature and identifying a gap, which this book attempts to fulfil, in understanding the experience of growing up without siblings and the repercussions this may have in later life. The central concern is to identify the meaning adult only-children themselves have of their experience and elucidate it through the idea of 'voice'.

Chapter 3 contains eight adult only-child experiences based on my interviews. They are written to offer a sense of what it is like to grow up an only-child and the meaning and impact that experience has on each person's life. The material that emerges from these stories gives a dramatic insight into the experience of being brought up as an only-child and spans 70 years.

Chapter 4 discusses my research findings, using three constructs of voice: the private, personal and public to analyse the data. The stories are then considered from a life-span perspective to show that there are certain challenges at particular stages of life that only-children face.

Part II, Chapter 5 describes the only-child experience using the World Wide Web as a research tool, specifically through the website onlychild.org.uk. Chapter 6 contains two adult only-child stories of Ivy, a student from China, and Yukinori, a lecturer from Taiwan. Both were brought up in China and Taiwan, respectively, but came to the United Kingdom as students. They give a rich insight into the experience of growing up an only-child in countries where only-children are common and reveal how that impinged on their subsequent development. Chapter 7 uses a selection from the hundreds of email life-stories I have received to illustrate some of the only-child developmental life-stage challenges introduced in Chapter 4.

Part III, Chapter 8 discusses the idea of an only-child archetype. This is illustrated through the folktale of the Handless Maiden which identifies themes that make up what I have chosen to describe as an only-child matrix of experience. Chapter 9 describes the formulation of the idea of an 'only-child matrix' and argues that both the social and psychological aspects of growing up an only-child are intertwined and need to be taken into account in understanding the only-child experience. Themes inherent in the only-child matrix are discussed and case material is used to illustrate both the way the archetype manifests and aspects of working therapeutically with adult only-children. Chapter 10 gathers the threads concerning adult only-child experience and discusses therapist's pre-conceptions. It concludes with some reflections on one of the central issues that the book seeks to address: the importance of witness in human experience.

Part I
Transcending the Stereotypes

1
The Politics of the Only-Child

Only-children are a growing phenomenon. In the United States, it is estimated that 20 per cent of children under 18 are 'singletons'. In the United Kingdom, the birth rate has fallen to1.48 children per woman, with 17 per cent of couples having only one child. This percentage of only-children is low compared to other parts of Europe: the Portuguese and Italians having 49 per cent, Austrians 43 per cent, Dutch 33 per cent and Irish 30 per cent (Office of National Statistics). In China it is estimated there are 40 million. The media have an increasing interest in the phenomenon of only-child families which they often refer to as the Beanpole family. Beanpole families are not pyramid shaped like family trees, but tall and thin vertical families. Articles reflect the increase in the numbers of only-children, due to later marriages, careers for women, a higher divorce rate, lower fertility and an economic desire to combine family and work. Having a child, and a career, is now a common expectation for women, and limiting the family to one child appears to avoid some of the disadvantages of increasing financial responsibility and dividing time and attention between children.

With an increase in population the only-child family has been advocated as a way to curb population, particularly in China. However, in the West, more concern has been shown in the falling birth rate compared with the rise in the numbers of elderly who will have to be financed by diminishing numbers in the workforce. The large family was the norm prior to birth control and there are undoubtedly underlying cultural messages that large families with lots of children are in some way superior to those families with one or none. A glance at popular TV programmes bears this out with the 'Little House on the Prairie' and the film 'Cheaper by the Dozen' containing the quintessential fantasies of an ideal family life. Politically, family values play an important role, but a 'family' in the popular sense is nearly always considered as 1+ child not just one child. My research revealed that being an only is seen to be a disadvantage by the majority of people, signified by statistical polls taken from people belonging to both sibling families and single-child families. The image of the only-child still carries with it the idea of the selfish, unable to share, isolated, socially challenged individual. Despite this, there is a growing trend to show the positive face of the only-child. Particularly in the United States, much effort has been made to raise the profile of the singleton and demonstrate the advantages. Only-child research has promoted a positive view of the only-child as outgoing, confident, sociable and successful. There are some understandable reasons why these two polarised views have arisen. However, whether you believe being an only is a good or bad experience, I hope the research that underpins this book will give a better understanding of how only-children experience themselves and the effect of society and culture.

To contextualise the study on only-child experience, this chapter will review some of the relevant literature that has been written on the topic. This comes from a variety of psychological disciplines, including psychoanalytic, birth order studies, evolutionary theory, genetic research, sibling research and family therapy. I have also included a variety of international studies and a review of the media perspective as they all impinge on the social view of the only-child. Whilst there are many divergent streams of research which encompass only-children there are few books, although these are increasing, written specifically on the subject of only-children, and still fewer contain a discussion on the developmental differences experienced by only-children. Instead there is a constant comparison of only-children with sibling children, which inevitably leads to a good/bad debate on the relative merits of various birth orders, a view that is reflected in the wider population.

My own experience of growing up an only-child led me to believe it is neither an inherently good nor bad experience. Rather I have increasingly come to view it as an experience that is 'different' from that of growing up with siblings. I am aware that for many people the idea of not having siblings is seen as a benefit, as it avoids sibling rivalry and means materially there are more resources and advantages, such as parental attention. However, many only-children themselves see it as negative, whilst books written for parents of only-children promote positive images. I will summarise the four different categories that emerge in the only-child debate reflected in the literature:

- First that the only-child state is inherently *negative*;
- Secondly that there is *no difference* between the only-child experience and that of having siblings;
- Thirdly growing up an only-child is *advantageous* compared to those with siblings; and
- Fourthly that *there is difference* but it is neither intrinsically good nor bad.

The research literature on only-children covers a variety of quantitative research from the United Kingdom, the United States, China, India and Japan, and some qualitative research which is undertaken less frequently. Another interesting way of viewing the research is from the perspective of 'behaviour' and 'meaning'. The quantitative studies are very much focused on the behaviour of only-children and how others, for example, teachers, assess that behaviour. In contrast, qualitative studies are more interested in meaning. This includes what only-children themselves understand, feel or sense about their lives that are lived without siblings. These two ways of researching only-children correspond to the three categories I use throughout this book. *Intra-psychic* experience which is about meaning and is subjective (qualitative), in contrast to the *inter-psychic* and *extra-psychic* experience which is how others perceive the way only-children behave and attempts to be objective (quantitative).

Psychoanalytic literature

The question of the significance of siblings to personality development has been a topic of debate amongst psychologists. However, the importance of sibling relationships has only recently become a topic of investigation in psychoanalytic literature. Freud did not develop the view that siblings are important to psychic development, even though he stated: 'Psychoanalysis has taught us that a boy's earliest choice of objects for his love is incestuous and that those objects are forbidden ones – his mother *and his sister*.' [my italics](1912–13, p. 17). Despite this statement, Freud later reiterates that the child's first choice of an 'object' could be anyone who is the major carer, but believes this choice will quickly transfer to the parents. Freud, therefore, stayed with the primacy of parents in the Oedipal phase, as the ones from whom all emotional experience is received.

Coles (2003) argues that Freud turned his back on the importance of siblings for earliest attachment (and people who were not parents), because of the centrality of the Oedipal complex to his theories of development. She also suggests that Freud had emotional reasons for retaining the centrality of Oedipal theory because there were many generational anomalies in his own family:

> The beauty of the oedipal theory is that it simplifies early attachment to nannies and to siblings and to the generational mix-up of attachments in Freud's family.... Brilliant though Freud's insight was into the importance of the oedipal complex, it has had the consequence of marginalising sibling attachment and reducing siblings to substitute figures in the oedipal drama.
>
> (2003, p. 38)

Adler (1928, 1962, 1964, 1992) is one of the few psychoanalysts who pioneered interest in the area of birth order. He moved away from Freud's emphasis on biological drives, believing human beings are primarily social. He advocated that the social environment and birth order were one of the major childhood influences from which the individual creates a style of life. There is potentially a favourable or unfavourable outcome from each birth order place; however, as we saw in the introduction the only-child state is seen as less favourable and he states:

> An only child is pampered by his mother. She is afraid of losing him and wants to keep him under her attention. He develops what is called a 'mother complex'; he is tied to his mothers apron strings and wishes to push his father out of the family picture.
>
> (1962, p. 114)

The rival for the only-child is not a sibling but a parent and the continual attention only-children receive causes problems in later life. He believed that only-children dislike the prospect of another sibling. If they are unfortunate to have parents of a timid and pessimistic disposition, they will grow up over-anxious. Adler was also concerned whether parents raise a child for their own gratification; an only-child would be particularly pampered and not given learning opportunities. As a consequence, these children would later discover that they were truly inferior, leading to problems in relating and being a good, contributory member of society.

Melanie Klein (1932) in her early writing, placed emphasis on the importance of sibling love on the development of the psyche. She developed the idea that siblings promote the process of emotional development and help in the task of separating from parents. Sibling rivalry and jealousy exist, but so does sibling love, and Klein sees this as a counterbalance to the hatred of the Oedipal conflict. She states that sibling or peer love is important as it enables the child to develop emotionally, and through identification achieve adult heterosexuality without the necessity of doing it through parents. Recently, this has been developed further by Juliet Mitchell (2000, 2003) and Prophecy Coles (2003).

Mitchell claims there has been a 'massive repression of the significance of all the love and hate of sibling relationship and their heirs in marital affinity and friendships' (2000, p. 77) She sees the birth of a sibling as both catastrophic and significant, a part of the 'lateral' sibling relationships, as opposed to the vertical one a child has with its parents. Siblings can act as a 'mirror' for each other, but Mitchell sees this as a distortion and thereby reduces the power of siblings to an internal negative and destructive influence on the psyche (2000, p. 107). However, in her next book (2003), Mitchell develops these ideas, arguing that analysts such as Winnicott (1958, 1978), and developmental psychologists like Boer and Dunn (1992), have rightly focused on the significance of sibling relationships and their interactions. She believes sibling relations need to be conceptualised as 'relatively independent and autonomous structures' (2003, p. 11) which are important to both social and psychic development. Furthermore, she also addresses the position of the only-child, who has no sibling, but does have an internal expectation of one:

> Yet psychologically speaking, siblings are crucial also to the only child who expects their arrival and fears what may have happened to them. An actual sibling is considered important in allowing the access to hatred in a way that can be resolved so that sociality results. Siblings provide a way of learning to love and hate the same person.
>
> (Mitchell, 2003, p. 225)

When there are no siblings, Mitchell believes, peer relationships can fulfil the same task of developing a 'we' psychology and not just 'I,' leading to a transformation from narcissism to object-love. Coles (2003) has also developed the idea that sibling relationships are important, stating that the significance of parents in the emotional life of the child is just half the story, siblings being the other half. She states that siblings shape our inner world, but more importantly, play a significant part in our emotional and sexual development. With regard to the only-child, on whom she focuses very little, she describes differences in their inner world compared to a child with siblings:

> I chose to leave out the only child as my interest has been in beginning to describe the effect of sibling *relationships* upon the psyche... I am aware there is a qualitative difference in the feel of the inner world of only children compared to those who have siblings.
>
> (Coles, 2003, p. 6)

Coles describes this qualitative difference as the 'texture of the inner world' of the only-child. Whilst a child with siblings has a noisier inner world, an only-child's is quieter with less populated dreams. Coles also suggests that only-children are protected from sibling jealousy and rivalry, so this is one less area for them to experience existential anxiety. Both Coles and Mitchell see the only-child experience as different from one with siblings. They both, in different ways, give an influential place to the development of the psyche through sibling interaction.

A lecture given in 1945 by Winnicott (pub. 1957) addresses more only-child issues than any earlier psychoanalyst. His views are very similar to my own research findings. In his opinion there are more arguments in favour of having larger families rather than one child, although he also believes 'if the immense disadvantages of onlyness are understood, they can be got round to some extent.' (1957, p. 111). He discusses both the economic, social and emotional arguments that people use for having one child, now popular in current parenting books. In contrast to them, he states that the disadvantages outweigh any advantages. From an economic viewpoint he says: 'If people like to speak in terms of money, let them, but really I think what they doubt is whether they are able to support a large family without losing too much personal freedom' (ibid: 107).

Western society has become much more individualistic and the idea of loss of personal freedom is a highly motivating factor for people choosing (as opposed to negative personal circumstances) to have only one child. Winnicott questions the validity of the belief, popular at present, that having several children is more of a burden emotionally than having one.

He sees the advantages of having one are the 'uncomplicated infancy' and the 'simplified environment' when a mother only has to attend to one child (ibid: 108). However, the disadvantages are lack of sibling opportunities which provide playmates and creative play, so for the only-child 'it becomes silly to play' (ibid: 108). The adult environment does not encourage 'irresponsibility and impulsiveness' beneficial to children, but 'precociousness' popular with modern parenting styles. More importantly he believes the value of a sibling entering into a child's upbringing cannot be overemphasised, particularly in terms of learning to deal with one's hate and aggression (ibid: 109). He says that 'only children are always looking for stable relationships' because they have not learned the necessary social skills sibling families provide 'and this tends to scare off casual acquaintances' (ibid: 110). Winnicott also highlights the problems only-children can have with the care of elderly parents, and how parents of only-children may have difficulties in letting go. He puts this in the context of war-time, saying it may be a good thing from the only-child's point of view that they have the opportunity to leave home! (ibid: 110). Finally, without a sibling, the only-child is locked into their parent's view of the world. If this view is hostile it can be very problematic to their development, a view confirmed by family therapists.

There are a growing number of birth order studies that have emerged in the twentieth/twenty-first century, which focus more on inter-relational development. Birth order research has contributed to the debate concerning only-children, although they are always comparative.

Birth order studies and evolutionary theory

The research on birth order and its effect on the development of aspects of personality, for example, intelligence, sociability, emotional stability and self-esteem are comparative studies containing the underlying assumption that these aspects of personality are measurable. These studies are often viewed as problematic because of the huge number of variables involved, but Sulloway (1996) reviewing the existing birth order research believes birth order is significant, although he states the findings are often contradictory and easily dismissed. He employs evolutionary theory to understand how family dynamics affect personality development and how they are the primary source for historical change. He argues: siblings raised together have more differences than people outside the family, because in evolutionary terms divergence maximises competition for scarce resources. He sees only-children as less predictable psychologically and freer to develop aspects of their personality. Sulloway (1996) regards sibling conflict as important in evolutionary terms, as each sibling represents a genetic insurance policy. The production of children entails both cost and benefits that vary according to the gaps between births. The greater the gap between siblings, the less rivalry there is for resources. A lesser gap leads younger siblings to minimise direct comparisons with older siblings by diverging their interests to maximise on parental investment. Differences in sibling personalities, he argues, are an expression of sibling rivalry, and an important process in order to guarantee parental interest in their well-being.

Sulloway (1996) found that only-children were the 'least predictable subgroup', in his family dynamics model, 'precisely because they have no siblings.' (p. 204) Lack of siblings, he says, allows them to be more variable and freer to occupy a variety of family niches. The absence of siblings also makes only-children more susceptible to influences such as parents' social values. His research showed that only-children were less extraverted than firstborns, because lack of siblings inhibits social practice. He also noted, unlike any other research I have viewed including my own, that only-children manifest greater conflict with parents than children with siblings. He believes that siblings may direct conflict towards one another because it is potentially less costly than directing it against parents. Sulloway (1996), like Mitchell (2003), believes that only-children experience an internal threat from unborn siblings, which causes them to find ways of maximising parental investment; however, he does not elucidate on this.

A study by Guastello and Guastello (2002) cited research completed in the 1960s–80s that reported some correlation between personality and birth order. However, their research found no differences across birth order, using GPP constructs (Gordon Personal Profile variables). These include:

1. assertiveness and dominance (ascendancy);
2. conscientiousness and a sense of duty (responsibility);
3. emotional control and anxiety (emotional stability);
4. gregariousness (sociability); and
5. self-esteem (a composite score of the first four).

They concluded that while possible relationships between birth order effects and personality are fun to discuss, and commonly accepted as factual, scientific evidence does not support their validity.

Barrett et al. (2002) reviewing birth order research found that parental bias and sibling rivalry for parental attention serves to promote differences amongst offspring: 'It pays siblings to try and differentiate themselves from their older sibs in order to alleviate the negative effects of sibling rivalry, and it then pays to encourage and amplify these differences so that each offspring fills his or her own individual niche.' (2002, p. 174).

An important statement, as it suggests that children without siblings are having a very different experience. They do not need to differentiate themselves from their siblings, as they already have all the attention of the parents. They do not need to amplify differences as there is no one to compare themselves with, except parents, which I would argue is more problematic. Thereby they avoid sibling rivalry, but at what cost?

An interesting statement about only-children is made by the neuroscientist, Lise Eliot (1999), writing about brain and mind development, and specifically early intelligence:

> Finally, one unexpected finding to come out of studies of family configurations is that children without siblings actually fare somewhat *worse* than first-borns from larger families; an only child typically scores about two or three points lower than an oldest child with one or two younger sibs. This observation seems to contradict the 'parental attention' theory, since only children should benefit from more attention than children with siblings. It suggests however, that oldest children *benefit from another type of experience the opportunity to teach their younger brothers and sisters,* which is often especially effective way of reinforcing one's own knowledge and self-confidence. [my italics]
>
> (Eliot, 1999, p. 40)

According to Eliot, the most important limbic tutors are parents, whose every moment of interaction activates specific neural pathways, locking in the limbic circuits that will be used throughout life. Although this may be true in infancy, the primacy given to the value on parent interaction appears to ignore the discussion of the significance of sibling relationships and the social and emotional learning they provide. Eliot hints at this in her reference above to *'another type of experience'* sibling children receive compared to only-children. Lack of sibling interaction surely means a whole spectrum of learning is unavailable to the only-child. Although the limbic system remains plastic throughout childhood until limbic wiring is complete, important social and emotional learning for the only-child will depend on interactions outside rather than inside the family.

It appears that studies showing evolutionary reasons for sibling differences in families are more accepted than studies attempting to show similarities across birth order categories. Let us look at the affect of sibling relationships and why they are considered important for social and emotional development.

The research focusing on sibling relationships

The lack of research specific to only-children led me to want to identify what might be important psychologically in sibling relationships. To what extent is there evidence that siblings do in fact affect the family dynamic? Are sibling relationships beneficial or detrimental to the children concerned? There has been a great deal of research in this area which suggests that siblings are an important resource for learning social and emotional skills. For example, sibling research indicates that parents' management of their children's disputes and quarrels is important in helping siblings to develop pro-social attitudes to guide their behaviour towards one another (Dunn & Munn, 1986; Ross et al., 1994). Parents intervene in a variety of ways with their children. They address issues that children raise, take positions on those issues, intervene in disputes and enforce rules for each child's treatment of one another. This interaction, observed by siblings, provides much social learning. However, when parents do not intervene, older siblings are likely to dominate and be hostile to their younger siblings. Mothers' discussions with siblings of preschool age, about their younger siblings' needs and feelings, have been found to be associated with sibling care-giving and friendliness leading to siblings becoming engaged in friendlier and more sensitive interactions (Howe & Ross, 1990). They learn how to listen to siblings, to empathise with siblings' distress and to engage in cooperative efforts to resolve disputes (Dubow & Tisak, 1989; Fabes & Eisenberg, 1992). This teaches sibling-children to have confidence in approaching sibling disputes and to expect that they can be solved through direct action. They are therefore less likely to cope with problems through avoidance and anger. Dunn and Slomkoski (1992) showed that sibling conflict which combines self-interest, emotional arousal and a close relationship are a powerful stimulus for the growth of children's social knowledge. Having repeated opportunities to see alternative solutions considered and problem-solving skills demonstrated are useful sources of social learning. Therefore, we may assume that parental conversations with sibling interaction help children to develop perspective and empathic competencies that enhance sibling relationships, but these are unavailable to the only-child.

There are less favourable sibling experiences in which sibling-children receive harsh parenting that includes unresolved parental anger. This can lead to the development of behavioural styles, emotion regulation strategies and cognitions that will feed sibling conflict. Sibling disputes may then lead to anger-focused coping strategies, aggression and coercive behaviours (Crick & Dodge, 1994). Parental pronouncements about the importance of not fighting and sharing resources will be rejected if there is a tradition of hostile responses, and conflict and hostility will continue (Brody, 1998). However, Stocker and Dunn (1990) proposed that siblings who resolved negative interactions facilitated the development of conflict-management skills which enabled them to maintain close friendships. Sibling relationships give an opportunity to balance pro-social and conflict training and may also yield clearer links between sibling and peer relationships.

Mueller and Vandell (1995) found that children with older siblings were more responsive socially to other children of their own age. Sibling interaction propelled them into social situations where they actively sought out playmates in settings away from home. Mueller and Vandell (1995) believe the foundation for developing healthy peer relations is laid in the home at an early age. This is then solidified through further exposure to siblings as they continue to interact through communal activities. Socialisation is seen to occur largely in the home through interaction with siblings. Acceptable social roles and acceptable actions within those social roles are learned. Siblings in close but non-enmeshed relationships, particularly with younger siblings, have identified their sibling relationships as important sources of emotional and instrumental support during times of stress and family transitions (Bryant, 1992; Dunn, 1996; Jenkins, 1992). Brody concludes his research by saying:

> Sibling relationships are, in and of themselves, important as children interact with one another and influence the social and emotional context in which they grow and develop. The psychosocial skills attained through sibling interactions are also used throughout life in a wide variety of other social relationships.
>
> (1998, p. 145)

An Indian study by Das and Babu (2004) compared sibling and non-sibling children's acquisition of a 'Theory of Mind' (TOM). TOM paves the way for important co-lateral understandings like the ability to engage in pretend play, distinguish between see-know, appearance-reality and lies and deceptions which help in the understanding of others (empathy) and successful social adaptation (sociability). They concluded that the presence of siblings was found to have a significant positive effect in all theory of mind tasks as well as free play. Perner et al. (1994) also concluded that children who have intense relationships with their siblings have a larger database for developing a theory of mind. A further study by Nelson et al. (1998) found that the larger the family the greater the potential for sibling social interaction which led to an increased efficiency in social and reasoning activities.

It is clear from these studies that there is a great deal of evidence demonstrating the importance of sibling relationships for social and emotional learning. Only-children miss learning through sibling interaction. We know from neuroscience that social and emotional learning, via the primary care-giver, influences brain development (Ledouux, 1999). It seems highly probable then that the important emotional learning and development gained through sibling interaction also influences the development of the 'social brain' (orbitofrontal cortex). The development of the orbitofrontal cortex depends on relationships with other people, initially parents but subsequently interaction with others. Important emotional learning is a consequence of sibling interaction. Without siblings the child needs opportunities to learn social skills *outside* the home, usually considered a less safe environment, which in turn will influence brain development. Let us now look a variety of studies that have been made specifically on only-children.

Quantitative research studies on only-children

Most quantitative studies compare only-children to those with siblings. They fall into three sets of findings. Those which say the experience is *negative* . These exemplify much of the earlier research. Recent research and reviews of earlier research state there is *no difference*, and a growing swell of opinion, based on the no difference perspective, is going further and stating it can be *beneficial* .

A brief overview of this phenomenon shows that early American psychologists like G. Stanley Hall are quoted as saying: 'Being an only child is a disease in itself' or A.A. Brill that: 'It would be best for the individual and the race that there were no only children' (cited in Falbo, 1984). Both psychologists express negative perspectives of only-children. Hall described the only-child experience as 'damaging', thus helping to stigmatise only-children in the United States. Negativity towards the experience of only-children led to an ongoing debate on whether only-children are the spoilt, self-centred, socially maladjusted people that early psychologists suggest. Many empirical studies confirm the existence of *negative qualities* in only-children and provide examples of only-child behavioural problems and personality difficulties (Blake, 1974; Jiao et al., 1986; Petzold, 1998; Rosenberg & Falk, 1987; Rosenberg & Leino,

1987; Thompson, 1974; Westoff, 1978). These and other studies focus on the only-child's:

- *lack of sociability* (Claudy, 1984);
- greater than expected incidence of *mental health problems* (Belmont & Marolla, 1997; Howe & Madgett, 1975; Makihara et al., 1998);
- persistent *egocentrism* and *uncooperativeness* (Jiao et al., 1986);
- *negative social behaviours* (Petzold, 1998; Thompson, 1974);
- *lack of friends* (Graham-Bermann & Gest, 1991; Miller & Maruyama, 1976); and
- *'disadvantageous peculiarities'* (Bohannon, 1998) particularly an inability to interact with peers was found in a study of 46 exceptional only-children.

This research shows that only-children are more likely to be thought of as spoiled and indulged as there are no other children in the family to divert parent time or resources away from them. This is the basis of the negative stereotype.

Research aimed at only-child self-report appears again to confirm only-child negativity, indicating only-children *feel less autonomous* than firstborn children (Byrd et al., 1993) and some appeared to *experience insecurities* because of their parents' protectiveness and apprehensions (Leman, 1985; Pepper, 1971). In adult life, the only-child may experience heightened *dependency on others* and, in the extreme, live a *self-less* kind of existence (Forer, 1977). Only-children have also been viewed as more likely to abuse drugs than people from other birth positions. Pitkeathley and Emerson (1994) state: 'In America, the majority of people who seek counselling help are first-borns or onlies' (1994, p. 123).

Much of this only-child psychological research has been conducted in the United States from the 1920s onwards. The research in the United States includes longitudinal studies, confluence models and large scale surveys. Similar surveys have also been carried out in China and Japan (Ching, 1982; Makihara et al., 1998; Meredith et al., 1989; Petzold, 1998).

Recent research, however, provides evidence that challenges these largely negative views of only-children. Of particular note is the work of educational psychologist Toni Falbo. An only-child herself, and mother of one, she disputes the significance of birth order and family size. Her book (Falbo, 1984) summarises research from the 1920s to the 1980s and further articles includes research from China. She uses empirical studies to show that there is little difference between onlies and non-onlies. She also traces the development of social views concerning onlies that reflect the popular mythology of them as self-centred, unlikable, selfish, lonely and maladjusted.

Falbo's aim was to conduct a comprehensive examination of all the existing research findings in order to produce reliable, definitive data. From over a 100 studies, she concluded that there is very little difference between children with siblings and only-children. She believes the research goes further, indicating that only-child achievement in educational attainment is *higher* than that of non-onlies. Some studies were inconclusive on attributes such as self-esteem; others suggested young child onlies appear to develop more social skills than those with siblings. Several studies indicated only-children are unrepresented in mental health and that onlies show a consistent pattern of affiliativeness (sociability). In contrast, other research showed a lower pattern of affiliativeness, but this was not associated with loneliness or unhappiness.

Whilst Falbo concluded that differences between only-children and other children are very slight, she believes that factors like parent education, emotional health and values, parenting styles and genetic predisposition are far more indicative of how a child will be than either birth order or family size. She has promoted the view that only-children are no more lonely, selfish or maladjusted than others and have certain *advantages*: higher achievement and higher self-esteem.

Only-children in China

Falbo's conclusions are reinforced by research in China funded by The National Institute of Health and carried out by Falbo and her colleague Poston (Poston & Falbo, 1990). China's 'one-child policy' had led Chinese psychologists to fear that only-children would not reflect the collectivist values of China, as they were perceived to be more independent and 'me'-orientated. A negative image resulted, as this article in *Asiaweek* illustrates.

> The world that China's kids inhabit is a far cry from that of their parents. The earlier hardships are scarcely fathomable to today's TV watching, French-fry chomping young. Having been denied education and material goods as children, many adults wildly overcompensate in doting on their kids. 'Parents have a hard time saying no' says Xia Ming, who teaches environmental studies at the Children's Palace. 'They had nothing, so the kids are their only hope'.
>
> (Reese, 1999, para. 7)

Poston and Falbo (1990) went to China and studied 4000 children in rural and urban settings in three Chinese provinces and Beijing. Self-descriptions were used and descriptions from peers, teachers and one parent. Analysis showed that only-children had a slightly higher verbal ability and were considered to be good students, not arrogant and self-centred as feared.

These results are in contrast to Hong Guo (2000). He reviewed the research on the psychology of only-children in China and traced the development of two decades of one-child policy in China. Hong Guo found that in the 1980s various Chinese research psychologists concluded that only-children were more likely to have personality and social behavioural problems, and be more egocentric and less persistent. To counteract these difficulties, as one-child families became the norm, collective activities such as pre-school and day-care were provided and parents were encouraged to change their attitude to be less doting and use more authority.

Recent studies in China show there is little difference now between onlies and those with siblings. Feng Xiaotian, a sociologist from Nanjing University, has carried out research on only-children since 1987. Between 2000 and 2002, his research found onlies to be more sociable than those with siblings, and able to make friends quickly in a new environment. He claims, however, there are some minor differences; only-children are generally lazier and pampering by parents is common, although this becomes less marked as parents lose their influence:

> At a young age when parents have an overwhelming influence on the child's behaviour, it is only 'natural' that the only child behaves badly because he is pampered by everyone. As he grows up, his parents' influence on him weakens and the only child behaviours become affected by more external conditions – be it the mass media, his university education, or work environment – which affects everyone equally, regardless of their family background.
>
> (Chua Chin Hon, 2003, para. 12)

Psychologist Sun Yunxiao and his team from Beijing University have also completed years of follow-up studies at the Chinese Youth Research Centre:

> Their results show that the contemporary younger generation has many attributes that the previous generation lacked: they are more

knowledgeable, outgoing, democratic, observant of laws and regulations, and conscious of self-development and environmental protec-
tion. As IT continues to develop so rapidly, they are keen to keep up
to date and gain access to the latest information.

(Zhang Hua, 2003, para. 4)

This is the 'positive' face of China's single-child policy. There are,
however, two areas that have been highlighted repeatedly in newspaper
coverage; the only-child's unwillingness to take on responsibility and
their lack of independence. Chinese parents put a great deal of emphasis
on education. A lack of higher education resources with few places available for students to study means there is strong competition. Parents'
primary concern tends to be academic scores rather than health, social
or moral development. The government saw this as a problem because
it is redressing the balance by introducing a number of projects such as
the 'Star River Happy Garden', the 'Happy Rural Farm' and the 'Happy
Camp' designed to create more opportunities for socialising in big family
groups rather than just the nuclear family.

In 1999, the government issued the 'Decision to Deepen Education
Reform and Promote Quality Education'. All schools were now required
to pay equal attention to intellectual, moral, physical, artistic and
social education. Western education systems were studied and parents
educated to value the importance of social interaction. Chen Huilu,
Professor at the Development Psychology Research Institute at Beijing
University, used Western knowledge to start the young child's 'Socialization Project' which focuses on children's sociability, teaching them how
to play and learn to both cooperate and look after themselves. Chen
Huilu believes this will counteract the inherent difficulties only-children
have whilst with their parents:

Many Chinese parents consider their children as physically attached
to them. They comply with their every demand, lavishing excessive
attention and care on them. This deprives their children of the capab-
ility and right to make decisions and take choices.

(Zhang Hua, 2003, para. 2)

It appears to me that Poston and Falbo's (1990) research at least in China
has been politically useful. She criticises the Chinese psychologists for
holding negative stereotypes of only-children but Chinese research
suggests that there have been social problems with only-children
into the twenty-first century, although these have been increasingly

addressed. The conclusion from research undertaken in China (Falbo, 1994; Falbo et al., 1997; Poston & Falbo, 1990) that only-children are not disadvantaged and even have a slight *advantage* over those with siblings is in contrast to Chinese research and literature. Evidence exists that there have been social difficulties for onlies, particularly with regard to independence, autonomy and separation from parents. Ivy's story (Part II) illustrates the difficulties one only-child had growing up in China. Chinese only-children are not necessarily worse off than those with siblings, but their experience is different and exemplifies many of the disadvantages revealed in the UK research when children are the sole repository of parents' expectations. In particular, they have to carry a continual level of parental focus and the responsibility to achieve and be successful. Falbo and Polit's (1986), Polit and Falbo's (1987) and Poston and Falbo's (1990) contribution has been to highlight the prevalence of the stigma about only-children, but her intention to negate the experience to a position of at worse 'no difference' at best 'better than' children with siblings, in my opinion, does a disservice to the experience of only-children which needs to be addressed.

Research critique

One of the contributions of this book to the field of only-child research is the consideration of the social, cultural and historical context, through the use of a storied approach. Much only-child research in the West is politically motivated although this is not discussed overtly in the studies. In India, the political and social assumptions are clearly defined, as this introduction to Sidhu's (2000) paper on 'Differential Family Climate with and without Siblings' indicates:

> Population is the major problem of our country. India is the second largest populated country of the World and the World's 15% population resides here. The crude birth rate according to National Family Health Service is 28.9. The major reason being a desire for a male child and taking children as God's gift. Voluntary agencies have for many years been supporting the small family concept and on 12th August 1997 the government decide to promote a single child family. It was decided the government would encourage it only gently.
>
> (Sidhu, 2000, p. 117)

Social and political views have a major effect on how people see themselves and, in my opinion, are crucial to examine when looking at the experiences of growing up an only-child. China is attempting to decrease population, but what is behind the one-child lobby in the United States? Looking more closely at Falbo and Polit's (1986) and Polit and Falbo's (1987) meta-analysis, I noted that some of the underlying assumptions reveal a particular view of only-children. This is important to note because their research has had an enormous impact on books written for the public, particularly for parents of only-children, and the media. They believe parent–child relationships are a powerful determinant of developmental outcomes and in this way only-children are *advantaged* because they receive more motivated and interactive parenting (Polit and Falbo, 1987, p. 310). However, I would question some of the so called advantages of this parenting, and some of the inferences in the language used in the meta-analysis. Before we do this, it would be interesting to look at the idea of cultural scripts with reference to Kaufman (1985).

Kaufman says that family, peers and culture all affect and shape personality. School and later work are the instruments through which 'meanings, values and taboos are transmitted' (1985, p. 28). He describes three cultural scripts which are endemic to American culture. The first is the *success ethic*, based on the ideal of the self-made man. Achievement is equated to personal worth and is a measure of self-esteem, so failure or lack of success produces feelings of inferiority and shame. Equally, competing for success devalues caring and vulnerability. The second is the injunction to be *independent and self-sufficient*. This is the image or archetype of the cowboy, pioneer or hero who proudly stands alone, and does not need anyone or anything. Neediness is seen as a sign of inadequacy and thus shameful. The third is the injunction to be *popular and conform*. Individuality is not prized; so being different, or seeming to be different from others, becomes shameful. Kaufman indicates that these scripts conflict and lead to a shame-based culture:

> It is virtually impossible to accomplish all three visions simultaneously: compete for success, be independent and self-sufficient, yet be popular and conform. These cultural scripts become additional sources of shame. Through shame, culture shapes personality.
>
> (Kaufman, 1991, p. 29)

Falbo and Polit (1986), Polit and Falbo (1987) and Newman (2001) emphasise aspects of the only-child experience which relate to Kaufman's (1985) cultural scripts. As most of the only-child research has been conducted in the United States, this is an important insight for understanding the context of the only-child in American culture. In the following discussion, we are reminded that US culture prizes such behaviours as 'high achievement' and being a 'little adult'. Only-children epitomise the potential for achieving the *success ethic* and are propelled into *being independent and self-sufficient*. At the same time, it is important to show they are *popular* and *conform* to what is expected socially.

In the meta-analysis, Falbo and Polit (1986) and Polit and Falbo (1987) documented that they believe only-children develop a greater sense of personal control:

> Under concentrated surveillance, children are more likely to learn that their behaviour elicits a reaction from their parents. Thus, we argue that only children have opportunities to learn at an early age that they affect their environments (i.e. their parents' behaviours), and are more likely to develop a sense of personal control, especially in comparison with later-borns and children from large families.
>
> (1987, p. 311)

My research found no evidence that onlies have a more developed sense of personal control. Rather they outwardly appear to be more mature but inwardly often feel lacking, borne out by other researchers such as Pitkeathley and Emerson (1994), Love and Robinson (1990) and Pickhardt (1997) who found that only-children had issues about needing to be in control because of continued overshadowing by parents. There appears to be no consideration by Polit and Falbo that 'concentrated surveillance' might not be psychologically appropriate, words more familiar to institutions or prisons.

Polit and Falbo refute the popular view that only-children are lonely or maladjusted, or suffer from parental over-indulgence and high expectations. In their earlier studies onlies were found to rate themselves as significantly less sociable than others (1987, p. 312), but when sociability was measured from peer evaluation the opposite was true. They concluded: 'these two opposing trends neutralised one another' (ibid: 312). How valid is this idea of neutralising conflicting data? The self-report overwhelmingly suggests that only-children know they appear confident to the outside world, but internally do not feel this way – confirmed by my own research. Peer evaluation also shows this discrepancy between onlies' sense of self and how others see them. Why do Polit and Falbo conclude that the meta-analysis indicates that the sociability of onlies and non-onlies is comparable, with no reference to the possible impact of the internal/external discrepancy?

Polit and Falbo believed that because only-children are closer to their parents, they would score lower on need for affiliation and extraversion when compared with sibling children. This is a result, they suggest, of onlies entertaining themselves through solitary activities and having mature social skills learned from interaction with parents. They argue that onlies need to be less sociable as a result of their maturity and ability to play alone. I would seriously question that only-children's closeness to their parents is preferable to that of their peers which underlies this idea of a lower need for affiliation and extraversion. My research suggests only-children have *high* affiliation needs because of their lack of siblings as they do not have built-in playmates. Whilst only-children may learn at an early age to amuse themselves, I have no evidence that suggests they feel more mature. However, they may appear so, simply because they spend so much more time interacting with adults, leading to the familiar 'little adult' role.

Parental attention was clearly an important factor in their research, but their findings did *not* support their belief that only-children have more positive character traits as a result of parental rather than sibling attention. Rather than seeing sibling attention as important they see it as compensatory to the lack of parental attention. Clearly the evidence from sibling studies has had little impact on their assumption that it is primarily parents who affect personality development.

It may be that parent-child and sibling relationships are compens-atory in determining development in these areas (*positive character traits*). That is, sibling relationships may 'compensate' for the lack of the close parent child relationships characteristic of one-child families, while only children may compensate for the lack of siblings through their interactions with their parents and thereby acquire comparable levels of sociability, character, and personal control' [my brackets/italics].

(1987, p. 320)

There is an underlying assumption here that parent/only-child relation-ships are inherently better than sibling relationships. Throughout their discussion they assume that close parental relationships between onlies and their parents is the norm and always beneficial. They see no poten-tial problems like neglect or enmeshment nor do they acknowledge the social and emotional benefits of siblings who are closer in age and experience to the child.

Whilst their research is important in challenging the negative only-child stereotype the research itself is more restricted in its scope than people may realise. Much of the research was undertaken on children with the mean age of 17 years. This is very young and certainly does not give insight into the internal experience of the only-child either as a child or adult. This research uses the dominant empirical research paradigm, which is comparative and focuses on behaviour, because this is deemed to be measurable. It does not address the subjective feelings of only-children nor does it include the on-going experience of living as an only throughout one's lifespan which later qualitative studies, like this one, attempt to do. Major preoccupations for the adult only-child, like the care of elderly parents, are hardly going to be an issue for onlies aged 17.

Family therapy and family systems therapy

Family therapists offer a range of views that state there are *differences* in the experiences of only-children growing up without sibling interaction. In an article exploring family therapy and only-child families, Feldman states:

> The only child and his or her parents may have special problems when it comes to settling the issues of parent-child identification and attachment. Children, regardless of birth order or number of siblings, cope more easily with the developmental tasks of the oedipal period if there is not a pressure to remain loyal to just one parental pair. The child without siblings and his/her parents face a continual oedipal triangle unless the parents maintain a comfortable and united partnership at best, or at least are able to encourage independence in the child.
>
> (1981, p. 43)

Feldman explains that the problem is the indivisible unit of three, created by the 'family romance'. The family romance is when the child becomes involved in the parents' interests, and the parents become too sensitive to the child's 'only' status and over-involve them in areas of their relationship that are not always age appropriate. She suggests this is motivated by guilt, a result of having one child, or avoidance of the marital relationship. She also found that in contrast to the views of Adler (1928) and Toman (1969), female only-children were more *independent* than those with siblings, not *dependent*, as they considered.

It is, however, the Oedipal triangle stage of development on which Feldman particularly focuses. The Oedipal developmental stage of separation and independence, attained through renunciation of the opposite sex parent and identification with the same sex parent, leads to internalised parental authority via the super-ego (Freud, 1923; Kohlberg, 1963). Feldman suggests that instead of a resolution of the Oedipal triangle for only-child families, 'the female child seems to remain fixated in her attachment to her father. The male child remains attached to a mother who reinforces dependency' (Feldman, 1981, p. 44). However, she is at pains to point out that this is not the norm, but it is based on her experience as a clinical practitioner. In her opinion, dependency and lack of separation are potential hazards for only-children whose parents have not separated from their own parents, or are avoiding problems in their own relationship. Independence and maturity are discouraged by these parents in order to avoid shattering the fragility of their own relationship. The inner conflict this causes may be expressed through ambivalence or open hostility. What is required, she believes, is for the parents to learn to cope with their own dependency needs and focus less on the child, enabling a sense of both attachment and separateness. These views coincide with my research findings discussed in the next chapter and are clearly reflected in the stories in Part II.

Bank and Kahn (1975) argue that sibling relationships are influential throughout the life cycle. There are more possibilities for a child to identify with siblings than with parents, and these can be more spontaneous and less encumbered. In their opinion, siblings help foster differentiations which can prevent fusion within the family. Brothers and sisters can provide a mutual regulatory process of an 'observing ego' unavailable to the child who has none.

Similar observations are made by Neaubauer (1982, 1983), but he also adds that siblings often share a similar psychic organisation and are particularly responsive to one another. In opposition to Falbo and Polit's (1986) and Polit and Falbo's (1987) view that parents offer the best learning environment, he states: 'Experimentation, sexual curiosity, and displacement of aggression, can provide special, shared non-traumatic experiences that go far beyond the identification with parents they share' (1983, p. 334). Neaubauer views issues of sibling rivalry, jealousy and envy as a *positive* contribution to emotional development and is in sharp contrast, which is discussed below, to the views of Newman (2001). In particular, he sees these dynamics as expressing the interactions of all psychic structural processes, enabling comparisons and facilitating differentiation of the individual.

An interesting study by Byrd et al. (1993) on the subject of separation and individuation for the only-child was set up to assess differences among adult only-children compared to the youngest and the oldest child with siblings. Sixty men and sixty women between the ages 18–45 participated to assess autonomy and cohesiveness in family interaction:

> The results therefore show that only children were less independent than oldest children. While last born children had a higher mean independence score than only children this difference was not significantly greater. It might be hypothesised that the 'dethronement process' in which the first born must relinquish only child status at the birth of a sibling is instrumental in fostering independence...It is also likely that the loss of exclusive parental attention reduces the later tendency for dependent and potentially guilt producing relationships.
>
> (Byrd et al., 1993, p. 176)

Like Feldman (1981), they were of the opinion that an important aspect of individuation and separation for only-children is the prolonged Oedipal triangle. This can create a fixated dependent relationship and lead to greater problems of separation. The parent–child relationship exclusivity inhibits the ability to neutralise aggression from the parent. Siblings give that opportunity through the 'rough and tumble' of relating, as well as a place to vent frustration and conflict. Similarly, Minuchin (1974) sees sibling rivalry as integral to the family system, offering a stabilising force. This lack of conflictual experience for the only-child may contribute to greater anxiety when dealing with aggressive feelings, and lead to greater dependency. I will now turn to some qualitative studies which also indicate there are real differences between only-children and sibling children.

Three types of only-children

An article from Genetic Psychology by Rosenberg and Hyde (1993) addresses one of the problems we have already encountered in only-child research. Looking at the research on only-children over several decades, Rosenberg and Hyde (1993) have attempted to account for the conflicting data by suggesting only-children are not a homogeneous group. After summarising the inconsistencies in the previous research, they suggest there are two opposing theoretical views. The first view states onlies suffer deprivation from lack of siblings and the learning experiences they offer and thereby are disadvantaged. The second view emphasises the uniqueness of onlies who are never dethroned and have all the parental attention. Rosenberg and Hyde's (1993) research suggests there are ' three distinct types of female only children'. *Type 1* is labelled 'normal, and well adjusted,' *Type 2* is labelled 'impulsive, and acting out' and *Type 3* is labelled 'first-bornish' (ibid: 269). They claim that these three types remain consistent over the lifespan from early adolescence to late middle age.

Rosenberg and Hyde conclude that the qualities associated with the three 'types' of only-child emerging in the study are understandable. They believe one type of only-child research reflects the outcomes and views of the 'disadvantaged category' whilst other types of research reflect only-children in the 'advantaged category'. It is interesting to see the similarity with attachment theory. Rosenberg and Hyde's *Type 1* is similar to a description of *secure* attachment that is normal and well-adjusted. *Type 2* and *Type 3* similarly shows some *insecure organised* attachment patterns. It could mean that only-children do show a higher pattern of insecure attachment, something that appeared to be the case in my own research. Rosenberg and Hyde end their research cautioning against seeing only-children as one distinct category, which I endorse.

Qualitative studies on only-children

Few studies of this nature are available, but I will refer to two, one from the United Kingdom and the other from the United States. One of the striking differences in qualitative studies is the lack of comparisons between only-children and sibling children. Rather their aim is to describe the actual experience and not quantify it or compare. The most thorough study is by Pitkeathley and Emerson (1994) who conducted interviews with over 60 only-children looking at their background, childhood, schooling, relationships and careers, also interviewing friends, partners, teachers and counsellors of only-children. Their basic premise is: 'being an only child is most definitely a special and very different childhood experience' (1994, p. 1). The book is divided into three sections. The first identifies the differences in being brought up as an only-child, the second part looks at difficulties in relationships and the final part explores what partners of only-children experience. In summarising the first section they write:

> From the only children to whom we have talked, it is clear there is a set of pressures felt to a greater or lesser extent by all of them. Having had to be everything to their parents, they have had to carry a heavy

burden of responsibility, expectation and blame. Because they lacked experience of what they called 'rough and tumble' of emotional life, they had difficulties with their self image and were inclined to be emotionally immature behind a confident, grown up exterior. Most of them felt that, in the end, the only child is always alone.

(1994, p. 152)

Pitkeathley & Emerson (1994) present a compelling argument that only-children are distinctive: 'Not worse, not better, but different' (1994, p. 1). The main theme throughout the book is the differences between the way only-children appear outwardly in the world: confident, organised and in control, and how they feel internally: unsure and insecure. The discrepancy, the authors believe, is a result of having too much parental attention at an early age. Only-children appear adult, whilst lack of siblings means there are few opportunities to develop the emotional skills that lead to a positive self-image and emotional maturity. Mixing with other children may appear to be offering the same opportunities, but in reality the only-child is already at a disadvantage. Having primarily interacted with adults, they tend to do the same with peers, appearing serious and less comfortable with what they perceive as 'childish' behaviour. This discomfort can lead them to seem different, not knowing the rules of the game, whilst there are no adults to monitor their behaviour. For many only-children, playing with others can be traumatic leading them to withdraw, thus exacerbating the problem of difference. This appears to be the case, even with children who had mixed with other children in a pre-school setting, because most still felt both alone and an outsider (1994, p. 156). They also claim that the only-child's experience of being brought up without siblings leads to the development of a particular outlook that influences and 'produces distinctly different patterns of behaviour that get in the way of successful relationships, confuse partners, create problems at work and produce a permanent sense of isolation' (1994, p. 10). They conclude that:

Relating to brothers and sisters and having to accommodate them, however reluctantly, is an invaluable training for later life. Sure, you can get by without it. Sure, you can often catch up on the experience later as many only children do. Sure, not having to think about others leaves you freer to achieve academically, to take on adult responsibilities earlier. But what siblings do provide is an emotional training for life that is difficult, if not impossible to replicate.

(1994, p. 76)

Research undertaken by Roberts & White-Blanton (2001) focused on the subjective experience of being an only-child, because 'little is known about the subjective experiences of such individuals' (2001, p. 125). From a sample of 20 young adults in the United States, in-depth interviews were carried out, revealing both assets and challenges in the only-child experience. The interview transcripts were analysed into four thematic units briefly summarised here:

Having no sibling relationships. Most participants were not upset by their lack of siblings, although some had a life-long wish for one. Many were pleased they did not have to share parental resources, or compete for parental attention. They enjoyed and valued time alone, but also missed the emotional connection a sibling would provide, particularly when there were difficulties in family life. Some also believed lack of siblings had negatively affected their relational development. Feelings of isolation and tendencies to become self-isolating and reclusive were expressed (2001, p. 130).

Closeness of the child parent relationships. The majority felt grateful for the close bond they had with their parents, often seeing them as 'friends' and spending more time with them than their own friends did. However, some felt the pressure to succeed, and believed the undivided attention they had received from their parents had negatively affected their development. This was seen in the need to control, both people and situations, whilst others felt they lacked life-skills because they had not been given enough responsibility for themselves (2001, p. 132–4).

Being a 'small adult'. Spending large amounts of time in adult company was associated with 'unusual maturity' and the basis for close parental ties. Conversely many had problems in relating to peers, preferring older friends and partners, some said they were accused of speaking and behaving more like parents (2001, p. 134–5).

Ageing parents. Ageing parents was the main concern for the young adults interviewed. They were also anxious about outliving their parents, and appeared 'to feel a lack of lifespan continuity'. Some regretted they would never be an uncle or aunt, and many felt pressure from their parents to have grandchildren. Many wanted only one child because they worried about how to parent multiple children (2001, p. 135–6).

Roberts and White-Blanton (2001) researching from an Adlerian perspective, were addressing the 1990 Gallup poll that indicated 70 per cent of US residents believe only-children are at a disadvantage compared to those with siblings. College students (Nyman, 1995, cited in Roberts and White-Blanton 2001) also rated the only-child position as the least desirable. The research concluded with recommendations for further research into the subjective experience of only-children. It also called for a greater awareness of the challenges parents of only-children face and the break down of negative only-child myths.

There is a growing range of parenting books, a result of increasing numbers of only-children. I believe these have arisen to counteract the negative stereotypes of spoiled, self-centred, selfish, immature, perfectionist, unfriendly and rigid only-children, and a result of a negative public image. They are particularly focused on promoting only-children as 'no different' or 'better than' children with siblings.

Parenting an only-child

The following material may be considered as less academic, although it is based on research, mostly that of Falbo et al. This literature is in the public domain and has affected public views about the only-child. Whilst there is a lack of current literature about the *experiences* of only-children, there is a growing literature on how to bring up an only-child to avoid spoiling and creating self-centred, selfish children. This is interesting, as one might assume from this that only-children are particularly prone to these negative traits (Hawke & Knox, 1977; Kappelman, 1975; Laybourn, 1994; Nachman & Thompson, 1997; Newman, 1990/2001; Peck, 1977; Pickhardt, 1997; Sifford, 1989). Many of the books are self-help in nature, and attempt to break down myths and prejudices, whilst offering advice to parents. The broadest ranging, academic and influential in the United States is Dr. Susan Newman's *'Parenting the Only Child'* (1990), fully revised and expanded in 2001. It reflects both a particular value system and psychological perspective and has a cultural bias. Newman is a social psychologist who describes herself as an 'authority' on only-children. A mother of an only-child, she was also a step-parent to four children in a previous marriage, and has two sisters herself. I raise this, because I think it impacts on her views, which stress the problems parents encounter bringing up sibling children. Newman suggests difficulties, such as sibling rivalry, can be avoided by having only one child. Parents of only-children in the United States are very political in promoting the benefits of having an only-child which is evidenced by the US website www.onlychild.com. Two statements that underlie Newman's thinking are of particular interest. I have italicised particular points:

> Conventional parenting as we knew it – Mom at home with two children, Dad at work – is ancient history. *And we know that sibling*

interaction is simply not required to raise a happy, involved, well-adjusted and productive child.

(2001, p. 241)

This last sentence appears to ignore the research illustrated above that shows sibling interactions are important for social and emotional maturity. It is much more in keeping with the assumptions I highlighted in the meta-analysis of Falbo and Polit (1986) and Polit and Falbo (1987). She continues:

Every one of us wants to be recognised, to be the centre of attention, maybe not constantly, but more often than not. Centre stage in moderate doses is a supreme luxury. Why not let your only – or planned only – *soar to his or her greatest heights with every benefit the singleton status provides?*

One child opens vistas not possible to the multi-child family. *Parents can fulfil their own personal dreams while raising, educating, and enjoying a child who will be loved, secure, and privileged, and feel, loved, secure, and privileged* [my italics].

(2001, p. 242)

The three italicised statements reflect Newman's position which I will briefly describe. Her audience are parents or would-be parents, specifically women. Her arguments are focused on *parental* needs, particularly *economic* and *emotional*. The *economic* argument centres on the cost of a second child in the United States. She sees this as prohibitive: pre-natal, natal and post-natal care, child-care, nursery, school and college education, summer camps, extra-curricular activities, sports, ad infinitum. The underlying assumption is that these things need to be provided for a healthy child and if you cannot provide them you cannot afford to have a second child.

The *emotional* argument is more complex but also focuses on parent needs. First, Newman argues that having a second child will have an adverse effect on the home environment with less time for personal pursuits, difficulties in combining a career and less attention for a partner (2001, p. 54). However, this apparently does not occur with one child. Newman also warns against the lack of status that follows if you have to compromise your career to bring up more than one child. She says it can lead to lack of self-esteem – a result of relying on financial support from a partner. (Perhaps she has personal experience of this.)

Already we can see the cultural scripts of being 'independent and self-sufficient' and 'successful'.

An assumption that pervades Newman's book is the idea that parents have children in part to fulfil their dreams (their own career being the other dream). Only-children are pictured as over-achievers who want to do the best for their parents. Newman spends some time dealing with the pitfalls of taking this to extreme. She suggests parents should not put too much pressure on their child, are circumspect about advertising their child's achievements, are careful that the child does not rule the home and balance receiving with giving. This is good advice. However, when she attempts to dispel the 'myths' of the only-child, I was left wondering what was really being addressed. Here are two examples: *Myth 10: Only children become too mature too quickly.* On the one hand, she agrees they do become more mature but says, 'Being comfortable with adults and acting mature enough so they do not mind having a child around opens vast opportunities for learning to the only child' (2001, p. 45). They learn to copy adult behaviour and speech patterns which 'can't possibly harm the only child'. She concludes the section:

> ... mature reasoning permits only children to react in more responsible and adult ways. They are better equipped to recognise and handle problems without going into juvenile tailspins and resorting to childish behaviour – a quality that wins the admiration of adults. This face of maturity, rather than being detrimental, actually helps ease many of the ups and downs children encounter.
>
> (2001, p. 6)

Is copying adult behaviour and speech patterns quite the same as mature reasoning? Only-children may appear more responsible and adult and may not go into 'juvenile tailspins' or 'childish behaviour', but surely this is an example of learned behaviour leading to the 'adapted child' or the 'false self'. Whilst this may win the 'admiration' of some adults, it would appear Newman sees having an only-child as a way of avoiding childish behaviour. Surely to be childish is to behave as a child, what can be more natural than that? Children need to learn social skills but this is different from behaving like a 'little adult'. Pitkeathley and Emerson (1994), Roberts and White-Blanton (2001), Pickhardt (1997), Feldman (1981) and even Winnicott (1957) all argue that precociousness or taking on the persona of the 'little adult' is detrimental to the personal development of the only-child.

Myth 11: Only children have more emotional problems; they are malad-justed, anxious and unhappy. I think her argument about psychiatric visits quoting Falbo is particularly unclear:

> According to Dr Toni Falbo, 'there are no differences in emotional health among only and non-only children.' Although onlies are 'more likely to be referred for clinical help and to repeat visits to the clinic' Dr Falbo points out the 'investigators suggested that the major reason for this relatively high referral and repeat rate was the overprotective attitude of the parents'.
>
> It is important to underscore that the closeness for the only child to his parents allows them to be in touch and notice if something is amiss'.
>
> (2001, p. 46)

What does this mean? On the one hand, we are told there are no differences in emotional health between onlies and non-onlies, and then we are told they are more likely to be referred for clinical help with repeat visits. The last sentence infers this is a result of parental over-protection, and the final sentence neutralises this by saying it is because parents are more 'in touch' with their child. What appears to be avoided is the fact that over-protection has its own pitfalls, indicates enmeshment and many of the issues highlighted by family therapists (Bank & Kahn, 1975; Byrd et al., 1993; Feldman, 1981; Neaubauer 1982, 1983).

I think these two points taken from Newman's (2001) book illustrate that she is more motivated in the political promotion of parents having an only-child than actually looking at what the experience might be for the child itself. Newman, I think, has gone too far with the pro one-child lobby. I believe this does a disservice to only-children. She appears to be more concerned with parental well-being and dispelling the negative stereotype of only-child traits than looking at what it is like to grow up as an only-child.

Dr Ann Laybourn (1994) has written one of the few books for the UK market. She is also at great pains to expose the myths around only-children, and leans heavily on Falbo's research findings. She acknowledges the power of the popular stereotype of only-children as spoilt, selfish and self-centred, but having surveyed much of the research concludes there is little evidence of difference between only-children and people brought up with siblings. She dismisses Pitkeathley and Emerson's (1994) extensive findings, suggesting their research 'may have alighted on a particularly problem-ridden group' of adult only-children

(1994, p. 7). The difference in opinion between Jill Pitkeathley and Ann Laybourn was debated on BBC Radio Four, Woman's Hour (2004). Laybourn referred to her own and Falbo's research and claimed there are no real differences between onlies and non-onlies. She believes the primary reason for only-children feeling different is a result of negative conditioning: being told from a young age they are different, rather than any real experiential difference. She did, however, make the point that only-child adults were more likely to divorce or separate. Surely this suggests some difficulties in relationships?

Returning to the United States, the most useful and informative book, now out of print, is *Keys to Parenting the Only Child* (Pickhardt, 1997), which is informed by Pickhardt's experience of running parenting workshops and counselling only-children and their parents. It is the most coherent book on the discussion of the benefits, drawbacks and challenges of the one-child family. His starting point is that both parent–child and child–peer relationships differ when compared with sibling families. He challenges the 'myth' that bringing up an only-child is easier; rather different to the myths addressed in other parenting books (Laybourn, 1994; Newman, 2001). Similar to Winnicott (1957), Pickhardt suggests:

> Because parents find themselves extremely preoccupied with an only child, the sense of attachment can become very strong, responsible decision making can become very labour intensive, separation can be very painful, letting go can become hard to do, and an extremely emotionally sensitized relationship can develop between parents and child.
>
> (1997, p. viii)

Simply written, this book covers many of the areas witnessed in my interviews and in hundreds of emails I have received from only-children worldwide. Unlike other books, Pickhardt explores adolescence in detail and the difficulties of separation and dependency. In line with my own thinking, he suggests that only-children are not necessarily disadvantaged by not having siblings, as long as the parents have a secure attachment with the child. However, when this is not possible, he clearly illustrates the pitfalls of exclusive attention, lack of separation, fulfilling parents' needs through the child and the sense of obligation and duty only-children can feel towards their parents. All aspects that Newman and Falbo appear to value as positive only-child experiences!

Media coverage

To contextualise the debate about only-children from a social and cultural perspective, an overview of typical media coverage gives an insight into how 'the man in the street' regards this phenomenon. Academic research is important but 'popular' opinion reflects what many people believe. Whether positive or detrimental, to ignore it is to ignore an important influence.

Magazines and newspapers are a source of a lively debate on the pros and cons of the only-child status. Many themes are also echoed on website message boards, chat rooms and the US journal: *Onlychild* – for parents of only-children. The most common theme, in articles written in the last few years, is loneliness and aloneness. Many articles have similar titles:

- *Only the Lonely* – *Guardian* (2004);
- *Sole Survivors* – *Guardian* (2002);
- *The One and Only* – *Observer* (2001a); and
- *Lone Stars* – *Observer* (2001b).

Letters I wrote to the *Telegraph* and *Times*, respectively were re-titled by the editors: *A Lonely Existence* – *Telegraph* (2004) and *Only the Lonely* – *Sunday Times* (2004), yet the point I was making was that only-children have different experiences than children with siblings, and I did *not* dwell on loneliness. I am left wondering why a sibling society needs to highlight the loneliness and simultaneously deny the different experience of having no siblings?

In the United States, newspapers, magazines and web journals reflect parallel themes and a variety of opinions similar to the United Kingdom. Here are a few examples in the last decade:

- *Only-children are people too;*
- *Myths of the only-child;*
- *No more 'lonely the only' Parents of onlies lose the guilt as the kids adjust, society adjusts;*
- *When you have just one;* and
- *Kids without siblings lack social skills.*

Many more articles in a similar vein suggest popular opinion sees the only-child in a disadvantaged place. This is borne out by an article in the *Observer* (2001b, June 10th) which noted the 'largely negative' newspaper coverage on only-children over a period of five years. The negative stereotype of being an only may be abating (Laybourn, 1994; Newman, 1990/2001) but the stigma remains, illustrated by the growing number of books for parents on bringing up only-children and media coverage.

Summary

In this chapter, four differing viewpoints concerning only-children were used as a framework to explore literature and research pertaining to the only-child and the importance of sibling relationships. The differences in an empirical 'behaviour'-orientated research approach that attempts to look at only-children from an objective stance is contrasted with a 'meaning' approach that tries to understand the subjective experience of the only-child's being-in-the-world.

Different views of personality development were discussed, with regard to siblings, and that a lack of siblings is thought by some psychoanalytic writers (Coles, 2003; Mitchell, 2003; Winnicott, 1957) and family systems therapists (Bank & Kahn, 1975; Byrd, et al., 1993; Feldman, 1981; Love & Robinson, 1990; Minuchin, 1974; Neaubauer, 1982, 1983) to affect psychic development on an emotional and social level. These writers see siblings as an important resource for both developing emotional skills, like coping with conflict, and social skills, like dealing with competition. They therefore fall into the category of seeing the only-child experience as being one which is *inherently different*.

Birth-order research has tried to find evidence of birth-order differences in personality. However, the problem with all birth-order studies is the problem of *comparison* and the presence of a large number of variables which often leads to inconsistent results. Falbo and Polit's (1986) and Polit & Falbo's (1987) meta-analysis highlights many of these inconsistencies in the field of only-child research, leaving them to conclude there are no real differences between only-children and those with siblings. Whereas Sulloway (1998), who reviewed all the birth-order studies, believes there is evidence of birth-order differences and sees siblings as having an impact on personality development.

The research on birth-order difference, although interesting, is easily criticised, but this does not mean that there are no quantifiable differences between people of different birth-order categories, it just means they are difficult to quantify. How useful is it to attempt to quantify, I think, is another question. I would suggest that the evidence from the two qualitative research projects (Pitkeathley and Emerson, 1994; Roberts and White-Blanton, 2001) gives us a much clearer view of the way only-children experience their world, without having to claim uniqueness for the only-child experience or enter into the problematic area of quantifying those differences compared to sibling children.

One of the difficulties in talking about difference between only-children and sibling children is that it quickly leads to comparisons of better or worse, positive and negative. In the early twentieth century, large families were the norm and the phenomenon of the only-child unusual. The latter led to a tendency to view the only-child negatively, particularly by psychologists like Hall and Brill who favoured the large family experience for psychological health. Some psychologists portray only-children in a detrimental light. This is particularly apparent in China, where psychology and popular opinion unite in the view of the phenomenon of the 'Little Emperor' which encapsulates the negative perspective of only-children. However, it is also true that there have been problems associated with child-rearing practices of Chinese only-children which Falbo's (1984) research seeks to challenge.

Media research both in the United States and the United Kingdom exemplifies conflicting views inherent in the only-child debate. Parenting books, although written to dispel the myths, also highlight the difficulties involved for only-children growing up in a sibling society. Most writers, except Pickhardt (1997), do not address this in a systematic way. The research by Falbo (1984) has broken down some of the prejudice surrounding only-children. This is to be applauded. However, I also believe it has gone too far when it claims there are no differences in the experience of onlies compared to non-onlies, particularly the further claim that only-children are advantaged, as that surely assumes a difference. I would also disagree with their assumptions on what is advantageous in parenting an only-child. These are based on questionable cultural values. In fact, I would argue these values can be seen as the root of difficulties only-children experience. I consider there is enough evidence from psychoanalytic literature and family systems theory to hold the view that the only-child experience is indeed different. Perhaps a more useful question might be: How is it different? In the next chapter, I will offer a different approach and a new way of understanding the only-child phenomena.

2
The Research Framework

In this chapter, I explore how a different approach to researching only-child experience reveals a more complex and multi-dimensional result. This book takes its starting point from an original in-depth study that has been the basis for continued research over the last five years. To understand this evolving process I will begin by outlining my original research protocol, describe the underlying epistemology and the theoretical concepts that underpin the research analysis. I used a flexible design that included a narrative inquiry, life-story approach with heurism and reflexivity. The philosophical underpinning is social constructionism and I used a voice-centred relational model to give a structure to my research findings. I will describe these briefly and outline the reasons for these choices, which are connected to both my interest as a practicing psychotherapist and the research subject of the adult only-child experience. Finally, I reflect on the stories that emerged from my findings and the themes that arose, these will then be explored more fully in a series of only-child stories which are based on the original longer stories of my research.

A qualitative approach

I was drawn to a qualitative approach because it values subjective experience and the aim of my research was to discover how adult only-children *experience* their onlyness and the meaning they have attributed to it. Whilst quantitative methods of collecting and interpreting data has its place, it left me with no 'feel' of what it was like for those participants to be an only-child. There is a need to understand the only-child experience in the context of people's *lives as a whole*. For this reason, a qualitative approach was suited to my research as it allows a more focused, in-depth approach and an opportunity to contribute to the research literature in a different, yet complementary way.

As qualitative research takes into account the *context* of the subject of enquiry under the headings of social, historical, personal and cultural, this fitted well with my therapeutic approach as an integrative psychotherapist who values the intra-, inter- and extra-psychic forces on the personality. Qualitative research also relies more on hypothesis-generating, rather than hypothesis-testing, and has a preference for meanings which is the focus of my study rather than behaviour. Observation is a key element (Silverman, 2000, p. 8) and the use of unstructured interviews rather than structured also suited the approach I wanted to take.

Awareness of the social construction of reality and an interest in feminist research methods were the impetus to look with fresh eyes at the only-child experience from the idea of a commonality of experience. Initially, I chose only female co-researchers to redress the balance of earlier studies in the United States, which were mainly with young children or men of college age. There was little specifically on women and I wished to offer a voice to women in this research.

A primary aim of qualitative research is to develop an understanding of how the world is constructed. The implication is that we inhabit a social, personal and relational world that is complex, multi-layered and can be viewed from different perspectives.

> This social reality can be seen as multiply constructed. We construct the world through talk (stories, conversations), through action, through systems of meaning, through memory, through rituals, and institutions, that have been created, through the ways in which the world is physically and materially shaped.
>
> (McLeod, 2001, p. 2)

As a qualitative enquirer, I wish to know and understand how the world is constructed, but paradoxically it is already known to me through my own cognitive and interpretive inward experience. How I make sense of the world influences how I see the world, and of course how I see others. As a researcher and as a therapist, I am interested in trying to comprehend how others make sense of their world, keeping in mind that the world is socially constructed 'of common-sense understandings' (McLeod, 2001), which rarely appear as either consistent or coherent. This is the heart of social constructionism which endeavours to deconstruct social reality, by acknowledging its place within an historical and cultural perspective. However, as McLeod states:

> Implicit in any form of qualitative enquiry is the realisation that, ultimately, we can never really know how the world is constructed. We can never achieve a complete 'scientific' understanding of the human world. The best we can do is to arrive at a truth that makes a difference that opens up new possibilities for understanding. This understanding is forever incomplete. The best thing we can do is perhaps to make a temporary 'clearing' within which some things may be better understood, at least for a while.
>
> (2001, p. 4)

My research, therefore, is not aimed to produce 'grand theory' (Silverman, 2000), but to illustrate the different ways of knowing and understanding each co-researcher's sense of being an only-child in a social and cultural setting over the period of their life. This type of qualitative research is what McLeod calls *'knowledge of the other'* (2001, p. 3). This is useful to counsellors and psychotherapists, as we are inevitably socialised into stereotypical views of groups of people and these can be detrimental to the people we serve. Only-children, I would argue, have in the past been disadvantaged by a negative stereotype. My research was designed to offer only-children a 'voice' allowing their life-stories and experiences to emerge, to benefit the knowledge base of my own and other professions. Initially, choosing women gave a voice to their experience and acknowledged the importance of the social construction of their experience in a gendered society where power is still predominantly controlled by men.

Witness

As an only-child and a woman, I had the opportunity to immerse myself in my co-researchers' worlds and in their understandings and experience. One of the obvious but profound issues for an only-child is that I/we have never had a sibling to compare experiences with, in the context of the family dynamic. That sense of 'witness', of how it was, is something I wanted to give myself and my co-researchers. The significance of 'witness' is a key element in therapy and it was my intention to bring this therapeutic aspect to my research, as Frank writes: 'Becoming a witness assumes a responsibility for telling what happened. The witness offers testimony to a truth that is generally unrecognised or suppressed' (Frank, 1995, p. 137).

Connected with witness is the issue of power, a key issue in feminist research. At each stage of the research cycle, my co-researchers had an active involvement. I was mindful of the tension between placing myself in the centre of the research whilst not marginalising the voices of my co-researchers. As Braud and Anderson state:

> Contributing to the appeal and power of the various feminist research approaches (e.g. Nielson 1990) are their emphasis on the voices of the Others, providing opportunities for unassimilated others (other persons and other experiences that have not been valued or privileged within the dominant culture) to speak their own stories with their own voices and opportunities for these voices to be listened to and honored.
>
> (1998, p. 45)

Braud and Anderson continue with the notion that unassimilated others lead to 'separation, fragmentation and dis-ease', an incompleteness of worldview. They suggest assimilating others through story-telling and story-listening, as this leads to integration, wholeness and health. I chose my methodology in this vein, to offer a voice to myself and all the people who have agreed to take part in my research in a spirit of participation and adventure. Starting from my own subjective experience, moving to an inter-subjective experience through interviews with co-researchers and finally offering a platform to all only-children by means of the onlychild website, I hope to offer you, the reader, some public knowledge of only-child experience.

Heuristic research and reflexivity

I chose an heuristic approach because the spirit of 'exploration and discovery' is central to my thinking, and as Kleining and Witt (2001) write: 'qualitative heuristics try to bring back the qualities of exploration and discovery into psychological and sociological academic research' (2001, p. 4). In particular, two aspects attracted me – one is the way it lends itself to the practice of reflexivity and the second is the use of 'self' and 'subjective experience'. Heuristic thinking is *not* focused on one solution but rather seeks to find a multiplicity of possible solutions, encouraging divergent rather than convergent thinking. Moustakas (1990) believes self-dialogue and self-discovery are the trademarks of heurism and the heuristic process. It can only be validated by the people who are involved in it and only they can verify that their stories are a true representation and have been appropriately analysed. The question he poses about *validity* is:

> Does the ultimate depiction of the experiences derive from ones own rigorous, exhaustive self-searching and from the explications of others present comprehensively, vividly and accurately the meanings and essences of the experience?
>
> (1990, p. 32)

Validity, therefore, is not based on quantitative measurement and statistics, but on 'meaning', gathered from the process the heuristic researcher has gone through. This involves processes such as self-dialogue, tacit knowledge, intuition, indwelling and focusing on one's internal frame of reference. Here all knowledge, however it is derived, whether implicit, explicit or tacit, needs to be understood by the researcher. Polanyi (1969) says: 'there are no ultimate rules to guide verification, it is the scientist who makes the ultimate decision based on their own personal pursuit of knowledge and judgement. They decide what is presented as truth and what is removed as implausible' (p. 120).

Life-story and narrative inquiry

A *life-story*, narrative approach was chosen because of an interest in stories as a means of illustrating ideas, thoughts and feelings whilst conveying messages, morals and myths. Using stories as a medium for communicating is an ancient one, pre-dating the written word. Oral traditions and the power of story-telling have always fascinated me and as a therapist, I am also drawn to narrative therapy, which I first encountered in the works of David Epston (1992, 1998), Michael White (1989) and White and Epston (1990). There is much diversity in the use of life-stories and one of my tasks was to find a way of using those that benefited my research outcomes.

Atkinson (1998) describes the *life-story* as 'a tool that has many applications', but the aspect that distinguishes this approach is the presentation of the life-story in the words of the person telling the story. He states: 'The finished product is entirely a first person narrative, with the researcher removed as much as possible from the text' (1998, p. 3). What is left is a mini-autobiography, co-created, but with no explicit recognition of the co-creation. This particular view of life-story has been challenged as the researcher is not illuminated in the process. Postmodern ideas are concerned with idea of a 'relational self', being more concerned with what goes on between people – the inter-subjective experience. Examples are McLeod (1997), Sarbin (1986), Mair (1989) and MacIntyre (1981) who write about inhabiting a 'storied world', whilst Gergen (1988) states people can be understood as a living 'text'. The telling of stories gives us personal meaning and is an opportunity to explore the way we see and understand ourselves. According to Spence (1982, p. 458) 'the core of our identity is really a narrative thread that gives meaning to our life.' As long as this thread is not broken by life-crises, our personal stories can sustain us:

> Part of my sense of self depends on my being able to go backward and forward in time and weave a story about who I am, how I got that way, and where I am going, a story that is continuously nourishing and self-sustaining. Take that away from me and I am significantly less.
>
> (Spence, 1982, p. 458)

The process of story-telling is a dynamic one involving both the teller and listener who through the encounter find meaning.

Birch (1998) suggests that 'It is the telling of life stories that gives the individual a sense of who he or she is, a sense of self' (p. 172). Like Burkitt (1991) and Wiley (1995), Birch talks about the 'self in dialogue' that leads to the construction of a sense of self-identity through dynamic interactions between the self and others, on an inner and outer level, private and public, social and psychological. A theme which I hope is reflected throughout this book. The reflexive stance can be set in motion by telling life-stories. Braud and Anderson (1998) outline three occurrences that happen when we ask people to describe their experiences in life-stories: First, new knowledge and information may emerge. Secondly, it offers the co-researcher opportunities to learn more about themselves through telling their story, as well as giving a space for integration and assimilation; this can be a healing experience. Thirdly, the relational aspect of the interview affects both the researcher and co-researchers, resulting in 'change and transformation' in the lives of each. 'These three processes occur simultaneously, and each feeds the others in synergistic ways.' (1998, p. 43). Life-story research seemed a very appropriate medium to gather and reflect on the only-child experience for both myself and my co-researchers.

Narrative research, like life-story research, is based on the idea of gathering lived-stories and through 'analysing' these stories gaining an insight into the story-teller's world of meaning. Narrative inquiry has many proponents, who emphasise different foci, for example, analysing the *structure* of the story, rather than the *power relations* in the production of the story, or the actual *language* of the narrative (Riessman, 1993, p. 19).

Etherington (2001, 2004) makes a distinction between 'narrative analysis' and 'analysis of narrative' – the former seeks to keep the wholeness of the story and can be termed narrative method and the latter, in contrast, uses a tool like discourse analysis or grounded theory to understand and deconstruct the narrative. The purpose of narrative method is to capture lived-experience, a process that also facilitates 'insider information' about what it is like to be that person and is a way of both ordering experience and constructing meaning. Etherington writes about narrative inquiry as 're-presenting people's stories as told by them', she continues:

> Because there is a complex interaction between the worlds the individual inhabits and their understanding of that world, narratives are suited to portraying how people experience their position in relation to a culture, whether on the margins, being part of, or on becoming part of a new culture. When people tell us stories we hear their feelings, thoughts and attitudes and the richness of the narrative helps us to understand themselves, their strategies for coping and how they make theoretical sense of their lives.
>
> (2002, p. 167)

Narratives are embedded within historical, cultural beliefs and practices (Etherington, 2002, 2003; Polkinghorne, 1995), but they also contain local knowledge, individual stories and personal experience (Etherington, 2002, 2003, 2004; Mauthner & Doucet, 1998; Miller, 1998; Ribbens & Edwards, 2000; Standing, 1998). Stories usually have a dominant 'voice' but this is often only one voice among many. Stories in Western culture most often reflect the dominant male value system, the 'mono-myth' (Atkinson, 1998) of the hero on a quest to overcome adversity or travail. This idea of a personal myth suggests that the self is somehow unitary and a coherent sense of self can be captured. Narrative inquiry uses the concept of 'a community of selves' (Josselson, 1996; Mair, 1977) which moves us from the view of a single-storied self to one of a multiple-storied self. The self then becomes a part of a 'multiplicity of narratives attached to different situations and relationships, places and people' (McLeod, 1997). Narrative methods attempt to allow other voices to emerge even when they are less strong and incomplete. Within each narrative a multitude of discourses compete, whilst resisting being reduced to a single voice.

Voice

The challenge was to find a way of facilitating these voices to emerge and to capture them in a written narrative. The 'voice-centred relational model' (Mauthner & Doucet, 1998) based on the idea of a relational ontology of 'selves in relation' (Ruddick, 1989) or 'relational being' (Jordan, 1993) was influential in the design of both the research and this book.

> The voice-centred-relational method... represents an attempt to translate this relational ontology into methodology and into concrete methods of data analysis by exploring individuals' narrative accounts in terms of their relationships to the people around them and their relationships to the broader social, structural and cultural contexts within which they live.
>
> (Mauthner & Doucet, 1998, p. 126)

Using the idea of private and public lives and personal subjective experience, the model centres on these three titles: private, personal and public. The *private* world is the world of the 'I' and other personal pronouns, and shows us the way a person sees themselves and their sense of agency in life. It is in the private world that we begin to hear the multi-layered voices, views and perspectives bound up in the 'I'. The *personal* world is the inter-relational world of parents, partners, children, friends and relations. The *public* world refers to the cultural context and the social structures; it is the broader picture and the context in which people live.

The voice-centred relational model felt more appropriate to heuristic and narrative inquiry because it facilitated the multiplicity of selves to emerge seeing them as selves or voices-in-relation. (A different approach like grounded theory would have been useful for the collection of themes and categories, but the final composite story would have failed to hold the uniqueness of each person's experience. Neither could grounded theory *demonstrate* the process of reflection and decision making, whilst allowing the researcher to have their own voice and perspective in the process, which is fundamental to a voice-centred relational model.) However, the terms private, personal and public are ones belonging to sociology. In this book, I have broadened their definition to bring a psychological perspective although the sociological aspects of this research are equally important. Thus my term *private* refers to the intra-psychic common to psychoanalytic and psychodynamic thinking, but goes further because it consists of the multiplicity of selves rather than the idea of a unitary self common to both humanistic and psychodynamic perspectives (McLeod, 1997). The *personal* is the inter-psychic and is affected by the quality of the primary relationship which subsequently affects later relationships. Sibling relationships are also significant as they provide valuable social and emotional learning that is important for peer relationships and later intimate relationships. Finally, the *public* sphere refers to the socially constructed world which I have termed extra-psychic. This holds the paradoxical view of the only-child as one to be both envied and pitied.

There are a number of different uses of the term 'voice' in this book. First, voice refers to the idea of relational ontology and the idea of a multiplicity of selves and voices and specifically to the voice-centred relational model of analysis, which I use as an attempt to explore my co-researchers' narrative accounts in terms of their relationship to themselves and the people around them in the context of their broader relationship within the social, structural and cultural contexts in which they live. In this form of data analysis, 'voice' represents the interconnectedness we have as human beings with others, a view that is also integral to a narrative approach. This is in contrast to the predominant ontological image of the separate self-sufficient, independent and rational self. The phrase 'three voices' refers to the private, personal and public which is the framework that holds together the themes emerging from the co-researchers' stories.

Secondly, offering a 'voice' to my co-researchers refers to the opportunity to explore the range of only-child experiences in relation to each of us. Thus, 'voice' in this context refers to the co-researchers' stories and includes the multiple voices of the co-researchers, the voices and perspective of myself as a researcher and the theoretical voices that underpin this method of analysis. My use of the plural term 'voices' in the stories refers to the multiplicity of thoughts, ideas and views emanating from my co-researchers' stories. Some voices are louder and more dominant, others are less formed or emerging, whilst others are in dialogue and may be contradictory articulating opposing positions, different viewpoints or ways of assessing a situation, (i.e. 'being an only-child is good' but the tale told offers other possible interpretations).

The term 'voice' also represents my attempt as a qualitative researcher to equalise the unequal relationship and power dynamics between the researcher and the researched. It is this element of voice that underpins my research on only-child adults who up till now have rarely had their voices heard in the predominantly quantitative research methods used.

> ...this approach respects the role of the researcher and indeed the necessity of the researcher having her own voice and perspective in this process. By providing a way of reading and listening to an interview text '...that takes into account both our stance as researchers and the stance of the person speaking within the text' (Gilligan et al. 1990:96) this approach respects and to some extent exposes the *relationship* between researcher and research.
>
> (Mauthner & Doucet , 1998, p. 135)

The stories we co-created give 'voice' to the only-child experience. The stories are a testimony of what we have shared and witnessed together (Frank, 1995) which produce the voices that encapsulate the only-child experience.

Finally, I have used the word 'co-researcher' rather than the more common 'research participant' for those people who were generous enough to give me their time to explore and reflect on the only-child experience. The word conjures the important aspect of inter-subjectivity that is central to this book. Specifically, it refers to the epistemological stance where I have attempted to be as transparent as possible and have endeavoured to include my co-researchers at each point of the research process thereby as far as possible equalising power and making the process one of reciprocity.

Thus, the rationale for the choice of a flexible design approach (Robson, 2002, p. 547) was the need to allow the design to evolve through the data collection and analysis stage, allowing me to use my own reflexivity alongside the subjective and inter-subjective interview experience of my co-researchers. This facilitated the emergence of multiple realities and multiple voices situated in a historical, cultural and social context. Choosing a life-story narrative approach offered a useful means for gaining insight into experience and meaning whilst being cognisant of issues of historical time and place and the social and cultural context that are embedded in the stories. A narrative life-story approach also became a useful tool for communicating these stories to others via the onlychild website. Stories encourage people, both lay and professional, to gain insight and are a rich medium for learning. The only-child experience, made public, gave an opportunity for readers to relate or resonate with that experience and create another feedback loop influencing the ongoing process of my research. Clandidin and Connelly (2000) state a narrative approach is not about knowledge so much as an opportunity to vicariously experience others' perceptions.

> The contribution of a narrative inquiry is more often intended to be the creation of a new sense of meaning and significance with respect to the research topic than it is to yield a set of knowledge claims that might incrementally add to knowledge in the field. Furthermore, many narrative studies are judged to be important when they become literary texts to be read by others not so much for the knowledge they contain but for the vicarious testing of life possibilities by readers of the research they permit'.
>
> (Clandidin & Connelly, 2000, p. 42)

Interviews

I selected eight adult female only-children from ages 20+ to 70+ from different socio-economic backgrounds who had responded to my request for co-researchers via friends, colleagues and interested parties. I had many more offers than I was able to use, and as I wanted as much diversity as possible I made age one of the main criteria in order to gain a generational perspective. Co-researchers all live in Southern England, although most do not originate from there. All are white, one is from Eastern Europe, another part-German and some were brought up in the North of England. Their social backgrounds vary from poor working class, both industrial and agricultural, armed forces, middle class and professional backgrounds. The other major aspect of selection was co-researcher time availability. I realised that anyone taking part in the research would be making a significant commitment of time. Some people were initially enthusiastic to take part, but soon felt unable to offer enough availability. Time was discussed with each co-researcher before we began and continued to be negotiated at different phases, as circumstances changed for them and me.

Before I began the interviews, my colleague interviewed me so that I could experience the type of unstructured interview I was going to use. This enabled me to be aware of the way the interview changes focus and how empathic responding enables the process of elucidating meaning. The non-directive approach on subject matter worked well for the first interview, but I adapted this subsequently in order to focus on emerging material in more depth, part of my flexible design. I also began writing a journal to monitor my critical thinking and personal reflexivity and to be aware of my biases, assumptions and values.

Conducted over a period of a year, interviews of 1 to 2 hours were followed up, by either a second interview, sometimes more, or an ongoing dialogue by post or email. These were taped and transcribed and returned to the co-researchers for comment. At each point of the process, informed consent was requested from each co-researcher and issues around confidentiality and identification were discussed. The first interviews were unstructured to allow co-researchers to discover what they thought were important only-child experiences. On the second interview, after they had received their transcript of the first inter-view, I took the process further, checking for clarification and meaning. I also asked the co-researchers to speak more about emergent ideas and anything else that had come to mind since the original interview. This is based on the view that stories are told to be received in a particular way and this can change over time. I was also aware that many stories could be general to any child, so I attempted to tease out what the co-researcher thought was specific to her as an only-child.

Analysis

By using a voice-centred relational model (Mauthner & Doucet, 1998), I was able to distinguish between personal, private and public voices. I re-read the transcripts many times to discover the voices, social and cultural settings and sense of the public only-childness as well as the thread of life-story narrative itself. During the readings, I made notes of when the three voices appeared. I underlined the intra-personal (private voice) or 'I' which is how a person experiences their innermost self and their agency. It is not one voice but a multiplicity of competing voices. The inter-personal (personal voice) is usually seen as the world of private, domestic and intimate lives. I saw it as the one that focused on how each only-child related to their parents, friends and subsequent partners and children and how they believed others viewed them. The extra-personal (public voice) is the world of work and the social and cultural milieu in which the stories are embedded. I included the messages each co-researcher had experienced growing up as an only-child in a sibling society whose view of the only-child is predominantly negative. Using this idea of voice, I have attempted to capture the co-researchers' experience of being an only-child, reflecting the unique characteristics of each of their life-stories. To be transparent, whilst encouraging a reflective stance, I included this 'analysis' of the different voices in their stories followed by their comments. A co-researcher's story is therefore a combination of stories, reflections, voice and my own reflexivity.

Ethical considerations

I was mindful of the impact of the research interview itself, particularly around sensitive issues and vulnerability. In my practice as a therapist, supervisor and trainer, I take seriously the ethical rule of non-maleficence and I was aware of the importance of maintaining appropriate boundaries in the research. McLeod (1999) and Bannister et al. (1994) state that qualitative and feminist researchers claim that the outcome of research involvement can be beneficial in the lives of participants. The important consideration is the empowerment of individuals, the concept of voluntariness and the equalising of the research process (Hughs, 2002). I have been mindful of this throughout the initial research with my eight co-researchers, as well as subsequently when interviewing new people and receiving stories from my website onlychild.org.uk.

In my interviews, it was not uncommon for my co-researcher to become tearful and at those times I suggested we took a break, turned off the tape recorder and spent time in silence. If they needed to talk, I would listen and if it felt appropriate, share my own experience in order to readdress the power balance, bringing back the sense of collaboration. Before the interviews, in the information sent to co-researchers, opportunities were offered for them to see a counsellor during any point in the research, which I had negotiated with a colleague who as a researcher and therapist herself was aware of the dynamics of in-depth interviews. No one took this opportunity, but I felt it was part of my ethical sensibility that this was offered.

I was also mindful of the issues of power when it comes to taking personal and private worlds and putting them into the public arena. The research process is one of inequality because I as a researcher have the most power with regard to the designing, administering, analysing and representing of the research. The use of my own reflexivity, my involvement on a personal level, as well as involvement by the co-researchers in the analysis and final stories, I believe, has kept the process of the research as transparent as possible. The co-researchers had opportunities to review each interview and dialogue with me. Where points of conflict and resolution emerged, they were included in the final stories.

Stories I received from the website I always acknowledged, thanking people for their willingness to share and on occasions when appropriate asking permission to place on the website 'Noticeboard'. Subsequently, I asked people's permission to use their stories in the second part of this book. Not everyone was willing but most people were pleased to have the opportunity to contribute to the body of knowledge on adult only-children.

Reliability and validity

Some qualitative researchers have argued that these terms of reliability and validity are not applicable to qualitative research, but clearly some kind of qualifying check is needed. Riessman (1993) suggests the importance of persuasiveness, coherence and insightfulness in story-telling. Many qualitative researchers have offered their own theories of validity and have often generated or adopted what they consider to be more appropriate terms, such as 'trustworthiness', 'worthy', 'relevant', 'plausible', 'confirmable', 'credible' or 'representative' (Denzin & Lincoln, 1998; Guba & Lincoln, 1989; Hammersley, 1987; Mishler, 1990; Wolcott, 2001).

Clandidin and Connelly (2000) write about good narrative as having 'an explanatory, invitational quality, as having authenticity, as having adequacy and plausibility' (p. 185). They also suggest narrative researchers develop criteria that work for them, such as Conle's (1996) 'narrative resonance'. When well done, the creation of texts should invite readers 'to imagine their own uses and applications' (Clandidin & Connelly, 2000, p. 42).

I believe the co-created stories I offer have been a learning experience for both my co-researchers and me. Furthermore, they have also inspired others who have resonated with the stories published on the onlychild website and as a result have written to me to offer their own. I would argue that *reciprocity* may also be considered as representing validity. We do not live in isolation; our experience is always inter-subjective, as Merleau-Ponty states:

> The phenomenological world is not pure being, but the sense which is revealed where the paths of my various experiences intersect, and also where my own and other people's intersect and engage each other like gears. It is thus inseparable from subjectivity and intersubjectivity ...
>
> (1962, p. xx)

In the early twentieth century, the dominant story about only-children was a 'negative' one; this has now turned full circle in the United States to a 'positive' one. My intention has been to go beyond these polarisations and seek new stories and new voices with which only-children may resonate. I have witnessed many stories in the process and have tried to capture the nuances and contradictions of different voices, all of which I believe is part of being an ethical researcher. The next chapter contains the eight stories from my co-researchers which begin to illustrate the themes that make up the only-child experience.

3
Co-Researchers' Stories

The following are eight co-researchers' stories, shortened versions of the original ones, containing the essence of only-child phenomena. In order to offer a flavour of the speech in the narratives, I have used stanzas. By using stanzas, I found small parts of text could be held as single foci of consciousness (Gee, 1999). These helped to link and elucidate the meaning of connected speech, by inviting the reader to savour each discrete thought. Stanzas also helped to capture a matrix of meaning and re-create the intention embodied by the speaker, and reveal both the power and the passion of the original exchange. My co-researchers preferred the sharpness of this way of speech, and I have continued to use stanzas as one way of conveying the only-child story themes on the website.

The only-child experience is multi-layered and unique to each individual and I believe I have captured something of the personal challenges of being an only-child that all the narratives encapsulate. I have contextualised each story and they begin with the youngest co-researcher. The words of each co-researcher are in a different typeface from that of the main text.

Georgina: dependent and independent

I met Georgina in her flat a few months before her wedding, so a great deal of her energy was directed towards this. She is in her early-twenties, the youngest of my co-researchers. I enjoyed the interview and the later email correspondence. I was intrigued because much of her experience resonated with my own thoughts, beliefs and feelings from my twenties and I realised how much I had forgotten! It was like going back in time and seeing myself again at twenty.

Georgina was born to elderly parents and believed her experience of being an only-child was positive but also a responsibility:

> I think being an only child
> is like teaching yourself to be independent
> kind of use your own ingenuity in a way
> I see that as a great strength
> in some ways it's a great responsibility –
> you have this weight on you where you think
> well it's me and just me and only I look after myself
> in contrast to other people with siblings

However, she is also aware of the stereotypical thoughts and expectations others have of her being an only-child. These she described as having a lot of attention and being spoilt, but she does not believe it happened to her.

> People now tend to go through the old story:
> 'you must have been very loved
> very special'
> I obviously got a lot of attention
> which I suppose is true
> but then adults
> have their own things to do
> it was a case of keeping myself amused
> out of the way
> whereas with siblings
> I could pester them for attention.

Georgina's parents expected her to be: *a good girl, not showing off, not making myself too conspicuous.* She has found it difficult to be a child with other children and much easier to be a child with an adult. She experienced other children as childish and this led us to talk about the issue of independence and dependence. At home she said: *I just fitted in with what there was, there was no way to be independent.* She also described her life at home as: *contained – there wasn't any chance to test how independent I was.* It was not until she left home that she could take control of her life and she recounted a story describing the pleasure she got from having her own door keys and how this gave her a sense of freedom and control over her own environment. Georgina's story depicts a tension between how she feels she is and how she feels she should behave in the world. On the one hand, she feels being an only-child has made her independent and responsible for herself, and on the other she describes herself as wanting to be dependent, stay a child and not enter the adult world.

> I do tend to take on
> a child role
> I like but I don't like it
> it's free to be a child and mess about and stuff
> that's the good side
> but then it's kind of child like
> I'm very defensive
> I won't let anybody do things for me
> then once I've been won over
> I get a bit taken over
> it's not their fault
> some part of me wants it
> part of me wants to be dependent and looked after
> not have to worry about things like that

Georgina has always felt more at home in her imaginary world than the real world, and she has had a rich fantasy life since she was a child. She longs to be the centre of attention but she also fears it, wanting people to know the real her, but also not wanting it. These contradictions were apparent throughout her story and were indicative of an inner dialogue, very familiar to me, that sees both sides and finds it difficult to either hold both sides at the same time or choose one. Here is an example when she talks about identity:

> if you're an only child
> you feel you've got so much for yourself
> yet in another way
> sometimes you feel
> you've got this strong identity
> then sometimes you feel
> you've got no identity
> at all of your own.

Georgina struggles to find an adult identity and this impacts on her relationships. She believes people would not like the side of her that is not sensible and conforming. To make relationships work, she feels she should take all the responsibility. She spoke about having to hide, adapt and pretend and I wondered whether this was primarily because she is not comfortable with herself. As an only-child, she felt special but as an adult she realised this is not a specialness that everyone appreciates. She used the story of the 'Mad Hatters Tea Party' to illustrate how both the adult world and being in large groups can seem difficult to understand or negotiate. There are sets of rules which seem both *weird and illogical*.

Although obviously an adult, I was struck by Georgina's child self and her fear of adult responsibilities like a career or learning to drive. She saw a correlation between never having had the opportunity just to be a child and her difficulties in moving into the adult world.

> Some of these things I am starting to see
> may be related to being an only-child
> not having the opportunities
> to fully be a child
> yet finding it hard
> to find the confidence
> to really take on the adult world.

Georgina is close to her parents and is closer to her mother although her father understands her better. She admitted to a time when she quoted her mother as a *fount of all knowledge*, and until relatively recently she adopted what her mother said and made it her own. I remembered doing the same, and later, finding it difficult to develop my own opinion or hold a contradictory view to that of my parents who were unable to hear any view but their own. Mixing with adults and being the least consequential in the family had the effect of keeping me quiet. I learned from an early age to be seen and not heard, to observe and listen, but not to participate. It appeared this was also true for Georgina.

As her parents grow older she has noticed the roles changing over. She admitted she did not like to think of the loss of her parents as she equates them with home and security and her greatest fear is being alone in the world.

> it's something I try and ignore
> I've got this thing
> That when I did think –
> well when both my parents go
> it's just me in the world
> and that's it
> I feel as an only-child
> if my parents died and
> I had no partner
> or family of my own

or anything like that
then it would just be me
that's quite scary.

As I was just finishing my final write-up, I received an email from Georgina. It was now over two years since our initial interview. The email shows both the impact of the interview and changes she has subsequently made in her life.

Serious child, sensibly irresponsible, quietly rebellious, calmly angry. These are definitions of myself that I feel, and I think, sum up what a paradox it can be to be an only-child and trying to manage being a number of seemingly incompatible things. No wonder at times it feels as though being oneself is squeezed out of the list. Reading my story has helped me have a little more understanding of these conflicts.

I see some of this reflected in my story, and it leaves me with the impression that I am a third person that most of my inner voices are discussing – even in myself I am often acting as an observer. I feel now that this is very much related to having spent so much time on my own, analyzing and thinking, looking at all the angles, playing out scenarios in my head. People with siblings would actually have been dealing with these scenarios for real, with real people in real time. This would allow them less thinking time and more spontaneity. Perhaps for them such situations would be less complex and tiring because they have not been so over analyzed.

As an only-child, I feel the reason it is so difficult to know who I am is because experiments to help discover who I am seem to be so serious and binding. I tend to treat very few things as 'play'. Your comment that on my feeling 'responsibility in everything' I do is very interesting. I had not really seen this before, but it makes a lot of sense and feels very true. This weight of responsibility leads to a fear of action – of being out in the world. Accompanying the weight of responsibility is also a secret question: Am I allowed to do/be this thing? In the adult world what is allowed and what is not, is not defined in the way the rules of childhood are. So many shades of grey are hard to deal with when as a child you have grown up in a world of black and white rules, set by adults.

Looking now I see that I have focused on the difficulties of being an only-child. I remember at the time when talking to you that I felt strongly that being an only-child is a good thing. A strength in fact. I still feel this way – but having been involved in this story my eyes have been opened to areas where things are more difficult. However being able to see as well as feel them has in some way made me feel better about them, and more able to challenge these difficulties or blocks. I may still not have a very clear picture of who I am, but I at least have an outline. It may be difficult to be seen and heard, but I now have a stronger belief that there should be a place for me in the world where I can be seen and heard if I choose. And I am learning to drive!

Anna: being in the middle

I met Anna in London during her lunch hour and she talked freely of her experience of growing up an only-child in Eastern Europe. She illustrated her story with many vignettes of her life in her country of origin, where being an only-child was the norm rather than the exception.

> It wasn't very special
> I was aware that I had friends
> who had brothers and sisters
> I had friends who didn't
> and that was that!
> I think there was a bit of a fashion
> for city couples
> not to have more than one child
> so there were always quite a lot of us
> in the classroom and in the playground.

Anna was born in the early1960s, when both her parents were in their twenties. Her mother was a middle-child of four children and her father the youngest of three. They came from working-class backgrounds, and Anna described them as university-educated professionals. Anna believes she had a very different experience as an only-child compared to other only-children in the United Kingdom. Her childhood was character-ised by having plenty of friends, with continual movement in and out of their homes. Only-children were common and spoiling them was accepted as a sign they were special to their families and no stigma was attached. Despite the fact that Anna had plenty of friends, she did spend time alone and this she believes had a significant effect on her personal development.

> I did spend time on my own
> I learnt to read very early
> So I used to read a lot
> I always read a lot
> I used to play a lot in my own world
> I had a very developed imaginative world
> that's something that's stayed with me
> it was something that I liked –
> books and reading and imagining things.

However, although being an only-child was not unusual, Anna was special as the only girl in her family. She was also much younger than her classmates having started school at five rather than seven, because of her early learning skills. Anna believes being special has good points, but also consequences that have been more difficult for her to deal with.

> There was a sense of being special
> because I was a girl
> so I had a lot of messages
> about being special
> about being clever
> of course that bit was difficult
> it also meant that later on
> it was quite a job for me to move out of
> that sense of being special.

Like other co-researchers, specialness has made later relationships difficult. Anna experienced the specialness as a responsibility and longed to be ordinary. She found the intensity of being in the middle of her parents' relationship suffocating and at an early age began to make boundaries. She believed she was given too much power in the threesome, treated more like another adult and experienced her mother competing with her, as well as expecting her to act as a confidant.

> I had to separate myself from her
> I think in many ways
> she was too much
> she was too close...
> it felt like she wanted to run my life for me
> we were so close
> and I didn't have siblings
> I think she projected
> a lot of her own child on me
> and tried to give me everything she didn't have.

Anna's mother had a great deal of influence over her, even choosing her career. This experience of a mother leaning on her daughter is probably common for families with only one daughter; however, in a family where there is only one-child, the attention is undiluted. Anna was continually being pulled in opposite directions by her parents which caused her to rebel.

> There was a power battle about who would have me on their side –
> that was very difficult for me
> I was on my mother's side as soon as I was able to...
> because she was a woman and she was with me more...
> She used me for her own support and I felt used.
> But I had to keep my relationship with both of them ok

when there were times when they really hated each other ...
that was really horrible
I knew much more detail about their life than I ever wanted to know.

Anna feels that her experience of being bound up in her parents' relationship has affected subsequent relationships, making it difficult for her to be close as she had learnt to retain her independence in order not to feel suffocated.

> I wouldn't let people be that close
> I mean I had close friendships
> but I really had difficulty with close sexual relationships
> I had to be independent
> I had to be strong
> I wouldn't be vulnerable
> I was also very angry
> particularly when I was young
> I didn't think that highly of men –
> to do with the relationship with my father
> So it was really difficult because
> I didn't respect them
> I had to keep them at bay –
> so I would often change partners.

Anna thought she has had difficulties in asking for help. She could not ask her mother as asking for help would lead to more intrusion – so she learned to look after herself. She eventually decided to move to the United Kingdom to separate herself from her parents. Although she has some regrets about leaving her country, especially as her parents grow older, she feels it is not her responsibility that she is an only-child. Anna has fought hard for her independence and as a result she has found it difficult to show vulnerability and is afraid of intrusion into her private world. Now married, she has chosen not to have children, but as she grows older admits misses the sense of having a wider family. Her final comments were interesting, as I had gained the impression from the interview that she had many friends as a child.

> I have now read your reflections and I find it interesting and insightful. I was curious about your notion that there were many children I had to play with!
>
> There was no compulsion or hardship about growing up an only-child – but you have certainly got the gist of it. I have felt well understood by you.

Lyn: creating the siblings she missed

Lyn was born in London in 1955. Her father was the eldest of three children and her mother was one of four. However, because Lyn's father worked abroad, she had to move house every two to three years. This meant that between the ages of four and twenty-one, she attended many different schools and colleges. Lyn's mother had three pregnancies; her first child was miscarried and then she had Lyn a few years later, followed by an ectopic pregnancy when Lyn was about three. Lyn probably would not have been an only-child if these events had not occurred. Her mother once said: *having an only-child is like putting all your eggs in one basket.* This seems a very significant image and mirrors much of Lyn's experience and her sense of needing to be *grateful* and *get it right.* Lyn has many nostalgic memories of hearing other children play whilst she was alone. As a child, she experienced her own house as *cold and dead* in comparison to those of her friends.

> My house always seemed terribly quiet
> and my dad always played music
> but there wasn't life there
> there wasn't people
> there wasn't lots going on...
> I think it was those sorts of experiences
> when I was younger
> that highlighted the fact
> that sometimes it felt very lonely.

She always wanted a sibling and hoped initially to get a large family through marrying someone with siblings. She had every intention of having a large family but found the demands of family life more exhausting than realised, and she stopped after two. She experienced being at home with children more difficult than she expected, particularly the responsibility 24 hours a day. She believes the difficulty lay in her lack of experience of young children or siblings. She had never been around children and recalls one of her mother's friends saying about Lyn that she had never had a childhood. I asked her what she understood by this and she replied it was because, as a child, she had always played the adult. Whilst she had enjoyed being included in the adult world, she now realised it had made her older, and she had lost out on the carefree side of childhood.

Her childhood was both lonely and dominated by her mother's attention. She experienced her parents as a unit, one she could not enter. From her mother in particular, she felt constantly observed and scrutinised, and received strong messages from her parents to be a 'good girl'.

> With the attention bit
> you're constantly observed
> That's something my mother is renowned for
> I know I'm being watched the whole time
> it's quite intense and
> I couldn't say
> 'It was him'
> It was always me –
> if a milk bottle got broken or something
> I think that the intensity of it is quite relevant.

Her parents were afraid she might appear spoilt and her mother tried to ensure this did not happen. In this way, Lyn felt she lost out. The scrutiny her mother has given her has made her very self-conscious. This scrutiny has affected the way she feels about her appearance and how she thinks others see her and goes deeper, leaving her with a critical view of herself and a sensitivity towards others.

> it was hard to just go and do something –
> because I was always watched . . .
> As the only one
> you're the focus
> therefore everything is noticed
> politeness
> saying thank you
> behaving properly –
> and because in my case
> my mother was concerned
> I didn't become spoilt
> I needed to be grateful.

Lyn has struggled to find her own identity and opinion separate from her parents. She is still very close to them and has frequent contact. However, although this has many positive outcomes for her and her family she still feels that she needs to work hard to be heard by them.

> And if I hadn't been prepared to battle
> I would have been pushed along in their direction
> but I do battle
> I stand up for myself
> but it is a fight
> and it's tiring
> and sometimes you just want someone to accept

> that's what you want to do
> You don't want to have to justify it
> and that still happens now
> as much as earlier
> I still have to fight my corner every day!

Lyn later wrote she thought:

> It is quite difficult to be too separate from your parents because you
> are their only focus and although they do other things and they're not
> around you all the time, there feels somehow – for me anyway, that I
> should be keeping in touch with them all the time. So that feels quite
> difficult but equally you can feel quite special.

Friends have been particularly important to Lyn, because of all her
childhood moves, and she has had to make an enormous effort to keep
them. Her parents saw this continual moving as a positive experience
and appeared unable to reflect on the difficulties this gave Lyn. She
acknowledges that as a shy child it was not easy to develop friendships,
so she was highly motivated to keep friends, even after they had left the
country. She describes this as a time when: *nothing was stable, nothing
was concrete, nothing was reliable.* However, not all her efforts were reciprocated and she had a sense that once she had moved, friends did not
keep her in mind. This left her feeling unappreciated and thinking the
sense of connection others have to their larger families was always more
important to them.

Lyn has always felt a great responsibility to live up to her parents'
expectations. She sees herself as very independent despite the very close
relationship she has with her parents and family. She really values her
independence but also recognises she does not want to be left out, does
not want to cope with things alone, as she has done in the past.

> I am independent
> I'm very independent
> I'm prepared to do everything on my own.
> and its only recently
> I've realized that's what I'm doing
> and that actually
> I don't want to do it all on my own
> I would rather do it as a team

As her parents become more elderly, Lyn finds it hard to imagine not being
with them. She has no plans to look after them in their old age but she hesit-
ated to say she would never do so. In connection to her parents, Lyn spoke

of the myth of only-children 'having it all'. In her case, she thinks she has always had to earn everything she has received as it has never been freely given. Her parents expect *a pay back*, meaning the money or gift would have to be used as they expected. Lyn made a distinction between what others thought might be the advantages of growing up an only-child, mainly material, with some of what she felt were the disadvantages: those of responsibility for parents and isolation as a child.

> Other people's reactions
> when they find out you're an only child
> they think its all good
> a very positive thing
> 'Oh that's alright you're spoilt
> – got everything – life's a dream'
> I think people also think
> you'll get lots of inheritance
> but the fact is you might not –
> And there might be lots of caring involved

The fact that both she and her partner are only-children causes even more comment.

Like many parents of only-children, Lyn's were afraid to spoil her, and as a result, Lyn believes they went too far the other way. She said she understood spoilt as: *being given everything you want – particularly materially*. However, her experience was different: *I wasn't given everything – especially what I wanted*. This sounded very poignant, the way she emphasised *I*, and how Lyn as an individual has often been overlooked.

> I think my mother had this thing about me
> being spoilt
> if she wasn't quite strict
> So, for example,
> I had friends in large families
> who never did their washing and ironing
> I did my own washing and ironing
> I began to realise that I was having a bit of a rough deal here!

Lyn's reflections on her story noted that some of the themes I had picked up were not necessarily the same as perhaps she would have emphasised. This is true and made me aware again of how any encounter will be seen in different ways at different times by different people. I did make some changes to the original, longer story in line with her comments. These were Lyn's final remarks after she read her story:

Overall, I was very interested to read about the themes that you had picked out, the way you sometimes linked these to others experiences, within the study, and your own. I found the story easy to read and interesting. The story naturally felt familiar! Yet useful to have it relayed through a third party, which seemed different to just being in therapy. May be it was something to do with it being written down. What immediately came in to my mind, was how the authors 'bias' or 'own experiences' may, or could, influence what was picked up and noted. Very interesting to read and think about. Thanks for including me. I have cursed the extra work sometimes, but once I get in to it, I find it very interesting. As I do anything on people's 'place' in the family. In a way, I suppose it feels self-indulgent to be so involved with my own story and feelings, but yet, it also feels rather nice!

Amy: her mother's carer

I had occasionally seen Amy at college where we both taught, but never to talk to on a one-to-one basis. We had a mutual friend who had often said how alike Amy and I were, in the ways we reacted to things, which she felt was peculiar to only-children. During the period the interviews took place, Amy's disabled mother moved in with her, although even before that Amy was her major carer. Amy is an artist and also trained to be a nurse in order to care for her mother.

Amy was born in 1954. Both her parents were only-children and her mother was of Irish descent. She was brought up in a small two-bedroom bungalow, which was separated by a garden and allotments from her maternal grandparents. Amy's mother did not get on well with her own mother, although Amy enjoyed her grandmother's company. Amy believed that her mother wanted a child for company as Amy's father was a journalist and was often abroad or working late in London. She had an elder brother who died when a baby. This is something her mother has never been able to talk about.

Amy described her childhood as lonely because she had few friends to play with. She had imaginary conversations with her dolls or pets and later her horse. She spent her childhood longing for a horse, who became her best friend, so when the horse died she was devastated and became clinically depressed. Interestingly, Amy characterises her childhood as one where she distracted herself from loneliness whilst trying to keep her mother at arms length.

> I was on my own
> I would be in an imaginary world with 'Kate' or
> I would be with the cat or

> an imaginary horse
> There was a lot of that
> playing out things with dolls
> doing imaginary conversations
> I read a lot – we didn't have TV.

Whilst she always felt wanted as a child, her mother also needed her for company; so she experienced a struggle to develop and maintain a separate self. She felt like Pinocchio:

> His parents were desperate for a child
> which is quite often the case with only-children
> so you definitely feel wanted
> I mean there's no way I have not felt wanted
> I have always felt wanted
> But it's about struggling
> to have secret places
> struggling to have places
> where you're not intimate with a parent
> struggling to have your own space to go to
> possibly even having to lie about things
> So the experience of being an only-child is
> struggling to keep your nose small!

Amy's graphic description of what it is like to be the centre of attention, an attribute often perceived as positive by non-onlies, shows its intrusiveness and how attempts to gain separateness can be foiled by the effort involved. *It's like being in front of a mirror all the time a two-way mirror that people can see through.* The two-way mirror meant there was no possibility of a secret place, nowhere to hide, because Amy was always visible. The triangular relationship she had with her parents still manifests as an adult and she finds them difficult to cope with. In the past, she either ran away or drank.

> This thing with the three people
> it's not good
> if I get in that position now
> if I feel as if I've got to choose between
> one of the kids and mum
> or a friend and partner
> or any of those three cornered sort of situations
> or the two kids and me
> I don't deal with that very well
> I get panicky
> I feel demanded of
> very stressed and my heartbeat starts to go

Amy is very aware of the financial advantages of being an only-child but she also experiences the responsibility of being her mother's full-time carer.

> We're having major alterations done to this house
> to have my mother come and live here
> that wouldn't be happening if I weren't an only-child
> This actually gives her a proper space
> to be a disabled old lady
> I've been saying I would do this for my mum
> for a long, long time
> there were times where she would have liked it
> to have happened earlier
> since I went through that sort of pain barrier of:
> Oh my god my life is at an end
> the difficulty has always been the emotional side of it
> feeling pressurized
> feeling demanded of
> feeling that I'm smothered
> by everybody else's needs

Amy has experienced a constant battle to find emotional and psychological space for herself. Both as a child and adult, Amy has felt smothered by her mother and under constant pressure to be continually available to her. At nineteen, Amy left home to escape her mother, had a son, and stayed away for ten years. She finally returned to give her son a better life. She has always felt very responsible towards both her parents and her two sons, but her intimate relations have been fraught with difficulties and she has spent much of the time living and dealing with things on her own. She has continually felt trapped by the demands of others. She gave up her career to look after her disabled mother and her partner left as a result. Despite this, she regards herself as very independent and selfish in getting what she wants but has brought up her two sons mostly on her own.

Amy has learned to deal with life by compartmentalising different aspects of it. She often feels trapped and in need of both emotional and physical space. She rides her horse which gives her a sense of freedom but inevitably has to return home to face the many problems linked to looking after her mother, who by the second interview, was immobile, blind, suffering from Parkinson's disease and needing care 24 hours a day. Eventually, Amy had to give up the battle of looking after her:

> It was absolute hell on earth!
> Terrible!
> she would not accept my authority
> yet I was responsible for her
> But she questioned everything
> on a minute to minute basis
> she became very abusive
> I couldn't manage
> and had to put her in respite care.

Two years later, Amy said: *I have been through hell and out the other side.* Amy is now living an independent life and I asked her if she had any regrets. She explained how she had tried to protect her partnership but not at her mother's expense and ultimately her partner would not wait. Amy had been responsible for her mother for ten years. Although in hindsight she feels the decision to become her full-time carer may have been mistaken, she does not feel she could have known the extent of the impact it was to have on her life. The abuse she suffered from her mother is now projected on the residents in the home, and Amy can retain a separateness she was unable to do whilst her mother lived with her. In particular, she finds great relief from the responsibility she has carried since her mother went blind. Amy feels she has found herself again and spends long periods on her own. During this time, she has reflected on her only-childness and, in particular, her own emotional intensity. She believes much of her creativity has grown out of her experience of aloneness and isolation as a child and adult. She is aware that others see her as calm and accepting although she sees herself as jittery and jumpy. Feeling alone and responsible as an only-child has been the pattern of her life. As Amy concluded:

> The story doesn't change
> I have had great benefit from it
> huge creative urges
> which are a big part of who I am
> God-I'm on my own and I always have been
> but when I forget that
> I can be very creative and energetic!

Poppy: a claustrophobic childhood

I met Poppy, an ex-counselling student, in the spring of 2003, at her house. I was aware that as an ex-head teacher many people projected power on to Poppy and although she was often appropriately assertive she had a soft vulnerable side that not every one saw.

Poppy was born in 1950, the only-child of her mother who married late in life and gave birth at the age of thirty-eight. During the pregnancy, she was very ill; so she was unable to have more children. Her father was the third of eight children from a working-class background in Newcastle, but moved south when he met Poppy's mother. The family lived in a flat until Poppy was sixteen. The only other occupants were adults. She felt she lived very much in an adult world, having no real friends, until her teenage years. Similar to Lyn, she has poignant memories of hearing the neighbours' children playing in the garden while she was isolated in her parents' flat. Her father worked away from home during the week, so during that time she was alone with her mother until her father came home for the weekend. She described her life as *boxed up* as her mother did not like her playing with other children or having them to visit:

> Even when I started school
> she didn't really want me to make friends...
> well you can't have them round to the house!
> we did have people occasionally round for tea
> but I couldn't run out of school and say –
> Can I bring Jane for tea today?
> It would have to be planned –
> quite a long time in advance.

Poppy has very strong feelings about being an only-child and expresses anger that her mother did not give her a sibling. On the surface, she believes her life as a child might seem idyllic, but in reality she felt constantly smothered by her mother who wanted to play with her rather than allowing her to have friends. Despite this, she spent much of her time alone, playing with toys and living in a fantasy world built around the story of Lady and the Tramp. Time spent alone taught her to cope and rely on herself which she has carried into adulthood. She feels her childhood did not afford her the opportunities to develop social relations because she was cocooned and mollycoddled by her mother and treated like a china doll by her father.

> She was so into me and so involved in me
> Her life just evolved around me really and dad
> but then because he was away

> there was like even more pressure on me
> on the days that he wasn't there
> she didn't want me to go off and do anything...

Poppy found the pressure of attention difficult throughout her life and felt it never went away even after she left home. She felt as if her mother had taken up residence in her head. During her mother's lifetime, she constantly felt she needed to consider her. *I think there was a tremendous pressure on me right until she died...I was the be-all and end all of her life.* Poppy admitted she also rebelled a great deal, particularly in adolescence, when she took up with a group of girls her mother felt were a bad influence, and despite Poppy's intellectual ability, she failed all but two of her GCEs. Poppy returned to school to re-do her O levels and met her first really good friend who became as close as a sister to her.

> She was an only-child
> in fact our birthdays were on the same day
> we were the same age –
> that was kind of weird
> She had also mucked up her 'O' levels
> we were really like in a similar position
> She wanted to teach and we just clicked,
> we got really really friendly straight away.

From an early age she played the role of the 'good girl' and at school she was given the responsibility to look after the less-able children. Poppy has always felt a lot of pressure to be the person her mother wanted and to fulfil her dreams as her mother had no life outside of Poppy and her father. Although she knows she meant so much to her mother, she also felt her mother put her own needs first, expecting Poppy to meet those needs. As a result, in adulthood Poppy has tried to control people, finding it difficult to negotiate and fearing that if she became angry dreadful things would happen. This has impacted on all her relationships. Poppy never felt her husband needed her in the way she wanted, so she devoted herself to her career in teaching. He did not support her in her wish to become a head teacher and she felt he got in the way by messing up her tidy house, so eventually they divorced. After a number of unsuccessful relationships with women, one of which was very violent, Poppy is now living with a woman with whom she can have the sort of relationship she has always wanted: where negotiation is possible – something she feels has been a problem for her since childhood.

> I suppose it's only now really
> I don't feel I'm in a relationship
> where somebody is actually controlling me
> or even trying to
> As a result of that...
> I've realised that I can't actually control other people
> that if I try and dictate what she does
> then it's not going to work anyway
> because people need to do what they need to do
> I still find that difficult

She believes that being controlling and finding negotiation difficult is due to being an only-child. When a friend said to her: *When people don't fit in with what you want then you just get rid of them,* she recognised some truth in this, knowing she is often functioning from a place where she feels she can cope on her own. When a person does not fit into that, she can be quite ruthless. Whilst all my co-researchers had fantasy siblings, they were also aware that people do not get rid of siblings like they can a friend – this is seen as positive but on the flip side it does mean a level of connection that cannot just be dropped. Poppy thinks having siblings might have made her childhood different.

> I think we would have talked about her (mother)
> so we would have said –
> 'Oh there she goes again'
> So we'd kind of get together
> tell her that's not what we want to do!
> We would have actually got together and said NO!

Poppy struggles with anger. As a child, her mother was never overtly angry with her and did not allow anger to be expressed by Poppy. Poppy also believes her anger and frustration resulted from not being herself and the legacy of this has been re-created in her relationships with other people. It is hard for her to express anger and feel safe.

> I mean it's affected me a lot –
> My actual belief is:
> that if you get angry dreadful things will happen
> of course that was borne out in some of my relationships
> that just made it worse!

She believed her mother would disintegrate if she showed that side of herself. She also understands that her mother, as the eldest child, had mothered her siblings and developed this pattern of relating from an early age. Interestingly, Poppy's favourite aunt had found Poppy's mother overbearing, controlling and bossy too, but at least she had four other siblings to dilute it! A constant sore point is Poppy's resentment towards her mother for having only one child. She talked about her mother being different and selfish compared to other mothers. I wondered, however, if she was displacing the difference she felt as an only-child onto her mother.

> I think – I thought she was really selfish...
> I don't think I actually thought it was to spite me
> or anything like that –
> I just kind of felt
> Why do I have to be different?
> and she was making me different.

Reflecting back on her life she concluded that her childhood had been like playing a game, or living out a fantasy. Once again I was struck by the fact that constant attention is not experienced as beneficial when you are the only recipient. It may be envied from the outside, particularly materially, but like Poppy I experienced it as extraordinarily restrictive and stifling. Overprotective parenting is not useful for any child, but when there is only one it is particularly restricting as there are no siblings to distract the constant parental focus. Poppy believes this had a detrimental effect on her developing a sense of identity separate from that of her mother's:

> I don't think I had a real identity
> I don't think I knew much about myself
> until fairly recently –
> no it was all struggling
> with what she wanted me to be
> and what was that?
> I don't think if I'd ask her
> she would have known
> it was just:
> I want you up there –
> I want to be able to look up to you
> I want you to be special.

Poppy said on reading her story:

> It's like reading a story about someone else!!
> However it makes so much sense to see it written like this – in some ways
>   scary

The fact that being an only-child can TOTALLY affect my life in so many ways
I recognise and that I still struggle with lots of these issues.

She then addressed five issues that had arisen from her life story.

Anger: This is only recently coming out. I think this may be why I now feel so angry about what happened to me as a child. I could not experience the true feeling of anger then – but I certainly can recently. At last I am not afraid to express anger and see that it has a positive side.

Enjoying self: I still find it hard to lose myself in activities really let go and have fun.

Independence: Yes I am and always have been independent, often not to my advantage. It is still hard to let my guard down completely. Yet it is what I find lately, in particular, what I desperately want. There is still conflict here for me and work to be done on myself. It is still frightening to let go completely.

Parents: It really struck me, whilst reading my story, how superficial a lot of the relationship with my parents was, particularly with my mother. Who was the real 'Poppy'? I don't think I had a clue and my parents certainly didn't. I am still trying to find her but I know a great deal of her now!

Real Poppy: Now I just want people to see what is behind my public image but I know I need to allow them in…It is hard to believe that being an only-child has had such a great impact, and it is interesting reading my story in this way. Things I knew are there, but now stand out in a slightly different way. Thank you for the privilege of doing this work with you. It has been really useful for me in my development.

Kate: spoiled not spoilt

Kate and I met numerous times during the two years of research and she shared with me some very intimate and painful details of her only-child experience. Although in many ways her experience differed from my own, I particularly resonated with the contrast she felt between her outward appearance of confidence, yet often feeling uncertain, inadequate and fearful of exposing her more vulnerable side. Kate was able to do this in the interview and like Poppy I saw a very soft and caring side.

Kate was born in 1947 in Manchester and was brought up to believe she was lucky to be an only-child by her parents who both came from large families. However, her experience did not feel lucky and she believes that her mother's fear of spoiling her meant that she was denied the opportunity to really be a child. A constant expectation that she would be a 'little adult' left her feeling she was not recognised for who she really was. As a child, she felt there was too much intensity and focus on her to be everything her parents wanted, but at the same time she experienced angry, hostile attacks from her mother. Although she had a better relationship with her father, in adolescence when she tried to separate and form her own identity, she experienced both parents as punitive.

> I never felt that either of them
> recognized me for who I was
> so it's not surprising in a way
> that I have chosen a lot of the time
> people who are unequal
> who clearly aren't going to value me for who I am.

Kate believes her experience of being a special daughter has not been helpful to her social development. She has constantly feared being swallowed up and annihilated by her mother which has led her, as an adult, to find intimacy difficult. She vacillates between wanting to be close and doing 100% to keep a relationship, to withdrawing, when she experiences relational difficulties, into a place where she is hard to reach. In adolescence, she rebelled and did many things of which she knew her parents would not approve. Eventually, she realised she had developed self-defeating patterns that she has carried into adult life. She thinks these patterns are a direct result of having to maintain her parents' illusions whilst fighting to have a separate identity. Her relationship with her mother was characterised by a battle, and it was not until her fifties that Kate finally stood up to her.

> When I stood up to my mother and said:
> I can't look after you any more!
> Well I remember her first reaction
> was to beat her fists on the bed and say –
> You've won! You've won! You've won!
> And it felt terrifying
> really terrifying
> a confirmation of my experience
> my terror of our relationship being a power battle
> that we couldn't both exist
> it either had to be me or her

This struggle with her mother has affected Kate and she has tended to relate from a defended place rather than a vulnerable place in her significant relationships. She thinks she had too much attention as a child, which has left her feeling overly sensitive to criticism from others. As adults, only-children lose their parental attention and find that other people do not appear so concerned with the minutia of one's life. When that occurs, it is easy for the adult only-child to believe something is wrong in the relationship rather than to accept a level of disinterest as normal. Kate believes having a sibling gives a sense of existential connection, even when they are not physically there, a connection the only-child never has.

> I know that's the sensitivity that I bring
> from being an only-child
> I think the sense of 'going on being'
> with a group of siblings
> when they don't give you attention all the time
> you are just all there together
> You've got a connection
> I never had

Her experience as an only-child has made it hard for her to trust in relationships and she feels she has been in a bubble much of her life, making it difficult for her to see other people's point of view. It has also led her to a somewhat naïve view of the world where people will always be honest and moral, and she experiences difficulties in learning to accept disappointment when this is not the case.

Despite the difficult relationship with her mother, she chose to have her parents live with her in their final years. Kate's partner, who does have siblings, was supportive but inevitably having two more adults living in a two-bedroom terraced house was a strain.

Kate and her partner have no children and she described her relationship as providing what she missed as a child from her parents.

> we can talk to each other and
> we do hear each other –
> that's not what I had as a child
> so may be that's why I have chosen John
> may be that's the most important thing.
> Often we say we're more like brother and sister
> and yes I think that's right actually
> I think that's what I do value in our relationship
> is that we're siblings.

I particularly resonated with this, having married two only-children. One significant aspect of these relationships for me, and probably them, has been to have someone to 'play' with. Like Kate, it has also been important for me to feel heard and be able to speak on an equal level.

I was often surprised at Kate's lack of acknowledgement of her own attributes. She appears calm and self-contained which belies her self-deprecation. She spoke about the shame she experienced as a child and adult when disclosing she was an only-child and expecting that people saw her as privileged. The shame is still something she carries and is linked to her parents' fear of spoiling her, in fact she says: *Well I was spoilt but not in the way that they meant!* Kate, now in her late fifties, feels she has been able to separate from her parents but only after their death. She is content with being herself, feels connected to others and no longer needs to isolate herself.

Kate's feedback, after she read her story, was interesting as it spoke of witnessing. This has contributed to my own view that only-children need their experiences witnessed and their voices heard. She liked the parts where I put myself into her story because:

> It's about being witnessed and a sharing that reverberation: Ah I am not the only one! You have felt like this too. You have been there too! It's a comfort, a link.

Carol: recapturing childhood specialness

I arranged to interview Carol in October 2002 in my therapy room, as she felt it would be more private. I have known Carol professionally for about two years, although it was not until I began my research I realised she was an only-child. Carol was born in the late 1940s. Her mother was ill for most of her young life and died when she was twenty-six. Her family lived with her paternal grandparents until she was eight. She recalled the relationship with her grandmother as being very special and she gave her a lot of security.

> I felt so special
> I had huge responsibility
> there was my parents
> my grandparents
> I was the only grandchild
> the only child
> and there was a feeling I think of being special
> which was so important
> and with that went responsibility

She characterised her early life as lonely despite living with her parents and grandparents as there were no children around to play with. Adored by both her father and paternal grandmother, her mother's continuing illness meant she spent much of her time alone with imaginary friends. She felt very responsible for the feelings of her family, keeping her own feelings to herself, particularly those of anger. This has led to difficulties in knowing and expressing her own needs because she felt, as a child, she did not have a right to express them.

Carol believes that being an only-child has reverberated throughout her relationships. She has always found intimacy difficult, although she longs for it, and the sense of being special that she once had as a child. She believes the lack of siblings has meant she missed out on learning to be with people of her own age, and as a result has found relating difficult. In particular, she has found difficulty in dealing with conflict and friction, preferring to withdraw if she cannot put it right, even if this is to her detriment. She tends to go from superwoman mode, where she can do everything and needs no one, to feeling lost and lonely and longing for a truly intimate relationship. Initially, in her marriage, she felt responsible for her husband's happiness. He had been adopted at eighteen months and despite his adoptive parents giving him everything materially, he felt an emptiness inside, which Carol felt it was her responsibility to fill. Later he traced his birth mother and found he had siblings towards whom Carol felt envy and resentment, a common phenomenon among the only-children I interviewed.

> It was very hard for me to come into his family
> I feel very jealous actually of his sisters
> it's been a real stormy relationship
> a rocky relationship
> over the last twenty years.

Friendships are extremely important, and Carol agrees in part with her father's accusation that her friends are more important than her family. She thinks that is because she can share with them in a way she has never been able to do with either her own parents or husband:

> My really close friends, my real friends
> I can really share at a very deep level
> and are actually far more important
> as I've never been able to do that
> with any members of my family.

Carol chose to have five children as she wanted to give herself the sort of family she missed out on. She has learned, through watching her children deal with situations like conflict, how little she herself had learned through her own experience in childhood. However, watching her sons deal with conflict has given her a different perspective and she now realises conflict can be useful and important.

> When I use to see the boys arguing
> I used to think that was just awful
> they don't like each other
> I've never experienced it myself
> if I've had an argument with somebody
> I've taken on the responsibility to sort it
> it's not been easy for me to hold the tension
> it's un-natural
> I have to sort it – put it right

Competition is another area Carol has found difficult and she linked this to being special and not learning as a child to share attention. We discussed this in the terms of dethronement, which naturally occurs when a child has a sibling and has to learn to share parental attention.

> I found that very hard –
> to be dethroned
> I was dethroned
> wasn't I in my marriage?
> I'm dethroned sometimes with friends
> I don't like that part of me
> I don't like that part that is jealous
> that possessive part of me
> my real shadow side

Like Kate and Amy, Carol rebelled in adolescence to cover some of the hurt and anger she carried from childhood. Her father was very critical towards her and as a result she became very self-deprecatory. As an adult, she rarely shows her angry side unless she feels very safe in a relationship and continues to be self-effacing and lacks confidence in her own abilities, although like Kate she is a successful psychotherapist and university lecturer. Carol spoke about how she hated the label that she was 'too sensitive' and thought that it was possibly a result of not having experienced sibling teasing or arguing as a child.

Carol has always felt there was a stigma to being an only-child. Carol has experienced shame in not having siblings, feeling awkward and

embarrassed and less valued. She feels she has missed out on something –
a way of relating – that people with siblings experience, know and
understand, which she does not. This comparison has left her feeling
less capable and stigmatised as an individual.

> I would not be able to relate
> in the same way as them –
> they would all relate
> in a different way to me
> my way was not as good as theirs
> Something was wrong with me
> something wrong with my family –
> it felt like a stigma
> that's what it felt like!

Admitting to being an only-child, with its image of selfishness and
indulgence, she has found particularly difficult. This has made speaking
about herself shameful as she is always aware she could be accused of
these negative attributes. Wanting to be special, she relegates to her
shadow side. Part of her is desperate to be special to one or two people,
but her other side believes she has no right.

> I swing backwards and forwards
> from this person
> who wants to have all this validation
> wants to have the relationship
> yet the other part of me thinks
> I'm being selfish
> I'm being like a typical only-child
> who is selfish
> indulged in a way

When reflecting on our interviews, she said the fact I was also an only-
child had an enormous impact on the way she felt during the interviews,
perhaps allowing her to share more than she otherwise would have done.
Like Kate, she also mentioned the importance of feeling connected and
witnessed.

> I was just amazed at how much came out. How much it made me look
> at relationships and how I can observe myself in the world, whereas
> before I pushed it down – Being an only-child felt a stigma, so I didn't
> really want to look at it, now it felt safe but quite painful. I think overall
> being an only-child reverberates on all my relationships. It's been really
> helpful to me that you are an only-child. Some of your insights and
> some of your comments have been really helpful and I think there is

still a lot more I have missed out or could expand upon! It felt like I was understood. Some of your comments just connected with how I felt – may be that's my judgment on the rest of the world that other people who are not only-children don't understand me – the too sensitive bit!

When you related it to your own experiences in my story it made so many connections. I felt it helpful how your experiences matched up with mine that's what made me feel: 'Ah – she understands, great! Some sort of connection a meeting of only-children!' I think you have just got the right balance. I think it's made me feel understood and given my feelings validation. I found it very helpful.

Magritte: alone and independent

I met Magritte in November 2002 and I was particularly excited to meet her as she was my eldest co-researcher. I soon noticed her story had different social and cultural aspects growing up as a woman and an only-child in the 1930s. Her story depicted a time of Victorian attitudes towards children. Magritte is a retired civil servant, the only-child of her mother, the daughter of a German baker who came to Britain in 1900. Magritte's father was an only-child. When Magritte was fourteen, her father had hung himself and her mother had found his body. Her parents met when her father was on the 'rebound' and her mother keen to escape looking after her own widowed mother.

Magritte gave a particularly interesting description of the only-child family triangle, which felt familiar to me, and has been illustrated in other stories but most clearly in Magritte's. I also had difficulties in asserting myself, a child in between two adults. Like Magritte, the feeling I could never be right, that my opinion was never really valued was familiar.

> I had fought hard to assert myself
> in the face of these two dominant parents
> First they were bigger than I was
> When it came to physical chastisement
> there was not merely the one
> but the two.
> who were bigger than me
> Secondly they were older than me
> so they had far more experience.
> Thirdly they had this approach
> where I was wrong and they were right
> any sort of exchange of views was a battle
> which they always won

> because if by any chance
> one of them didn't know the answer
> well the other one did!

The experience of being small, a lone child, compared to two adults has had the effect of leaving the only-child feeling powerless even into adulthood. Most people interviewed seemed to experience difficulties in being able to separate psychologically from their parents. Certainly, Magritte thought that she had won the battle for independence by leaving home. However, much later, in her fifties, when her parents were elderly she was finally able to assert herself and be heard.

> They would pursue a policy
> that each was talking to me
> but not talking to each other
> but we reached this point
> where I was in silence in my own home
> Then the worm turned!
> The next time they talked about coming to stay
> I said: In future you can come one at a time
> or not at all!
> My mother didn't come again...
> neither did my father for some time!

Magritte's childhood was one of isolation, only mitigated by her own attempts to go out and meet people. Her parents banished her to her room whenever she was 'difficult' and never invited other children to play. Magritte became extremely independent of her parents, valuing this above anything else. So much so that she did not want to marry as she realised that she would lose a great deal of her independent status, which had been hard won. Notwithstanding the disadvantages of her childhood upbringing, she still feels that being an only-child made life more isolating for her as a child and this has impacted on her subsequent relationships. Throughout her story, her overriding dilemma is of wanting to be close to others and yet fearing a loss of independence. Brought up in an era where women did not have independent status, she succeeded in a male world as an independent woman with a career and has preferred friendships to anything closer. Reflecting on whether it would have been different in today's culture, she said:

> It's difficult to put myself into the modern world
> I can imagine that I would possibly have taken advantage
> of the fact that you don't have to marry now
> I mean you can live with somebody

> I can see that appealing to me
> there wouldn't be such a degree of commitment
> if it didn't work
> all would not be lost.

Magritte was adamant that she did not want to appear a victim, despite the difficulties of her childhood, as she had learned to be very self-sufficient and overcome her past disadvantages. I wondered if this self-sufficiency was partly a result of her being an only one. She appeared tremendously resourceful, extremely energetic, with a very lively mind. However, the lack of intimacy in her childhood relationships with her parents may account for the fewer opportunities she has encountered in her life for deep friendships.

> I think being an only child made me independent –
> too much according to some!
> I know a lot of people
> but there are not so many
> with whom I am intimate
> A close friend of thirty years said –
> I was difficult to get to know
> The fact we have both suffered from depression
> and are both interested in psychology
> has probably deepened our understanding.

There are many reasons why people choose not to have children and being an only-child was probably only a factor for Magritte. The decision to never marry is one she does feel is linked to her only-child experience. Friendships have taken a priority but she has found other people have not always reciprocated. Even today when friends prioritise their families, it affects her negatively. She described women of her generation as being slaves to their families. There have been many occasions where she has been let down by women who have put their family first, ringing her and cancelling because a family member, such as a son, has subsequently asked them to lunch. Not surprisingly Magritte has found this marginalisation of her friendship difficult to accept. She says she thinks this behaviour stems from Victorian times when women were not supposed to have friends after they were married, so a family should be enough and be put first. Her own lack of family has meant she has created a life around her interests and friends. However, she is also aware of the double-negative in a family-orientated society of having no family and no children. Despite this, she realises she was never emotionally ready to have children.

> I feared I would do to a child
> what my parents did to me
> I think my mother very much proceeded on the basis of
> I had to suffer therefore so can you
> I think I was too immature
> at the age when one normally has children
> to have the understanding
> which I hope I have now developed
> which would at least have inhibited me
> from making the same mistakes

When reflecting on her social milieu, she talks about 'the general assumption that only-children were spoilt' as one she experienced but also one she would query. Her view is that:

> It is possible to have parents who are so frightened of spoiling an only child that they bend over backwards not to as a result never do. Whereas in a larger family the parents can spoil little Johnny today in the knowledge that tomorrow it will be little Billy's turn.

This is borne out in the other research interviews that led me to realise that parents as well as only-children are susceptible to the accusation of spoiling rather than being spoilt and the inherent shame that this word carries.

Magritte wrote me a letter and her reflections began:

> My reaction to most of your comments is – spot on. As to having a fantasy about what it would be like to have brothers or sisters. My fantasy (if such it is) is not so much about brothers and sisters as about the whole network of active relationships thus providing for plenty of choice and opportunity.

Magritte ended her remarks with these two quotations. I believe they illustrate her feelings that she has lost something by not having siblings. Siblings she values over partners or friends because of the networks they can potentially provide: *Siblings for solidarity and companionship*. However, like Margot Asquith, it is a sister that she would have really desired:

> I can't even imagine a future husband being so much to me as my sisters'; they are the salt and essence of my existence. I would rather talk to L. than anyone in the world because she understands me. *Margot Asquith*

4

Only-Child Voices and Life-Stages

This chapter will look at the themes that emerged in the co-researchers' stories, through the three constructs from feminist theory based on the idea of 'voice', to reflect upon the only-child experience. The process demonstrates those elements which appear to be common to the only-children I interviewed. Although none of these descriptions are unique to only-children, I would argue that a combination of these experiences is common to the adult only-child, which has been constantly reiterated and confirmed in workshops I have led, letters sent to me in response to my website and Internet message boards dedicated to the only-child. Furthermore, there appear to be a number of re-occurring issues that adult only-children bring to therapy and workshops, about their sense of self and their difficulties in relating to others. Again, this is not unique to only-children, but I am continually surprised by the intensity of the concerns and have realised how much they resonate with me and my own experiences of being an only-child.

The three voices

The first voice construct is the intra-personal voice and is about the person's relationship to their innermost self, including their self-image and feelings about the person they are. This includes a number of ideas around key words such as 'imaginary worlds', 'special', 'responsible', 'different', 'sense of self', 'alone', 'lonely', 'personal space'. The second is the inter-personal voice because it deals with the way each person relates to others in their life. It is often primarily about their relationships as children with their parents, and in later life with friends and partners. Finally, the extra-personal voice is how a person relates to the world and work. This category incorporates the social and moral aspects of the way people view themselves in the world, and I include here the public stereotyping and social stigma concerning only-children. There is a natural overlap of all three voices as they are inter-connected. So for example: the fear of spoiling only-children, which is very apparent in the public (extra-personal) domain, effects how parents treat their only-child (inter-personal) and how that child and later adult will view themselves (intra-personal). The inter-connectedness of the three voices illustrates common only-child experiences from different relational perspectives. The voices hold the complexity of experience by not reducing them to simple themes and are the foundation for the only-child matrix described in Part III.

An interesting aspect of my early and subsequent research has been to look at the reasons why an only-child is one and the family 'story' attached to it. This is an example of how a subject crosses the intra-, inter- and extra-personal voices: a person's own view of their only-childness, their parents' view and the cultural view which impinges on the other two. Family stories are powerful and influence the way a person sees themselves. I will discuss this further in Part III under 'shame'.

My own family story (personal) is that I was premature. Subsequently, as a result of this research, I realised this was untrue. I was conceived very early in my parent's relationship (private), before they were married. My mother told me I was an only-child because she did not like babies and found the dependency of a child difficult. I now realise it was also because she wanted a career and at twenty-four was not ready to be a mother. As an only-child, my parents neither wanted to spoil me (public) nor make me feel responsible for them (personal). Elements of this 'story' are central to my experience and the development of my own private story. This includes never feeling central to my parents relationship; always concerned that I would not appear spoilt and let my parents down; and feeling the need to be independent at an early age, so my mother in particular would 'see me but not hear me'. My co-researchers had similar family stories which have affected their private stories.

- Georgina's family story was of an unexpected though longed for pregnancy. At her birth, her mother was forty-one and her father an only-child at thirty-seven. She knew she was considered particularly special because her mother conceived her later in life. Outside the family, she was aware of being thought of as spoilt.
- Amy had a father who was an only-child. Amy, however, was a second child but her elder brother died when a baby and his absence, though

constantly felt, was never referred to, except later in her mother's dementia. Yet the shadow of him was always present.

- Poppy's mother was older (thirty-eight) and she was unable to have any more children after her difficult pregnancy with Poppy. Poppy believes she focused all her time, attention and ambition on her to compensate.

- Carol's mother was also unable to have more children due to illness and subsequently died. Carol believed she was in some way respons- ible for this.

- Lyn's mother had three pregnancies, a miscarriage and an ectopic pregnancy. Lyn was born between them, aware her mother thought one should never 'put all your eggs in one basket'. Her parents were fearful of spoiling her and she feels that they went too far and she lost out.

- Magritte's mother came from a large family although her father was an only-child. She believes her mother in particular never wanted children and Magritte feels she was never given any real mothering.

- Both of Kate's parents came from very large families and continually told Kate she was lucky to be an only. They were also fearful of spoiling her and she feels this led to her being more harshly treated than if she had siblings.

- Anna's parents chose to have one, which was popular with the profes- sional class they had entered in Eastern Europe. This is reflected in Anna's experience that only-children were considered special and 'precious' and gave her a positive sense of her only-childness.

These stories illustrate the impact of society's views of the status of the only-child, which we have seen in the United Kingdom is largely negative. This affects the parenting that a child receives and is subsequently reflected in the individual sense of being an only one. Let us look at the voices in more detail.

The intra-personal voice

The co-researchers' intra-personal voices spoke of very rich imaginary worlds and involvement in creative activities, a result of spending time alone. Time spent alone was not always welcome, but for many an inevitable part of childhood. In early childhood, few went to nursery or met other children on a regular basis. They were often home with their mother, some left very much to their own devices (Amy, Magritte), whilst others experienced their mother as too demanding of their attention (Poppy, Kate). In later life, the ability to have both a rich imaginary world and to be alone was seen as a useful personal resource and a positive attribute of being brought up an only-child. All co-researchers felt wanted and special, except Magritte, but paradoxically most also felt alone and intruded upon. Some felt particularly lonely as children, envious of other children with siblings to play with. Initially, aloneness and loneliness was rarely at the forefront of co-researchers' minds (except Lyn), but when they began to think back to their childhood, the stories became vivid and a great deal of feeling was expressed. The experience of aloneness and loneliness became articulated more frequently when the co-researcher spoke about growing up. Talking about this was often painful. However, being with others was no guarantee of not feeling lonely; in fact, it was in the presence of others that loneliness was felt most acutely. Contrary to this, some co-researchers found being alone was a safe and familiar place to be and did not necessarily mean loneliness but more aloneness.

There was a tension between the ability to enjoy aloneness and a longing for intimacy and friendship. Carol, Kate, Anna and Magritte believe their ability to be alone gave the impression of independence and not needing others. Most co-researchers said this was not real; they did want others around but also needed 'space' which could be physical or emotional:

> I don't need you
> I don't need anyone
> part of me feels
> I don't need anybody
> part of me says –
> I can do this alone
> I don't need anybody
> that's the paradox of being alone
> there's part of me that wants to be alone
> be able to think
> I am quite independent
> I am quite fine on my own
> I can do all this
> But the other side of that is
> I am desperately lonely
> I want to have an intimate relationship (Carol)

All said that needing space, whether physical or emotional, was important and a way of getting back in touch with the 'self', which is described as the person they feel they are rather than the one they feel they 'ought' to be. A sense of self, separate from parents, was often difficult to establish. Most co-researchers felt very attuned to the expectations and ambitions of their parents and some like Poppy, Anna, Lyn and Carol went along with these, at least initially.

As children, positive fantasises of having a sibling is common. These fantasy siblings are there to play with and talk to but also protect them in the school playground. Attending school, traumatic for some co-researchers, was often the first opportunity they had to mix with groups of children. Pets were very important, along with toys and imaginary friends to both talk to and in some cases vent anger.

Feeling special and for some privileged, was a common theme:

> When I was little
> I always use to have
> incredible daydreams
> about being rather grand
> in the centre of things
> I know it sounds really arrogant
> but it was kind of the natural place
> I should be (Georgina)

Being thought to be special by parents was a significant part of the experience of having no siblings. Unlike sibling children, the only-child is never dethroned by a sibling birth so they remain special. However, when dethroning and the loss of specialness does occur; often with the onset of adolescence, the loss can be experienced as traumatic.

> I lost my specialness
> at about eleven or twelve
> I went completely
> off the rails for a while (Carol)

Some co-researchers rebelled in adolescence (Amy, Carol, Kate, Anna and Poppy) whilst Magritte waited until she was older. Despite an adolescent rebellion, most co-researchers remained strongly attached to their parents. Carol describes losing her specialness as coming in contact with her 'shadow'. Her narrative has a powerful theme in adult life of wanting to recapture the specialness of childhood.

> There's a part of me
> that wants to be very special
> has a right to be very special
> the shadow part of me
> is saying no
> you're just a member of this world
> you don't have a right to be anything
> you're just on your own mate (Carol)

A common theme that creates a tension for only-children is knowing you are special and having difficulty in expressing needs and asking for help. Most co-researchers felt special, but they also felt very responsible towards their parents, believing they should look after themselves and make few demands. Independence was the one label they all attributed to themselves, seeing it as a very positive statement and one they connected with their only-childness. However, this was often juxtaposed with feelings of dependence which some wanted (Georgina, Carol) and others feared (Magritte, Anna).

Isolation was frequently mentioned (Lyn, Poppy and Magritte) and was linked to feeling unconnected with other children. Other feelings expressed, as integral to their experience as only-children, was a sense of being powerless and voiceless (Carol), claustrophobic (Poppy, Amy) and ignored (Georgina). Feelings of being 'smothered', 'boxed in', 'molly-coddled', 'swallowed up' and 'scrutinised' were common in one form or other to all the co-researchers. They were linked to being the central focus of the family, where attention could never be deflected onto a sibling, the blame always falling on the only-child.

Perhaps as a result of being unable to deflect attention, co-researchers spoke of themselves as overly sensitive and emotional, experiencing anxiety particularly with regard to others, despite appearing outwardly confident. The gap between how each person views themselves and the way they believe they are seen by others is very marked. Poppy, Kate, Lyn, Georgina and Carol found the contradictions between how they feel and how they are viewed particularly difficult to come to terms with. Is this linked to social messages about only-children? I noticed that the label of 'spoilt' was ever present in most co-researchers' lives, their parents trying hard to avoid it, leaving some of them feeling they had a raw deal as children (Lyn, Magritte and Kate). Has the negative stereotype had the effect of creating self-consciousness which they overcompensate for when presenting an outward persona? As interviews and other exchanges progressed, I became increasingly aware of the discrepancy between the voices that said they were independent and self-sufficient and others concerned about who they really are and what they really want. There was a dominant voice that focused on trying to have a separate identity from parents and was described most often as a battle, usually with their mother, during adolescence. Poppy, Kate, Amy and Anna rebelled, whilst Carol, Lyn and Georgina became increasingly angry but continued to find difficulties in expressing this to their parents. In adulthood, all but Georgina (who is still in her twenties) have stood up to their parents, but generally not until their forties. It was only after her parents had died that Kate felt able to develop her own identity, a theme common from onlychild website emails.

The inter-personal voice

Most co-researchers had voices that spoke about feeling different to other people and expressed anxieties about their ability to relate to others. The words co-researchers used to describe themselves were 'different', 'weird' and 'not fitting in' and reflect the difficulties experienced in inter-personal relationships. As children, there was evidence of a very close relationship with one parent (Anna, Amy, Poppy and Kate), who may have used them as a confidante, giving inappropriate levels of personal information. This left them caught in the middle of the family triangle. Knowing one is the repository of parental hopes, ambitions and fears gives a sense of responsibility towards them, which is perhaps the reason for co-researchers' separation difficulties.

> I had to separate myself from her
> because I think in many ways
> she was too much
> she was too close...
> it felt like she wanted to run my life for me
> the fact we were so close
> and I didn't have siblings
> she projected a lot of her own child on me
> and tried to give me everything she didn't have
> She also competed with me
> there was this dynamic in the family
> where the competition was
> who was the top woman in the family. (Anna)

> I think it is quite difficult
> to be too separate from your parents
> you are their only focus
> although they do other things
> they're not around you all the time
> it feels somehow –
> I should be keeping in touch with them
> all the time
> so that feels quite difficult
> but equally
> you can feel quite special (Lyn)

All my co-researchers had, in my opinion, some characteristics of enmeshed family relationships, particularly with their mother. Less clearly enmeshed, Lyn and Georgina continue to spend a great deal of time in contact with both parents. Anna escaped her parents by leaving the country and Amy became a carer for her mother for many years. Carol has a very problematic relationship with her father and like the others experiences much guilt. Kate invited both parents to live with her until their death, despite a very difficult relationship with her mother. Poppy's maternal relationship was equally problematic and caused her enormous guilt and anger until her mother died. Magritte, although extremely independent, has struggled throughout her life to psychologically separate from her very Victorian parents, only achieving this through their death.

Whilst the main difficulty was separating from mother, co-researchers often felt peripheral to their parents' relationship, both unseen and unheard. Many had high expectations of themselves, though not necessarily a strong sense of who they are, tending to be defined by parental hopes and expectations. Poppy describes her experience:

> People saw this little girl
> doted on by her mother
> doted on by her father
> they thought
> I was really happy
> I was taken here – there – and everywhere
> I was lost in it somewhere!
> I don't think I stuck up for myself
> I wasn't encouraged to
> I just played the role of
> a good little girl (Poppy)

Playing the role of 'good girl' is an expectation that most co-researchers felt they had to follow. Being responsible, polite, not answering back, seen and not heard were all attributes they felt their parents required. With no siblings, they did not have an opportunity to engage in childish behaviour and some remember thinking it was neither what was expected of them nor something they wanted or were able to do (Lyn, Georgina and Poppy).

Siblings provide opportunities to learn social skills such as sharing, negotiating conflict, arguing your point of view and generally mixing with others. These were all areas that my co-researchers found difficult in navigating relationships. Sometimes outside relationships were made more difficult because parents, usually the mother, resented them. Many co-researchers had a sense of being different, feeling separate and isolated, especially at school where some experienced teasing and bullying.

Although school was often the first occasion to mix with other children, it seemed for many 'fitting in' was a problem. For others, school was a great opportunity to make friends and a way to escape intrusive parents. A common voice with co-researchers was their oversensitivity to others. This was viewed as unhelpful in relationships and the tendency to blame themselves when relationships became difficult. Missing out on the learning from the rough and tumble of sibling relationships led them to avoid conflict, competition, anger or assertiveness, fearing their relationships would not survive if these feelings were expressed.

A dominant voice concerned pleasing and placating in relationships as a way of 'fitting in' with peers, although most had discovered this is a problematic way of relating. Perhaps fitting in is learned in childhood as a result of a high level of adult interaction where the child learns that parents always know best and opportunities to assert one's own point of view are rare. Being overly responsible for the feelings of others was a common view, again possibly as a result of being the 'good child'. This affected friendships as there was usually a very high value placed on friendships and a morbid fear of losing them. Co-researchers felt you never lost a sibling like you could a friend. You might fall out with a sibling but the relationship remains, even if distant. Pondering this, I realised the importance of a sense of connectedness and how this is part of what a sibling relationship offers. Connection to a parent is different from that of a sibling and although co-researchers admitted having overly positive fantasies, siblings do offer a continuity of lived experience in a family, which is missing for the only-child. Once parents are dead, siblings still carry that continuity which I believe is a significant difference in the life of an only-child and the reason why the only-child always feels alone.

Problems in keeping firm boundaries were characteristic of the difficulties onlies said they experienced in their relationships. Naïvety, gullibility, sensitivity and taking things too literally leading to much embarrassment were cited a result of not having had enough interaction with children early on. The importance of friendships and the loyalty felt towards friends is common and usually spoken in terms of substitute siblings. Kate, Carol, Lyn and Poppy spoke about the significance of good friendships, but they also described how they could lose themselves in the process. Georgina, Anna, Amy and Magritte had felt badly let down by incidents with friends, but rather than finding ways of working through the conflict they cut them off.

Another dominant voice was high expectations of others, including themselves. This was particularly associated with needing intensity in relationships and paradoxically space, both physical and emotional. High expectations of friends often led to disappointment and a sense of not feeling good enough. All my co-researchers said asking for help was very difficult and appeared to be based on an inherent sense that problems or tasks must be solved alone. Allied to this difficulty was the effect of both parental neglect and intrusion that prompted the need to separate and become independent. However, this battle to become independent from parents was also perceived to be self-defeating (Kate, Poppy and Amy). When the need to be independent was taken into other relationships, particularly intimate ones, it could be disastrous. The fear of becoming too close and thereby losing a sense of 'self' meant some co-researchers kept themselves distant (Carol, Amy) or separate (Magritte, Georgina). Others like Kate are aware of the effect that parental expectations has had on their growing up.

> I feel very, very sad
> the half life I've had
> has been a self-defeating one
> in order to maintain
> my parent's illusions (Kate)

Laybourn (1994) mentioned a higher divorce rate for only-child adults and I had been intrigued by the fact that all my co-researchers had talked about difficulties in their relationships to do with levels of intimacy. Magritte was the only one who had chosen not to be in a relationship. The most frequent difficulty expressed was accommodating a partner's siblings. Lyn, married to an only-child, appeared to have less relationship dilemmas compared to others. Difficulties with partner's siblings emerged as a major discussion point on Internet message boards and focused on jealousy of the sibling relationship. This was very poignant for Carol who married her partner who had been adopted and then subsequently found he had a family:

> All of a sudden
> he had this large family
> he had a mother
> he never found his father
> but he had a mother
> he had three half sisters
> who he immediately struck up a rapport with
> became very close to
> I felt pushed out – pushed out (Carol)

It is apparent that lack of siblings meant that an opportunity to learn social skills was missing for co-researchers. In theory, this could be learned later in school and with friends. However, a frequent voice was that social occasions were threatening and most preferred one-to-one conversations rather than dealing with groups (a similarity with Internet message boards).

The extra-personal voice

The extra-personal voices focus on how co-researchers view themselves in the public arena. The previously discussed discrepancy between intra-personal and extra-personal experience of self will be examined as a possible link to the negative only-child stereotype and the subsequent stigma that leads to shame. In Chapter 1, it was demonstrated that the image of the only-child has gone through several changes. Prior to the late-twentieth century, only-children were viewed negatively both socially and psychologically, whilst the current position promoted in the United States is primarily positive. In the United Kingdom, I would argue, much of the negative stereotype remains. At best, there is a move towards non-differentiation in the experiences of onlies and non-onlies but this seeks to ignore the evidence that siblings are important for social and psychic development. I chose my co-researchers to span a fifty-year period in their growing up as I wanted to see if there were any similarities and differences growing up in an only-child family at the end of the millennium.

Magritte (the eldest co-researcher) speaks about living in a family-orientated society that values family life over friendships. Many of her stories are about being overlooked by her friends once a family member is on the scene. Her frequent experience of being 'blamed' for not having family has been very painful for her. No husband, children or siblings has led to her feeling on occasions ostracised. She yearns for a sister above all else; believing they give a sense of belonging to a family unit. The freedom to be independent, which she values so much, is not compromised by sisterhood.

Georgina (the youngest co-researcher) feels insecure in the public world, preferring home. Although still in her twenties, she is finding the transition to adult life difficult. Not learning to drive and not focusing on a career are indicative of her wish to remain in the secure base she calls 'home'. Lyn, Carol and Amy have put their children and parents first, not pursuing a career except where it fits around these responsibilities. Poppy, Anna, Kate and Magritte have chosen not to have children

and have all had outwardly successful careers. However, I was particularly aware with Poppy and Kate, the discrepancy between how they felt
in the public world compared to how they knew they were perceived.
They appeared confident and outgoing in the public sphere but inside,
as Poppy describes, the opposite is often true.

> At times that's felt quite hard
> that people have thought –
> Oh god that hard professional woman!
> which actually isn't what I'm like
> but I know that I can come across like that –
> that quite cut and thrust thing again (Poppy)

The power the only-child stereotype holds in UK society is more
powerful than people realise. Chapter 1 reflects on the negative stereotype attributed to the only-child in the family by early psychologists and
psychoanalysts, for example, Adler (1928, 1962, 1964, 1992). Although
much of the birth order research shows differences between onlies and
those with siblings, and between different birth orders, it is not a popular
concept. Books for parents of only-children are at pains to minimise
difference and maximise advantages. However, the effect of a negative
stereotype became evident in my interviews. The following stanzas illustrate the power of the only-child stereotype both in the past and in
the present. They centre on the idea of being spoilt and illustrate fears
parents have of spoiling their children:

> The stereotypes that I used to get
> when I was younger
> from friends who had siblings
> was the spoilt aspect
> of course you're spoilt! (Georgina)

> (Mother) use to say
> You're an only child
> everybody's going to say you're spoilt
> Well you're not going to be spoilt
> Just because you're an only child
> don't think you're going to get anything more
> And it almost felt as if –
> because I was an only child
> I was going to be deprived
> I wasn't going to get anything
> I didn't get anything
> It was like there was an over compensation
> there was that assumption you'd be spoilt (Kate)

Fear of spoiling is as prevalent today in the United Kingdom as in my own and co-researchers' childhoods. Anna, living in a culture which prizes the only-child, experienced positive connotations around the concept of spoiling. This positive public view of only-children made Anna's experience a different one, and the popularity of one-child families meant more effort was put into social opportunities. Anna has chosen not to have children, but she volunteered she would not have just one child in the United Kingdom (although she would in her own country) because UK families tend to be more socially separate and the extended family is rarer.

Another aspect that emerged in my interviews is shame linked to the expectation that only-children are potentially spoilt. This 'fear' of spoiling or being accused of being spoilt leads to shame at being an only-child:

> I was the only one
> who was an only child
> I actually felt
> awkwardness and embarrassment
> I actually felt
> ashamed
> I felt like
> I was different
> not as good
> there must be something wrong
> with me
> my family
> I actually felt ashamed (Carol)

I will discuss this more fully in Part III, but I believe shame is an important aspect in the lives of many only-children and adults. Shame was mentioned by Carol, Kate and Poppy, all of whom I interviewed extensively. One of the difficulties is the gap between what people assume only-children are like and how they experience themselves. The stereotypical assumptions that co-researchers have experienced were the common ones of spoilt, selfish, self-centred, lonely, unable to share, bossy, arrogant, independent, privileged and lucky. Running workshops for adult onlies entitled: 'Surviving the Stigma' explored this more fully. Whilst the negative stereotypes were very much in the room, another reality emerged that gave a very different picture. Words and phrases used by the participants about themselves were shy, a swot, observant, quiet, polite, responsible, high expectations of self and others, jealous, possessive, moody, introverted, naïve, defended, sensitive, emotional and reticent about saying they are an only. This last is connected with shame:

> there's that girl
> who hasn't got any brothers or sisters
> that poor girl!
> that's the shame
> something about when people are saying
> poor her
> she is an only child
> shame comes in there (Carol)

The power of the only-child stereotype was one that I had not expected but it became stronger the more I explored a number of different media. Internet message boards for parents of onlies and one for onlies themselves became a rich source of material. It was not until I began to study Internet bulletin boards for parents of onlies that I realised the level of parental anxiety for those who chose or had no choice but to have one child. These focused primarily on the attitudes of others who are vociferous in questioning the validity of having one child. A common refrain on the bulletin is '*I feel guilty for having only one child*'. The two major reasons given for their guilt are: the child will not have anyone to play with (and be lonely), or the child will get too much parental attention (and be unsocial and spoilt). In my opinion, neither of these is an inevitable consequence of being an only-child; but I do think it is a greater concern for parents of onlies, because of the lack of sibling relations and has an effect on how they are treated by parents even if this is not overtly conscious.

> They (parents) were quite strict
> and I think my mother
> had this thing about me
> may be –
> being spoilt
> if she wasn't quite strict (Lyn)

Since completing my research, I have been interviewed for a number of magazines and local Radio programmes. From these interviews, some underlying assumptions have arisen from the writers/presenters which are indicative of a common view of the only-child.

- Only-children are spoilt because they get so much parental attention.
- Only-children must be lonely with no siblings to play with.

- Only-children are socially inept and constantly crave attention. (A website for only-children proves this!)
- Only-children can't share and are therefore selfish.
- Only-children tend to be social isolates.

Whilst all of these have a basis in reality, I endeavour in the interviews to re-frame these assumptions to facilitate an altered perception of what it is to grow up an only-child in the United Kingdom.

Reframed response

- Only-children can receive much parental attention but this can feel both intrusive and claustrophobic and this attention does not necessarily mean they feel or have been spoilt.
- Only-children can be lonely but they also learn to be on their own and appreciate aloneness.
- Only-children can have disadvantages growing up without a sibling and parents need to provide a lot of compensatory peer play.
- Learning to share is a challenge for someone who is brought up without the opportunity to learn to share in the safe environment of home. They may appear more selfish until that skill is learned.
- Some only-children may become isolated if they have not been given enough social opportunities, but this is not inevitable.

At the heart of many of these assumptions is the idea that only-children are perceived to be both 'lucky' to be an only-child and potentially 'spoilt'. These two perspectives underlie the envy I and others have experienced from people with siblings. Overall, I would argue that an only-child is more often perceived as potentially spoilt than children with siblings, as evidenced in China's so called 'Little Emperors' (although the youngest child is also prone to this). This has a powerful effect on both parents of onlies and onlies themselves. I believe it is the reason behind the attempt to 'normalise' the only-child experience whilst promoting the view that only-children's experiences are essentially the same as those with siblings.

Only-child life-stages

Having used the construct of private, personal and public to understand the only-child experience, I will develop this further from a life-stage perspective. Various writers have used life-stage developmental models such as Gould (1978). Erikson (1950) uses a psycho-social model; Sullivan (1953), a model of developmental epochs; and Levinson (1978), a theory of adult development. These all emphasise an inter-relational model which is also fundamental to my own perspective of only-child development. However, I will offer a model which is both inter-relational and based on my research findings and suggest that only-children have certain challenges at different stages of their development that can be attributed to growing up without siblings. Through the idea of voice, I have highlighted the importance of the internal world (intra-personal) of the only-child; the inter-subjective world (inter-personal) that is constantly being re-created through our interactions, specifically with people; and finally the public world (extra-personal) that includes the social and cultural values that impinge on the other three. In the only-child life-stage approach, I will attempt to show how these three worlds interact with one another, through the medium of significant others with whom we engage throughout our lives. Initially, this is parents (as there are no siblings), then peers, teachers, intimate relationships and one's own children. Of course, not everyone experiences all these stages but that in itself is an interesting factor in the experience of growing up an only-child.

Childhood concerns significant relations between the child, its parents, peers and school, which facilitates, if things go well, trust, autonomy, initiative and industry (Erikson, 1950). My research reveals that this stage leads to a well-adjusted only-child if they have experienced attuned parenting from parents who are not attempting to merely fulfil their own emotional needs by having a child, and are able to offer opportunities for their child to engage with other children in and outside the home. However, this is not always the case, some of my co-researchers' childhood experience was characterised by intrusive (Amy, Poppy, Anna and Kate) and neglectful (Magritte) parenting. Intrusive parenting occurs when a mother's (sometimes father's) emotional needs got in the way of allowing a level of separation and development normally attained by the child through parents permitting an exploration and manipulation of their environment. Neglectful parenting is when the child's needs are not taken into account because the parent is more concerned in meeting their own, often unfulfilled, emotional needs and therefore have nothing to offer the child. In these cases, the child does not have a problem separating but has no support in that process and can become isolated as their own emotional and social needs have never been prioritised or contained. Both intrusive and neglectful parenting is detrimental to the development of self-esteem. Kate's and Poppy's mothers prevented any attempt they made to explore and become independent. Both children rebelled and became very angry in adolescence but by then the seeds of shame and doubt had already developed.

By *school-age*, children with siblings have learned a good deal from interaction with each other. Recent research has estimated that on average siblings spend about 33 per cent of their free time with a sibling (Kluger, 2006), which is considerably more time than they spend with parents, friends and teachers or even alone. As a sibling, they have acted as playmate, collaborator, co-conspirator, tormentor, an object of both envy and pride and as a vehicle to cultivate empathic feelings. Conversely, each sibling has been on the other end of that learning, experiencing all of those roles from their own sibling. Thus, siblings model different behaviours and facilitate opportunities to learn and to choose to copy and be like their sibling. In Chapter 1, we saw how significant siblings are for learning and practicing social interaction. They teach us how to and not to resolve conflicts, to be angry and make up, to share secrets and to learn ways of dealing with the opposite sex (if you are lucky to have an opposite sex sibling!) ad infinitum. But siblings also form a buffer against parental difficulties and can become closer and supportive of each other when parents are particularly abusive or neglectful. All this social and emotional learning is unavailable to the only-child who has only adult role models. One of the difficulties of only experiencing an adult role model is the power differential which can lead some only-children to feel inferior. Linked to this, the only-child must enter the social world of teachers, peers and other members of the community whilst learning, sometimes for the first time, social skills required by society. They may therefore enter this new world in deficit which leads to a greater danger of developing a sense of inferiority or incompetence. At this stage, if not before, they may also become aware of the social stigma surrounding their 'only-childness' which can continue to engender a sense of shame (Carol, Georgina and Kate). Often the stigma becomes apparent because of the only-child's lack of social skills, their difficulties in sharing, knowing the rules of the game or even standing up for themselves. The website has indicated a high incidence of bullying of only-children because they do not 'fit in'. Again this is not inevitable and many only-children are very popular because they are well adjusted and prepared to be different. These only-children appear more comfortable in themselves, have interacted with a lot of children from a young age and are often the ones who really appreciate their experience of being an only-child.

In *adolescence* the task is to achieve what is usually described as 'ego identity': knowing who you are and how you fit in with the rest of society. Adolescence itself is a relatively new phenomena (Mabey & Sorensen, 1995) and as a stage was more influential on the younger co-researchers who have had more experience of the 'cult of youth' than older ones like Magritte. However, peer groups are particularly significant at this stage and many co-researchers were still experiencing difficulties in peer-relating, although there was a tendency to have found at least one close friend, more often than not another only-child. It is also a time to separate further from parents, part of the process of finding an identity; a task which many only-children find difficult because of enmeshed parental relationships. Enmeshment occurs when parents are unable to separate their own identity from that of their child, seeing the child as an extension of themselves. One result of this is for the child to become a 'little-adult' because they pick up the subconscious messages to both be like the parent and do what the parent expects. This leads to the only-child phenomenon of appearing mature whilst in fact feeling insecure. The discrepancy arises because the only-child is playing the role learned as a young child, rather than being themselves. Aware of this role, they also feel insecure because they know it is something that is not really integrated; rather a false self taken on to fulfil parental expectation. Feelings of insecurity may enter subsequent stages until a sense of a separate identity emerges which for many only-children can be after the death of parents.

Young adulthood is characterised by achieving some degree of intimacy, as opposed to remaining in isolation. Sibling relationships give vast opportunities to be with another human being. We saw earlier that siblings spend more time together and relatively little time alone. Whilst sibling children spend 33 per cent of time playing together, only-children have spent this time primarily on their own, playing with toys, imaginary friends or pets. I will explore this further in Part III, but one of the overriding difficulties common to all my co-researchers (and myself) is the balance between dependency and independence, which can lead to difficulties in commitment and intimate relationships. If, in adolescence, you have not developed a clear sense of who you are, you fear losing yourself in relationship. The only-child, who is paradoxically familiar with both intense relationships (with a parent) and being alone, can end up fearing commitment. Carol craves intimacy whilst wanting to be 'superwoman'; wants to be isolate, yet is desperate to be loved and cherished. Georgina is fearful of taking on adult pursuits and fluctuates from wanting to be dependent and wanting to become more independent. The difficulty many of my co-researchers have grappled with is self-exclusion, which refers to the tendency to isolate oneself from love, friendship and community. This is true in part of Magritte and is certainly the case for many of the message board writers and email respondents to the onlychild website, who both feel isolated and excluded from the social world of families and siblings.

Middle adulthood includes the period during which we are actively involved in generativity which could be raising children or contributing to the welfare of future generations in some other way. It is at this stage many of my co-researchers took on the responsibility of caring for elderly parents (Kate), alongside care of their children (Amy, Lyn and Carol), whilst others had continued to progress their careers and interests and had chosen specifically not to have a child (Magritte and Anna). All my research suggests that this phase of caring for elderly parents is particularly challenging for onlies, who often have strong feelings of responsibility toward parents and at the same time no one to share these feelings with. It also means that for some only-children the projected responsibility of elderly parents has coloured their views about having children and some cases even partners. A common theme from the website is not experiencing being a child when a child, coupled with a dislike of growing up an only-child, which can lead to the idea they cannot relate to children and many choose not to have them. Others prefer to try and create the family they felt they missed out on and have several children. Whilst some only-children who really appreciated their only-child upbringing are happy to have one child, they appear to be in the minority.

Late adulthood is seen by Erikson (1950) as a time when people come to terms with their lives, reassess what they have done or achieved as they move towards the end. It is a time which can be particularly difficult for only-children who by now often have very little, if any, family. The sense of despair can be greater particularly if there is no wider social interaction and this can easily be the case for onlies who have spent a large part of their adult life caring for their own elderly parents. Linked to this is the fact that many only-children do not develop a clear sense of themselves until their parents die. When I interviewed Magritte, she was at this stage of re-evaluating her life, whilst Kate was moving into this stage. In Part II, I will explore this stage in more detail using stories from the website which illustrate the fear of losing a parent and the aloneness many only-children feel when parents have died. They are alone in the world, with no siblings to share memories and even when they have children of their own, this does not always alleviate the isolation.

A lack of siblings affects only-children throughout the lifespan, in particular their early emotional and social development but later it can also impact on intimate relationships. When parents are the major source of psycho-social development, the process of gaining separation, self-identity and self-esteem, can be problematic for the only-child. More seriously is the effect of intrusive parenting and the rise of shame and guilt. All these themes come together and form the basis of a matrix of only-child themes discussed in Part III.

I have attempted in this chapter to analyse only-child experience through the concept of voice, which highlights various themes that have arisen from the data, and have overviewed the stories from a lifespan perspective. I have *not* argued that these experiences are exclusive to only-children, but that a combination of these experiences are common to onlies and include elements that are experienced as different by people brought up with siblings. I have argued that the social impact of being brought up an only-child in the United Kingdom is both significant and detrimental. It affects the only-child's sense of self and plays into the fear parents have of bringing up a 'spoilt' child. Onliness and spoiling appear synonymous and can lead to parents being fearful about the way they treat their only-child.

Part II considers more stories which have been received through the onlychild website. These stories continue the only-child themes identified in this chapter and offer stories from different cultures and genders which are particularly focused on a life-stage perspective.

Part II
A Multiplicity of Voices

5

Research Data and the World Wide Web

Part I described the history of only-child research and my contribution. Part II introduces how the findings were made public. Going public was an integral part of the research project and by using a narrative life-story approach, it was always intended that the stories would be available to a wider audience, primarily adult only-children, but also anyone interested in only-child phenomena. Having collected my initial data (the stories) and discovered the areas of similarity and difference in only-child experience (the findings), I was now interested in promoting this knowledge and gathering a response from anyone who might be interested. This was done in a number of ways. The first was by publicising the stories on a website, the second was to write articles and simultaneously to offer workshops to adult onlies and attend conferences to promote the work further. This chapter reviews some of the results of going public and some of the less-expected aspects of this process.

Using the world wide web

During the research interviews, which might be viewed as a more conventional phase of the research, I began thinking about setting up a website as it appeared an ideal tool to publicise the research and ensure feedback. Web searches on only-children had proved useful in discovering some material which was primarily from the United States. The US website www.onlychild.com, initiated to support parents of only-children, fired my curiosity to see whether setting up my own website would be able to achieve the widespread dissemination I wanted. Despite my lack of knowledge about websites, I made some enquires and found I could buy a package and design my own. The choice and availability of a name: onlychild.org.uk seemed opportune, so in January 2004 I began designing and launched the site the same month.

Onlychild website

The primary reason for this website is to offer a feedback loop between those people who discover the resource, usually a result of personal curiosity to see what is available on the subject of only-children, and to provide them with a possibility of sharing their own stories either publicly (on the website) or privately (to myself). All postings come to me via email (*adultonlychild@gmail.com*) and I undertake to answer all emails received. It is both the accessibility of *www.onlychild.org.uk* and the fact that people know I will answer their emails that has made the website so popular. It has also led to an unexpected source of publicity, as I frequently receive requests from local radio and TV programmers to provide only-children for research purposes or to talk myself on radio shows that focus on only-child issues.

The website is a simple format of five pages. It consists of a home page which outlines my research interest and encourages people to read the stories and respond. The newest stories are also posted on this page, chosen for their differences from existing stories. Fortunately, not everyone wants their story featured but I do still have a lot of choice and this means older stories are replaced by newer ones. The second page has some of the stories from my original research, some in stanza form and others in normal text format. These stories have been changed from time to time to show different perspectives on the same issues. The third page has an abstract of my research and some of the activities I have been involved in such as the British Association of Counselling and Psychotherapy (BACP) Research Conference. Material from only-child workshops is also featured here and has led to further enquiries about ongoing workshops. An overview and brief synopsis is available on only-child literature which is perhaps why I also get a number of requests for help with research. The fourth page is 'About me' to offer some background of my own personal journey, and the final page is the 'Noticeboard'. This has a selection of emails from contributors and useful links for only-child resources.

When I initially launched the site, the first email I received, to my surprise, was from a pensioner, which immediately counteracted my fears that the website would only be seen by young people! Since then the number of visitors has grown from ten to twenty visits a week to as many as two hundred a day, particularly when my research has been featured on the radio.

23.2.04 An Only Child Pensioner

I was born in 1937, an only child of a very possessive mother, and a henpecked father. Both parents' professional people, so from the age of five I was a 'latchkey child'. I had to cook my father's supper at the age of 11years, as mother did not arrive home until late in the evening. Although I had school friends, I suffered terrible loneliness at weekends and evenings. I always thought that I was adopted, as my mother never once showed me any affection, and my father was very official towards me.

I married and had 2 children (I was determined not to have just one). I had to divorce after 31 years of marriage because of a violent and abusive husband. I had no brothers or sisters to support me, and I became even more isolated.

I am now a pensioner on my own, caring for my now 94yrs old mother, for whom I have no love whatsoever, only doing my duty. I do not burden my children with my depressive thoughts I have in my innermost being. I have always been extremely lonely and felt 'different' from my few friends and on occasions very jealous of their extended families. I have never been able to voice my feelings of complete isolation until now.

Although this was my first email, it has within it the themes encountered in the stories and discussed in Chapter 9. These are a sense of aloneness, feelings of being different, isolation, problematic relationships, caring for a parent and jealousy of extended families. However, what particularly excited me was the last sentence: *I have never been able to voice my feelings of complete isolation until now.* Up to this point, I had sought people to share their experience with me. From now on, I was to find that literally thousands of people from across the world resonated with the stories and wanted to share their own story, sometimes just to me whilst others were happy to share theirs on the website too. This interest in sharing led me to look more closely at the idea of witness. As a therapist, I believe the witnessing of a client's experience is a healing aspect of therapy. Similarly, parents are an important witness to our growing and maturing, as I believe are siblings. When parents die, people with siblings still have that witness, but only-children do not. I am often struck by the fact that many of the emails I receive are from only-children with very elderly parent(s) or who have just had a parent die.

They have now lost that witness. In answering the emails I receive, I have realised that for many people it is the writing and the witnessing by me of their life-story that appears to be both cathartic and healing. I occasionally have an email dialogue, but in the vast majority of cases a few lines from me responding to their story is enough. This idea of witness and reciprocity is fundamental to the success of the website and I am often very touched at the responses I get from having responded, even briefly to an email. Here are a just few of the types of responses received:

> It was a comfort stumbling quite accidentally upon your site, having never had encounters with other only-children or their experiences. (Mark)

> I suppose I was compelled to write to you simply because I have never encountered anyone who wanted to know, in some depth, what it felt like to be an only-child. (Eileen)

> I just found your website and have to be honest, I am amazed, I never realised other people found being an only so bad. I must admit I haven't found it so good myself – thank you for a very enlightening read! (Holly)

> I have gained so much from the stories I have read on your website – here is mine... (Heather)

> Thank you so much for responding to my story its such a comfort to know that other people feel like me and I found writing my story so beneficial it was the icing on the cake to get a reply! (Jim)

Correspondence by email has been stimulating and at times critical but it has also lead to interesting dialogues. The range of emails I receive are from adult onlies; young people under eighteen; parent's of onlies; occasionally partners of onlies, therapists and people requesting articles. I have attempted to keep a balance in the ones published on the website, but the polarisation that being an only-child is either good or bad is common. At other times, there is a real attempt to look at both the positive and negative as illustrated by the following email received in 2006 from Australia, entitled: *Not such a bad thing!*

> I was reading with great interest your findings and peoples stories re: growing up an "ONLY!" It amazed me the amount of negative comments people had about the matter. I grew up an only child (I have a half brother and sister from my Mums' previous marriage

but they did not live with us.) and I have never felt any different from anyone else I know, siblings or no. It just never occurred to me that I may be different growing up on my own as I felt everyone is different in their own way anyway.

At school I was bullied a bit, no more than any other tall, skinny girl with big feet. But I feel it made me stronger and who I am today. In fact whenever anyone else told stories of their brothers and sisters, good or bad I used to feel slightly smug that I never had that problem and that I could choose who I wanted to have around me. I left home when I was 18 a very independent, well adjusted woman and travelled from the UK to the Mediterranean and now live in Australia.

The only negative remarks I could make about being an only child is that still, 28 years on I seek approval from my Mum and mostly my Dad (and anyone else for that matter). My dad was also a very strict when I was growing up. I suppose being his 'little girl' and all that! I don't have many significant childhood memories a few from holidays, Christmases, etc. And I'm not a big fan of spending too much time on my own nowadays, I get bored very quickly.

I found your website as I was searching for a few answers. We have one child who is now one. I obviously don't want him growing up lonely or unhappy like some other only children I've read about. I just wish I knew if giving him a sibling would guarantee his happiness! How can I ensure that he grows up as happy to be an only child as I was. Thanks for the web site, a great and insightful read. Keep up the good work. (Tammy)

Tammy also requested hearing my views about her son and this is part of the reply I sent, based on my findings and the fact that I really do not believe only-children always suffer!

Dear Tammy,
Thank you for your email which I found very interesting. I think an only-child can be perfectly happy without siblings as long as the parents are aware of potential difficulties which are primarily around the child needing to please the parents which often means that separation (psychological) is more difficult. In fact this is what you refer to when you write: 'The only negative remarks I could make about being an only child is that still, 28 years on I seek approval from my Mum and mostly my Dad (and anyone else for that matter).' If you can separate from your parents i.e. not need to seek their approval

then you will not pass this need on to your own child. Otherwise I really would not worry especially as he has plenty of cousins!

Occasionally, I have had emails from people whose partners are only-children, which is interesting and has made me reflect a great deal on the effect growing up an only has on later relationships. Mary talked about how, throughout her married life, she had been plagued by her husband's only-childness. In particular, he is jealous of the attention she gives to her own brothers and sisters and is unable to share 'his toys' with them or her. Mary puts this down to her husband being 'the apple of his parent's eye' and that he finds it difficult to relate to the rest of her family in a down-to-earth fashion. Instead, he needs to be the centre of attention finding it difficult to share attention with his son even at the dinner table when neither of them has seen each other for some time. Another email correspondent talks about the difficulty her partner (who has siblings) has understanding her need for time alone:

> I also cannot get my husband to understand that I am quite happy on my own, I am used to being on my own and like my own company now and again but he thinks we should do everything 'together' and I sometimes find it suffocating, sweet but suffocating.(Julie)

From the myriad of emails I have received, many people have thanked me for posting the stories with which people have identified. For example, Carole, a Masters student and only-child, contacted me because she wanted to do her research on literature for only-child adults. Carole had found my website during a web search and contacted me because she was excited to find on-going research on the subject. Carole got me thinking about books I had read as a child, and I began to notice that many of my favourites were in fact about only-children, although I had not been aware of thinking that at the time. I used some of these stories to illustrate the website with quotations and pictures. I have also had requests for information from the United States, India, Australia, Europe, the Phillipines and New Zealand. All have been thought provoking and an opportunity to exchange ideas and articles which led my research to become more internationally orientated.

'Beinganonly': Internet message board

Ann Richardson, an only-child and therapist, set up the 'Beinganonly' message board which provides support to onlies of all ages. I carefully followed the message board postings during its first year and have been both interested and affirmed that the material from my own research has also been important concerns for other onlies. In that year, there were over six hundred postings from one hundred and sixty-five members in the United Kingdom, the United States, Canada, Australia, Taiwan and Malaysia. The realisation that there is little documented research on the issues of adult only-children prompted me to make an analysis of these postings. It is not necessary to give one's age, country or gender to be a member of 'Beinganonly', so the following statistics only give a flavour of the age range, gender and country of origin. An analysis showed that out of approximately 25 per cent who gave their age, it ranged from eighteen to seventy-six years, the majority between twenty and forty years. Approximately, 50 per cent gave their country of origin; the highest percentage is from the United States, 38 per cent; followed by the United Kingdom 36 per cent, Australia 5 per cent, Canada 3 per cent, Taiwan and Malaysia 5 per cent. Out of one hundred and forty-two members, 61 per cent were female, 20 per cent male and 18 per cent of unknown gender.

The following categories are based on the themes that have emerged from the messages posted. I have not included subjects like 'times of chat' or 'places' people live in the United States or the United Kingdom. I think it is interesting to note, in the top six categories, the most influential theme is *difficulties in friendships, 32 per cent*, which covers topics like feeling let down, 15 per cent; trying to please, 12 per cent; too high expectations of others, 14 per cent; letting go of problematic relationships, 12 per cent; taking too much responsibility, 12 per cent; and intensity in relationship, 10 per cent. The next category focuses on the *importance of the message board and chat room, 30 per cent*, as both a support and witness to other onlies as well as parents of onlies. *Loneliness, 29 per cent*, is a continuing theme and emerges particularly around issues of dealing with *elderly parents, 25 per cent*; being *orphaned, 18 per cent*; and *sick parents, 10 per cent*. A frequent theme is a *difficulty in functioning in groups*. It is related to difficulties in both child and adulthood at family gatherings, 16 per cent; Christmas gatherings, 12 per cent; and in groups in general: feeling a scapegoat, 15 per cent; not fitting in, 12 per cent; bullying, 10 per cent; and difficulties in verbal expression – being heard, 6 per cent.

Tips are offered to only-child parents, 12 per cent; and reasons why people are only-children, 19 per cent. In a poll, 68 per cent said they would have preferred to have siblings and 31 per cent preferred to be an only. A further poll showed 47 per cent of onlies were single with no children; 10 per cent were in a relationship but had no children; 18 per cent were in a relationship and had one child; whilst 13 per cent were in a relationship and had more than one. Although these polls are not completed by everyone, they do give an indication of some issues onlies have.

Whilst the message board may not reflect a cross-section of the only-child population, for example, the high number of single female onlies, the issues and the support offered to new and old members do indicate that adult onlies appreciate some medium to air their differences. 'Beinganonly' is one place where they feel they belong, a forum for bringing issues they feel are peculiar to them. These can be tested out and discussed with other onlies. But it is not just supportive. Challenges are made by members who feel things go 'too far' in being attributed to an only-child status, thus bringing balance back to some message board threads.

> I've always wondered why I was so 'defective'. From reading the posts on this list and looking into the social and psychological ramifications of being an only child, I've finally been able to figure out why I am the way I am...and that in a way makes me feel less 'defective'. (Amber)

> I couldn't believe what I was reading when I came here. I've lived my life never thinking about being an only child. I've had an incredibly close relationship to my dad, not to say that my mom and I aren't close also. I grew up in the same town my whole life, and have been fortunate enough to find life-long friends early on. Well I've examined my relationships more closely since coming to this website and have found that my life has started making a little sense. (Chuck)

> Nancy, we are not here to whinge and whine about how terrible life is as a result of being an only child. We do know that there are far worse things that can happen to people. Actually, I am fortunate that my life is pretty good. For me this is a wonderful opportunity to compare notes with other onlies, as I don't know any otherwise. All my friends have brothers and sisters. It is amazing to realise that there are people out there who have shared similar experiences. That is all! (Paula)

The idea of existential witness is at the heart of the popularity of 'Beinganonly' and has led to two conferences in the United Kingdom dedicated to the only-child in 2005 and 2006. The purpose of these conferences is to increase awareness of the only-child experience amongst therapists; give adult onlies the chance to meet and support each other; and offer parents of onlies support and information on the particular needs and challenges of bringing-up an only-child.

Articles, workshops and the media

Interest in only-child issues is increasing and the website has helped to disseminate information about not only this research but other only-child research. Articles written on aspects of only-child phenomena have been published which have enabled another feedback loop to emerge from therapists working with children (Sorensen, 2006b), adults (Sorensen 2006a) and people interested in only-children as a social phenomenon (Sorensen 2006c). As these are also available through the website, people outside of the United Kingdom have access to them. Here are two responses which illustrate the sense of witness and reciprocity:

I enjoyed and appreciated your articles a great deal. Please, do send me any other articles you have written. Your articles were cogent and powerful reminders of the 'only child' reality. I am facing certain medical issues with my husband right now and the increased clarity about my own perspective helps me with understanding his own responses to his crisis. No matter how much therapy or meditation I have had to try to get clear of a too narrow perspective, I find my expectations still wander back to old 'only' assumptions about the world. Thank you so much for sending your writing to me. Your site is terrific and also quite balanced. Rachel (US)

I found your article in Therapy Today and your website so interesting. Some of the statements from the workshops reported on the site left me breathless, it was as though I was reading my own thoughts Like your male correspondent on the noticeboard, I spent a lot of time talking to myself, talking myself to sleep at night and amusing myself by playing all the characters in my own plays. I also had two imaginary friends, one was a good girl, the other naughty but charismatic.

My childhood was not an unhappy one, I think being an only child has made me resourceful, independent and happy to be in my own company. I am never bored, even in traffic jams. However, like many of your contributors, I feel different, and can recognize some grandiosity in the way I think about myself sometimes, which is very annoying! I find it difficult to form friendships which go beyond the small talk stage. I have few close friends. I also find staffroom chat and parties very uncomfortable. Pamela (UK)

Running only-child workshops has led to further exploration of certain themes, such as the negative and positive only-child stereotype, shame, the parental triangle and enmeshment. The knowledge and information gained formed the ideas in Part III of this book. However, perhaps the greatest response is from radio programmes where I have been asked to comment on the research which has led to more people writing to me to share their story.

The next two chapters focus on stories from around the world that I have received as a result of 'going public'. They illustrate that the issues emerging from the original research are also confirmed by only-children from different parts of the world. Although there are cultural differences, many of the experiences are very similar. However, I would invite you as reader and witness to the following stories to decide for yourself.

6
Stories from China and Taiwan

Both Ivy and Yukinori have had an opportunity to leave their own culture and live in and observe another. I think this has given them a unique standpoint to reflect on their experiences of growing up as an only-child. They have been able to step outside and reassess their own experience in a way which would not have been possible from home. In my experience, living in a different culture offers a whole new perspective. It allows one to look anew at those things you previously took for granted in your own homeland.

Ivy is twenty-four, Chinese and living in the United Kingdom, whilst studying and working. Yukinori is thirty-three, Taiwanese and a lecturer in the United Kingdom. Despite being only-children from two different nations, they had many similarities growing up in the shadow of a dominant one-child policy. They both come from relatively wealthy families and this has given them the opportunity to study abroad. Their families know the importance of education and have invested heavily in their child. The investment is not just financial; it is also emotional when there is only one child to carry all the family's hopes and dreams.

I thoroughly enjoyed interviewing both Ivy and Yukinori. They were very open and honest about their experience of growing up as an only-child in a culture where it is neither unusual nor stigmatised. I wondered whether the fact that growing up without siblings being normal had enabled them to be more critical of their experience. So much of what they describe has similarities with my original co-researchers' stories. In particular, the themes of specialness, aloneness and responsibility; feeling dependent and yet yearning for independence; valuing friendships and a growing concern for their ageing parents; and feeling the need to be successful and fulfil their families' expectations, which they both experienced as a duty and a burden. Neither felt they were ever able to be a child as they grew up. They were not free to play and had a great deal of responsibility to succeed. This has affected them both. Yukinori still tries to make up for this in his adult life and Ivy clings tenaciously to her independence.

The stories are primarily in the words of Ivy and Yukinori, and the words in italics are my questions.

Ivy's story

Ivy is a student in her final year studying accountancy, an only-child because of China's one-child policy. She was brought up in Tianjin, south of Beijing. Her own parents grew up with siblings, her mother the eldest of five and her father the youngest of four. Since she was eighteen, Ivy has lived away from China initially in Malaysia and more recently in the United Kingdom. She has no plans to return but does expect to work to her thirties before she gets married. Ivy is adamant that she would never have only one child and she regrets the pressure of her own childhood but does not blame her parents. She is close to them and has a very equal relationship since she cut the ties of her childhood dependency. As they get older, she is concerned for their well-being and is adamant she will look after them in their old age. Ivy is engaging, lively and very open. She talks about her only-child upbringing in China and how her experience has affected the way she is now. She laughs a lot but she also becomes very emotional when thinking of her parents' later years. The interview was very moving for me and Ivy was happy with her story and did not feel she needed to add any more. Ivy begins with her childhood and although she is smiling throughout, quite bouncy and emphatic, I heard a real sadness in her voice as she described the pressure she was under as a child.

Ivy began by talking about her childhood

I was so unhappy as a child, so unhappy! All my parents' attention, from every side was on me. I feel it was too stressful, too pressured. I spent too much time on homework and things like that; I never had time to play. They expected me to do a lot, learn a lot of things and play the piano. There was an enormous pressure to achieve.

As a family we rarely played games. Occasionally, when I was a young child, my mum read me a story at bedtime. My father was working but mum was there all the time cooking, cleaning etc. Most of the time she spent finding out and dealing with my physical needs: hunger, thirst, and clothes. I was on many own a lot of the time, as my parents did not bother me when I studied. If I needed help they got a private teacher, but we never spent time as a family.

When I was little my school bag was so heavy! I could hardly pick it up, hardly carry it, there were so many books! I just had to study or play the piano. The piano was seen to be my relaxation. (she laughs) I don't think so! I used stay in all day; sit in front of the piano the whole day! I wanted to go out in the fresh air, play on the grass, but my parents said: 'No, you are a girl you should stay in and do girly things' – singing, ballet dancing, music, and drawing. If I said I didn't like it, my mum told me why it was good for me. 'When you grow up you can go anywhere, play or travel, do anything you want, but now you have to do the right thing'. This is a typical Chinese family! You can't play with other children, though some children did. Perhaps 30% may have played with other children but the rest carried the expectations of their parents. If you're a boy it's different, they expect even more! But many boys are naughty and do go out and play, as long as they study hard, and have really good results, they are allowed.

In China the pressure is very great to study. You are given a ranking out of so many people, and you have to keep up with your marks or you fall behind in the ranking. You must study, that's all, just constantly think about your results. You spend six years in primary, three years in middle school, and three years in high school. Then there is a very serious examination, so parents spend a lot of time ensuring you do well. This is perhaps because of China's population problem; the competition in education is so high. The good thing is that when you are older you have got more ability to face the competition in society because you are used to working so hard. Parents worry about your future – which is good. It's just you don't have a childhood – that's all! (Ivy laughs)

That sounds so sad

Yeees it is! But I know more compared with other people the same age – but so what! (Both triumphant and self-effacing, Ivy laughs again)

However, I really enjoyed my childhood, apart from the pressure. I didn't have to share with people! This does sound quite selfish, every thing for me and me only! Like the majority of people my parents work for the government. My mum is an accountant. My father does not have a high position but works for quite a big company, as a department manager, and he has his own business.

Did they want more than one child?

They can't because of the one child policy – but yes they would have liked to. When I came to England I saw people with brothers and sisters. They sometimes argued but often they really enjoyed each other, really laughed. I felt quite jealous and I rang my parents and asked: 'Why don't you give me a brother or a sister?' My mum laughed and said she had enough with me! They gave me so much love, but if they had the chance they probably would have one more child, company for me. I feel lonely as well, very lonely. I will have children of course, but I promise myself I will never ever have one child only, at least two or three! My parents knew as a child I was under too much pressure and they felt so sad for me, but they had no choice. You have to compete; you have to see the future. If I am not learning I can't compete with people. If you want to have a place in society you have to have your own skill.

I came abroad because my parents did not think studying in China is the best educationally. They realised it was hard for a little girl to spend all her time in study, study, study. They just wanted their daughter to be like normal people. Going abroad helps with both English and Accountancy. This way I did more – they planned it! So when I was 18, I moved away and went to study in Colombo and in Malaysia. I was taught in English and the books were in English, but everyone was of Chinese descent. In school we were all speaking Mandarin and Cantonese. I did not learn to speak much English, only listen!

I found living with other people so difficult! I had to learn to share and stay on a student campus. I had to learn how to get on with people because I hadn't learnt how to communicate. When you go out and are with other people, you have to be nice or how will they be nice to you? It was all so difficult. In my family you ask and they just give it to you. It was very difficult because mum never told me how to interact with others. In Malaysia I stayed with a Chinese girl. I got into mixing socially, but at first I found everyone really strange. These students liked going out in a group of say five to six people to eat, or play, or shop, or even cook together, that was so strange to me. I was on my own, but they always asked me out, they would say: 'Come and join us'. To start with I said no, but after awhile I did and I liked it. They helped each other in study which I really liked and I began to enjoy the help. Before I was always on my own, I was very independent, but now I know one person can't do everything. I need others and if everyone uses team work it is quicker and makes life easier. So I had to change a little bit, find out things, but now it's ok.

I finished my first degree, and at that stage most people would want to stop. I did as well! But because I came from a one child family, my Mum and Dad persuaded me to do more, even more, so I had to do a Masters. When I finished my Master's, I said: 'Ok Mum that is all!' But Mum said that it is not enough so now I am doing certified accountancy.

I don't blame my parents; I think the pressure comes from living in a society which is over populated. People here in the UK enjoy an easy life but in China everything is fast, everyone rushes all the time, never stopping. A lot of people can't afford to come away or even study at university. In the countryside a really good student with good results wouldn't have a chance because their parents have no money. Some people go abroad like me, but not a lot compared to the population. It is hard to get into university in China, but not so hard once you are in, so it is more challenging to go abroad.

When I went back home to China, this summer, I was treated like a princess – I was so happy! I don't have to think about anything. My parents asked me what I want to eat, where I want to go. I don't have to think about anything when I'm there. Here I have to think, plan what I eat, what I do and it all depends on whether I have enough money. But in China parents worry about everything for you. I was a princess as a child, I complained a lot but my parents spent a lot of money on me, bought me a piano, paid for tuition and private lessons for school. Even at school teachers tell you exactly what you need to do, to get a good result. Yes, it's about learning what you are told, not about curiosity. I was not happy with this way, it's learning from the outside. Now I learn from the inside. I said to my Mum one day in high school, when my results had dropped: 'I spend a lot of time doing this studying, and my results are not that good. So much effort and no return.' I used to get really upset about that. Now I come here, to the UK, I do my own work and I feel happy. I do it and get results, good ones, and I feel happy to have found my own way to learn.

Nowadays students are getting so spoilt, so spoilt. They don't have to work; they have no pressure at all. This was my experience before, when I first went abroad, and all my fees were paid. When I came to the UK, I got a part time job and now I am independent. I am so happy to be financially independent from my parents. It is quite important! When I realised I could make money I phoned my parents and told them: 'I can make money I am independent' and they were so happy too! Perhaps even more happy than me! They thought: 'Oh my god our girl has grown up'

When I was little I did not care about money I could buy anything I liked. A lot of Chinese students, even though they are older than me, are in that position. Whereas when I came here, I saw that all English boys and girls get a part time job, even at 16! I did not start until I was 21, but lots of Chinese students are not working at all. They don't do so because their parents plan for them already. They plan for their future, their study, their job, even marriage.

I used to be fed up as a teenager as my parents made me dependent. That's why I wanted a job to make money so that I could become independent. Now it feels I have an equal position with them. Before they told me what I should do. I had to do it and I didn't always want to. Now we can talk and we are like two adults, quite comfortable. Before I had had enough, really enough. I listened to everything from my parents. First you are going to do this, the next step you are going to do a Masters, and after a job and then marriage. This includes the sort of man. He has to be rich and highly educated, like me!

Do you have a boyfriend?

I don't have boyfriend as I don't have time. I work 4 days a week and study. I'm also influenced as a result of my childhood. I like the way I am, I like to be independent all the time. So I don't want to be with anyone – it's not good but it's me. I had a relationship three years ago in Malaysia. He was a nice guy and I got on with him but I was not happy to be in a serious relationship. You have to change and I am not happy to change. I feel like this is the way I am, I am happy for that. I don't mind changing little things but I like the way I do things. I am independent and I do the things I like to do. If I am in a relationship I have to ask permission and I don't like it!

Why permission?

Guys are like that. If you are their girlfriend you have to tell them everything you do.

If you are going to make a decision, like I am going to go here or there, you have to ask if you can go or not. Oh I have had enough of that! I want to be on my own, that's all!

Marriage is a very big concern, like studying, a big issue. A job is a big issue and marriage is the last one of the big issues. You can't get divorced, Chinese people don't do that. In China if people marry and have difficulties they do not divorce. It's because of pressure from outside, the reputation of the family. In my case, if I marry over here, my parents don't care where he is from, but he has to be the same as me: highly educated, not poor. My father expects me to find someone who will take care of me, so that one day when I have a family and I am at home with our kids, my husband can look after me. Yes, I do feel pressure from my parents about marriage. I am 24 and the normal age of marriage is 24 or 25. All my classmates are getting engaged or are already married.

How do you feel about that?

I don't care – that's why I ran away, so they can't control me!

My Aunts and Uncles ask my parents about my boyfriend. So they are a bit worried about me but they can't control me because I am so far away! (Ivy laughs)

I would like to get married at 30. I'd like to settle my career first. I have no work experience so I must go out and work. I can't just be a housewife. Before I settle down I must try everything.

Is that a result of your childhood?

Yes. I am jealous of people with a sister or brother. They take care of each other.

I don't have that so I'm close to my parents. I will look after them when they are old. They don't mind if I have to stay here, but in Chinese culture, when parents get old its payback time. I will definitely go back to China or if I don't, I will do my best for them if I've got money. My parents come from very big families. Every kid helps to take really good care of their parents. But with an only-child it is all my responsibility.

Do your parents see it that way?

No – They have their own plans! If I have a family they think about me and my career. I don't have to take care of them. They keep some money so they can go into a nursing home. I feel so sad when they say that. I feel so sad.... I can't just leave my parents behind and have my own life, it's too selfish. No I can't do that.

The pressure Ivy felt as a child to succeed is evident in the next story. Neither Ivy nor Yukinori blame their parents for the isolating childhoods they both experienced, rather they see it as a condition of the social climate. Ivy finishes her story, similarly to Yukinori, concerned over the well-being of her parents, especially as they grow older.

Yukinori's story

Yukinori now lives in the United Kingdom, but was born in 1974 and brought up in Taiwan. He has a PhD in Business and Management and he lectures in a number of universities. Initially, in the interview, he seemed very serious possibly because he was unsure of what I wanted. However, I soon saw another side to him which was playful as well as intense and thoughtful. He speaks of a lonely childhood in Taiwan, with few friends. This has made him very appreciative of friendship and also independent. At fourteen, he moved to a public boarding school in the United Kingdom. He believes his experience of solitude and aloneness as an only-child prepared him for the isolation he encountered. He has a strong sense of responsibility towards his family and others. This is evidenced by his generosity in giving up his time to be interviewed, despite a very busy schedule.

Like Ivy's interview, it was both fascinating and enjoyable and I was struck again by the similarity of the many only-child themes I had encountered in my earlier interviews. In particular, the burden of being the only-one and the expectations that this role held, particularly being an only son. Similarly, his need to be successful in everything whilst being supportive even to strangers like myself to whom he had no obligation. Despite his confident exterior, I often met the little boy who never had the opportunity to be a child and now loved going to work in a baseball cap and playing PlayStation 2. His is charming and yet fearful of not making the best of his life, not fulfilling all his potential. Underneath the confident exterior, he does not really know what he wants, although he yearns for the opportunity to be a good son to his parents in Taiwan.

Yukinori began by talking about Taiwan

It is a free, democratic country, so to have an only-child is a parents' choice and not imposed by an external government. As a former Portuguese, Spanish, Dutch, Japanese and Chinese colony, siblings were common. Children were needed to work on the farm so there is a long tradition of large families. My grandad had six sons and three daughters;

perhaps this had a part to play in my father's decision to have one child! I think it was partly social pressure, but mainly financial reasons. My mother had two brothers and three sisters.

I found growing up as an only-child difficult because my mum was a primary school teacher and I went to the same school. This did not help, as other kids did not want to play with me, because they would get additional attention. Some kids don't want to get this particular type of attention, so as a kid I was very isolated. I am the only son and so I got extra attention for what ever I did.

Success was the only option available to me. I did not get an opportunity for personal preference. What is best is always according to other people's expectations, other adults, the family, my grandfather and the hopes and aspirations of my dad. I have only one chance, I have to get it right first time, so when I was a kid I was under an enormous amount of pressure. I believe this pressure may have stimulated my potential, but psychologically it may have done the opposite. Sometimes I do feel very rebellious!

My childhood is quite sad actually. Nobody to share a toy with me; nobody to fight with me for a toy; in fact nobody to talk to me. I had to pretend I had someone to play with. No friends to visit, but I had to go to school, so when I was in school I was rather active in terms of sports, and in other bad ways, which I don't want to mention. Sometimes I would chuck stones into the school pond to frighten the fish or throw a pair of keys in the sky and pretend to be amused.

I treasured friends and friendship; other people took companionship for granted, but I took it far more seriously. When I have friends, even now, I consider that to be a privilege. If my friends are in need, or want help, I will try and help them, academically, socially, what ever they need.

It must have been difficult to leave your home and friends to come here.

Yes. I came to the UK at 14, on my own, to join a boarding school. There was no family, no friends, no relatives and it was my first time overseas in a foreign country. It was totally alien, with different weather, different culture, a different race. It was exciting and at the same time tricky. I was extremely homesick at the beginning. There are two different types of kids that go to boarding school. Smart ones whose parents think they have got potential and problematic ones where parents are less inclined to give them attention. I had to adjust myself to the environment so that I could pick up the language.

Before I came, my dad told me it was his grandfather's dying wish, to have been able to study here – so I have been given this opportunity and it is an honour for me, but I also carry the burden of the family. I have been given this fairy tale, of how England and France actually contributed to the industrial revolution, in earlier days, before Japan. Perhaps if I can acquire sufficient knowledge – I can be of service to the greater good of the civilisation of man – that is his hope.

For me, Britain is a socially divided society. Families send their kids to state schools, some send them to private boarding. In the latter, they are taught in a very different way, about manners, pride, honour and traditional English values. I had to accustom myself to the very traditional ways, that the English think and understand. I had my study not a dormitory; it was posh. I was a foreigner and because of my hair colour and my skin colour, I was different. My main difficulty was the language barrier. I spoke very little English and I had no idea, of what is what, and I couldn't make out what was going on a lot of the time. On my first day, at boarding school, I realised that in three and a half years time I would have to compete with English students to get to the top university. Yet, I had no idea of what was a top university so I took it as the best university: Oxford, Cambridge, London and Edinburgh. I might aim high and achieve low, so I applied to go to these universities but I was also prepared to go to a polytechnic. My first choice was London as it was the capital and the political and commercial centre.

I did not go home for the first ten years because of National Service. Taiwan was under constant threat from China, so all men had to do national service. Taiwan has always been a colony and is not very good at governing itself. Legislation, as a result, is not developed and is often fragmented. The legislation does not reflect what is happening to individuals. So even half way through my O levels, I could have still been called up. I had, at fourteen, to leave the country to avoid National Service. My father did not want me to avoid it but do it differently; he wanted me to serve my country as my duty, in a foreign land.

As China has a lot of influence in Taiwan, my father did not want me to be acquainted with a fraction of the reality a Chinese dominated education would have given me. I came to Britain and learned about Taiwanese history. At first I was gobsmacked when I realised Taiwan had been a colony of Western and Eastern super powers for 400 years. We had been slaves for 400 years! I learned about the massacre by Chiang Kai-shek – I couldn't believe it! At that time in Taiwan the political party in power was the Chinese National Party, which was opposed to communism and the reason Taiwan remained separated. Speaking in Taiwanese was discouraged in 1980 so I started learning Taiwanese in England. I was taught by an English professor who had lived in Taiwan as a doctor. Democratisation in the last few years means we have a new president now.

How has being an only-child affected you?

I learned independence as a result of being an only-child. I don't have any siblings so I don't have anyone to cry out to when trouble occurs. Sending me here, when I was 14 years old would have been suicide, had I been used to siblings. Having no siblings prepared me, ever since I was a kid, for when no one spoke to me. It was just like when I was a child. It didn't bother me, because I had a clear set of objectives. If anyone was kind enough to be friends with me I would relish this friendship. If they didn't really care – then tough luck. I used to be the sort of kid who would toss my keys in the corner of my room – nobody cares or knew. Yes – There were other Taiwanese in the school but I did not have contact with them.

As a result of being an only-child I have been through a lot single-handedly. I also have an expectation that other people can do things on their own, like me. I think that it's because I can do it without others help – so why can't you! I do consider myself less privileged having no siblings. If you have brothers or sisters, you have friends, so you should be able to succeed. This has influenced some of my expectations of my students working on group projects. I think: 'How difficult can that be? It's just about organising oneself'. I tend to have this expectation, that other people are going to be able to perform because I have, I don't find it difficult to get on with people, so why should they?

As a result of being an only-child, I cherish opportunities to be with other people. When there are other people around I would like to consider myself to be the star! In a group I feel it is my responsibility for the whole group to be harmonised. Normally no one pays attention to me, so when I am socialising with other people, or working on a specific task with other people, I demand their attention. My strong character comes through. I not only demand attention but I also make them feel safe. I let them know I am intellectually capable, I am experienced and they are in safe hands. I naturally acquire this leadership style or status within a group. Now, instead of being an isolated kid, suddenly it's like I have got a lot of brothers and sisters! People think I am very much like their elder brother.

I wonder if you are a bit of a parent figure?

Parent figure? – No I don't tell people off.

Oh you see parents as telling you off?

Yes, yes.

What about a nurturing parent, isn't this what you are doing?

Oh woops! (laughs) that sounds bad!

(We both laugh and I explain:)

It's just I thought you described a nurturing parent role, to enable other people to fulfil their potential in the group. May be more to do with a parent than a brother? So what happens when someone else wants to be a leader?

Yes such circumstances have occurred. I become quite submissive, very silent, an observer. I participate but not as vigorously as I would like to when I am leading. I tend to be more cautious, only 80%.

You avoid confrontation?

Yes, I do my best to avoid any sort of confrontation. Confrontation is a tactic of problem solving. But it's not the only choice of tactic, it's a last resort – and I have to win, so I tend to take other more strategic approaches.

What happens if someone is confrontational towards you?

Perhaps it's because I have left them with no other options. So I would open some doors for them. There must be other ways which would be mutually beneficial, or a compromise. I see confrontation as very negative, even as physical aggression, verbal or ridicule.

So what happens when you are angry?

I lock myself in a room! Isolate myself – because aggression means you are not in the best control of your conscience. My responses, at that time, may not be in my best interest.

(I realise Yukinori is speaking here primarily in terms of work)

So what happens in personal relationships?

I make sure my significant other half is equally rational, as I am, in behaviour, emotion and speech.

What about your emotional life? It seems like emotionality versus rationality.

Yes! I do have emotions, I am not a robot! (We laugh)

This society is all about who you talk to and what you say to them. It's important to say the right thing, to the right person, at the right time. If you can do that you are a social success. Otherwise you are seen as not so trustworthy, unpredictable, less likely to be given any duties of responsibilities. I decided to make way for my rationality by putting my emotions away. When I feel upset I try to control my emotions. When I am very stressed, I don't sleep for more than 4–5 hours because there are so many things I need to have done. Plus I have to do this and that, as a favour to a friend. If I don't do this I will displease this person, so it's a complicated life.

(I smile and ask somewhat jokingly) *Are you ever spontaneous?*

Spontaneous? Well if that means going mental, walking into a garden and going mental – No! (I realise we understand this word differently, so I change the question)

Were you ever a child? (Yukinori smiles)

The reason I like working at the University is because I can turn up in baseball cap and jeans, and students find that acceptable. I can go down to the pub with them and listen to rock music, like I used to. I feel I never grew up and I am still deeply in love with childhood, I myself, have neglected. I even went to buy PlayStation 2 (he smiles looking shamefaced) and I play it at home. I was so surprised when my students did not have one! I realised even more how I had missed out. When I told my girlfriend she said 'Are you looking after your friend's kid?' When I told her the truth she said: 'Are you ok? Shall I come to England? Are you insane?' We have been apart for three years. We see each other every year and will marry in one or two year's time. She has two brothers in her family. She can behave childishly and so can he! (Yukinori's girlfriend is a sales executive in Taiwan with a Master's degree. They are deeply in love, and she has been very supportive whilst he struggled with his PhD.)

It's first the time I felt a failure when I did my PhD. I had spent all the family savings and I still had not got it because of my unsupportive supervisor. My girlfriend was the one who pulled me through and believed in me. Even my mum said if it's so difficult I should give up. I had a Masters so I should just go back to Taiwan. There was no support; all I heard was give up, you have reached your limit! For me the only way out was to finish. I have to accomplish what I started. I did, but it took six and a half years which makes me feel, even now, not good enough. Even though I have a PhD, I consider this to be a failure because it took six and a half years when I should have done it in four and a half years. I have never said this to anyone – for me failure is not an option. But it's different with my students. I tell them it's ok to fail. It's the way you learn. I want my students to enjoy their life. I did not have that option. I have so little time left. I don't want to die old – in my 40's or 50's – so I have little time to achieve.

Why die young – is there so little you can achieve with age? Sages were old!

True very true. I don't know, it's a presumption. Youth gives you emotion, age gives you wisdom! What am I expecting out of myself?

Will you have children and would you have only one?

It's probably better not to have kids at all, but one is better than more. Life has been hard for me, I prefer none. My partner wants children; I will probably do what she wants. I found it very, very difficult to grow up, to become mature and to take up responsibility. I have this responsibility to achieve something and I cannot face the possibility of failure. Getting my PhD almost killed me. All this pressure, all this burden, everyone looking at you, with great expectation. I don't want to be the individual that eats, shits and dies! I have lived a distinguished life for a foreign student. I have been asked to do many things and I have felt what an honour at the time, but now it's just another day. I want to be a star I don't want to be a sparkle!

A sparkle is not an everlasting brightness!

Is this to do with being an only-child?

Yes!

Grandiosity?

Probably! If had my life again, I would have an elder brother to share part of my responsibilities and things that I can not do because of the eleven years I have been in England, pursuing a career of my own. I want to be a good son when I return. I want to take out the rubbish for my mum, help my father move furniture. Seeing them in their 60s doing it on their own, it just kills me. I am a perfectionist; I want to be a good son as well as a good individual. If I had a brother, who could do those things for me, I could pursue my dream and ambition without worry. But I would always be special to my parents. One of the biggest questions puzzling me is: Do I go back to Taiwan? I have this fear of going back. In England I have a very British type of credential, and when I go back I will have to start over again. What I have on paper will be recognised but society is very different, it's not just about qualifications, but who you are acquainted with. Who can pull the strings! I don't know anyone in Taiwan like I do here. I have a phobia about going back. My girlfriend believes I will be able to improvise. But will she leave me when I don't! It's about confidence. Responsibility needs to be proactive; if it's reactive there is no other way of dealing with it, except by taking up that responsibility. Responsibilities are burdens, a lot of the things I do are responsibilities, but they are also burdens. My dream for the future is particularly reactive – am I going to be the Prime Minster? If I go back to Taiwan, what is it that I want? My only wish is to spend time with my parents in the countryside, fish with my dad, not worry about financial circumstances and take out rubbish for my mum. I don't really know myself.

Reflections

I hope, in these stories, I have given a flavour of the interviews. They are written to give a sense of the interaction between myself and my interviewee. I have kept in some of my questions to show how I focused the story to enable both the cultural context and the only-child issues to emerge. Before interviewing, I had no idea of what Ivy's and Yukinori's stories would contain, similar to my original co-researchers' interviews. I was often amazed at the similarity these stories had with those of the co-researchers'. For example, the loneliness and isolation they both experienced in not having siblings. Whilst both Ivy and Yukinori would have liked siblings, I believe Yukinori has reframed his only-child experience positively seeing it as enabling him to achieve greater things.

Ivy and Yukinori both experienced pressure as children to achieve from their parents and the wider family. They appreciate the necessity of this pressure in order to succeed in their culture. They also acknowledge the limitation this has had on them to mature, separate and become individuals, when the family dictates everything down to the person they should marry. Studying abroad revealed their lack of social interaction and acquisition of skills in this area. Whilst both value their friendships, Ivy is concerned with maintaining her hard-fought independence and does not yet want to have a boyfriend and Yukinori has a long-distance relationship, with a view to marriage when he decides to return to Taiwan. Independence and dependence have been important issues in their lives and Yukinori, in particular, is aware of his difficulties in growing up and maturing. Ivy recognises, when she goes home and her mother takes over once more, she is the 'princess'. She is also aware of the price she has had to pay by 'running away so they cannot control' her.

Yukinori tries to deal with life from a rational perspective. Nonetheless, he finds confrontation and anger difficult and he isolates himself, fearing failure above all else. Emotionally, he appeared to be at times in an adolescent stage. This was evidenced, I believe, by his wish not to die young and his need to prove himself; feeling a failure for taking longer than he felt he should over his PhD. He was aware of his grandiosity; being a star not just a sparkle. However, my impression of his remark about becoming a prime minister was meant seriously. I understood his ambition, but his lack of confidence was obvious and I think demonstrates the outward appearance of the confident, successful only-child that belies the little child which is very evident inside.

There were occasions when I misunderstood what Yukinori was saying. I have highlighted these in the text. In particular when he spoke about being a brother and I changed it to parent, I think I lost something important, although his response was also quite revealing, equating parents with 'telling off'. However, I think he has a strong need to be the elder brother that he would have liked to have had. His wish to demand others' attention but also offering them a safe place is interesting, as he becomes easily submissive if his leadership is challenged.

I noticed with both Ivy and Yukinori a slight lack of empathy toward their fellow students; Ivy saying how spoilt they were nowadays and Yukinori how he expected them to be able to do everything he could do because they had the benefit of a sibling, whereas he had not and had coped. I wondered if the harshness of their own childhoods was showing through or they were just envious of the greater freedom they perhaps saw in the next generation.

They both end their stories focused on their parents. Yukinori in particular misses his parents and feels he is not doing his familial duty. However, I was aware of the dilemma they both had. On the one hand, they were expected to fulfil their parent's dreams and expectations, and on the other they needed to separate and live their own life which appears incompatible with going home. The next chapter contains more life-stories that reflect both similar and different issues providing an insight on only-child experiences across the lifespan.

7
Life-Stories and Life-Stages

In the previous chapter, we heard the stories of Ivy and Yukinori, both young people. This chapter offers a voice to adult only-children who have contacted me through the website to share their life-stories. I have used these stories to illustrate that certain life-stages hold particular challenges for only-children as discussed in Chapter 4. The life-stages have been divided into six headings which denote the inter-personal relationships that are central to each stage.

Six only-child life stages

1. Childhood without siblings;
2. Friendships and peer relationships;
3. A significant other – intimate relationships;
4. Becoming a parent;
5. Ageing parents; and
6. The latter years.

The stages are not dependent on age, neither are they necessarily experienced by every only-child. What is important is the first stage; growing up without the benefit of sibling relations to develop social and emotional skills can impact on each subsequent stage. However, I would reiterate that the challenges of each life-stage will be fewer when the parent(s) of the only-child have offered them opportunities to interact with children of their own age to develop social and emotional skills.

The following stories demonstrate that for the adult only-child who does not develop adequate emotional and social skills, subsequent relationships can be problematic. This lack of social and emotional development can impact on the quality of peer relationships and lead to difficulties in maintaining relationships with a significant other. It may lead to a series of partners or none at all. Others who found their own childhood a negative experience choose not to have children or ensured they had more than one. Many adult onlies become very involved with caring for an ageing parent. Some of these life-stage choices can result in the only-child adult feeling alone and isolated in their later years, especially when they have no children or partner. For those who have cared for parents, rather than develop other relationships, this can be a particularly difficult time as there are now fewer opportunities to find a partner or develop a sustaining social life, and some fear what life will be like after the death of their parents.

All these stories have been offered by people who have read the 'onlychild' website and have written in to share their own. The stories are used to illustrate life-stage challenges; but with so many stories from so many people, it has been difficult to choose which ones to use. I have tried to keep a balance between those stories that come from adult only-children who are positive about their experience and those who are not. This has not always been possible. For example, there is a wide mixture of both positive and negative experience in childhood and early friendships. However, for those adult onlies who had particularly isolated childhoods, we find this isolation continues and is evidenced more forcefully as they grow older and many find themselves alone or caring for elderly parents. I am not arguing that the latter years are necessarily problematic for adult onlies, but I have received stories illustrating that the continued impact of social and emotional difficulties, begun in childhood, may be a direct result of being an only-child in overprotected or neglectful childhoods. Overprotective and neglectful parenting will be detrimental to a child with siblings, but at least they have another person to dilute the attention, compare experience or even receive support. They will also have someone to share, even in a minimal way, the decisions concerning ageing parents. Finally, they have someone who is a witness to their own childhood and important experiences, as discussed in Chapter 5.

Whilst most people wrote emails to me as a result of resonating with some or most of the stories published on the website, telling me small parts of their own experience, other people sent me their entire life-story. These can be many pages long and they have the feel of many of my initial co-researchers' interviews. The flavour of these longer stories clarified the life-stage aspect of my earlier research. All the stories represented here have the only-child experience as their focus. I did receive some stories which, although interesting and often poignant, were not written with an only-child focus and these I have chosen not to use. The following stories range from across the world, including the United Kingdom, Australia, the United States, Canada and Sweden. What is particularly interesting is the similarity of only-child themes which were also echoed in the original co-researchers' stories and in those of Ivy and Yukinori. I have chosen not to comment on each story as I have left readers to attribute their own meaning. However, I have introduced each person and highlighted the major themes within the story. The ten stories range from John and Kim in their twenties to Gunnar in his late seventies. These stories demonstrate the issues that emerge throughout the lifespan. Although my original research focused on women, I later began collecting stories from men to see if their only-child issues had similarities or differences. The stories selected for this chapter illustrate some specifically male issues from a life-stage perspective and also ones that deal with a sense of self.

Kim: indulged but positive and confident

Kim was born in 1982 and enjoyed being an only-child. Her experience has not impacted negatively on her friendships and that may be a result of the energy her parents put into ensuring she met up with friends. Kim describes herself as an indulged only-child which she feels has given her confidence. She is extremely close to her parents and sees them as making up for her lack of siblings. She is unmarried, but living with a partner and has no children yet. When I asked her about the care of her parents, when they are too old to care for themselves, she said:

> I haven't thought very much just yet about my parents' future care. Dad will be 78 this year, and although he suffers from arthritis and sciatica which limit his mobility, he is still completely 'on the ball'. Mum is 11 years his junior and has more energy than me! It's not something we have had to worry about as yet. One stipulation is – I will never allow either of them to go into a care home, or a prolonged stay in hospital. I would 100% prefer them to be looked after in their own home and would readily do this myself.

Kim is only twenty-four but her devotion and closeness to her parents and the responsibility she feels towards them is very typical of adult only-children. She was also able to resonate with many of the stories from the website, for instance, jealousy towards people who have sibling relationships.

I am the only child of two devoted older parents, I am now 24. When I was a child I felt in many ways alone, but never for long. My Mum had longed to have more children, but had left it too late and so she and my father went out of their way to drive me to friend's houses and organize activities for me at home.

Of course I envied my friends who had sisters and brothers of their age, but I also recognized siblings as a hindrance as well. Throughout my childhood, I was particularly good friends with two sisters who lived next door and I saw them warring and raging at each other; I didn't envy that! My childhood home was peaceful and as I was only 'one'. My parents made a concerted effort never to be angry with me at the same time so I always had one friendly face to find in our house.

My friendships have been made more durable as a result. My friendship group comprises of friends found in both primary and secondary schools and then throughout university, I am confident that I could confide in any of them my deepest darkest secrets, no less than I would a sibling, and perhaps even more. Boyfriends and partners have not even mentioned my non-sibling status. I have no annoying younger sisters to embarrass them when they came to the family home, or no older brothers to give them the once over when they walk through the door. Only occasionally did I get called a spoilt only-child, but then I think that it's due to envy from my peers rather than anything else. My parents didn't have the financial restraints of a larger family, although they were both retired by the time I finished school. They have always given me their time and understanding willingly, trying to relate to a teenager tearing in and out of their house and the trials and tribulations that came with my adolescence.

I was admittedly, an indulged child. If I were to say spoilt; my father would laugh and my mother disagree. But I know in truth I was. I was the centre of my parent's world, the result of their life together, and all their energies were channelled into me. That is true even today, but I idolize both of my parents despite the rows and disagreements that still occur. I would not replace them for the world, even though in younger spiteful moments I longed for a family the opposite of my own, with young parents and copious siblings. As I've got older I've realized that I wouldn't want any other family life than I have known and you have to make the best of what you have unless you want to be constantly haunted by dissatisfaction. My mother would never stand for me to feel sorry for myself, and made me realize that if I didn't enjoy my own company who else would?

I have read your website and its postings with great interest. I can relate to many of the observations, not being able to play board games alone (although I had a bloody good try), the worry of ending up alone should anything happen to your parents (I live with this to this day), and the jealousy of others and their relationships with their siblings. I never thought anyone felt that way, as I did, and as I expect we all have at one time or another.

John: actor and self-critic

John writes eloquently about his life as an only-child from the perspective of someone in their early-twenties. He describes himself as introspective and he has been able to reflect deeply on his character and the elements which he attributes to his upbringing as an only-child. He focuses on how he behaves in a social setting and his difficulty knowing at times how to act and interact and how close or distant to be. Relationships with women are particularly difficult and he hides behind the façade of a gentleman. He speaks about the two 'me's' the 'actor and critic' which dominate his life and lead him to feel angry and even depressed. I think John's story concisely describes the internal dilemmas only-children face. For men, in particular, the lack of social and emotional interaction as children can lead them to feel particularly isolated.

I'm a university student, in my early twenties. My childhood was split relatively evenly between North Africa, Malaysia, England and America. My upbringing, by two intelligent and motivated parents has left me with several quite useful traits, allowing me to be an independent and occasionally lively thinker, self-reliant and resilient. However, I feel that being an only-child has put a layer of emotional insulation between me and the world, especially the world of adult relationships.

There are three key issues which I think are pertinent here: a lack of the sense of commonality which others enjoy; a degree of emotional repression which makes any relationship difficult; and an inward looking navel-gazing approach to life.

When I'm in a public setting, in which I'm comfortable, I am often gregarious, funny and engaging. However, I have a constant problem with feeling out of bounds in the conversation, being first hesitant and then often too heavy handed with my speech and my mannerisms. Whereas others seem to slide into social interaction easily, I've always felt like I've been handed a guest pass. This may be due to being an only, and also has a lot to do with not having a consistent group of best friends throughout my childhood. When I do make close friends, I often have great difficulty in deciding whether or not they reciprocate the intensity of feeling. There is a constant pressure to be the funny one, the sparkling witty me, not the introverted, quiet me.

This gets worse in my relationships with women. With male friends I feel indebted to them for their very friendship, but with women I simply cannot understand why they would be friends with me. Having gone to an all boys school, in addition to having lead a relatively sheltered life, I never know how far to take relationships with women, and what is and isn't acceptable. So instead I opt for the 'pose of the gentleman', being polite and keeping a wall of relatively decent manners between myself and them. That's not to say I'm not genuinely trying to be a gentleman, but I suspect that the social rules involved have become more of a crutch than a worthy aspiration. In certain circumstances, it gets even more extreme with politeness giving way to intense self-deprecation, portraying myself as a monster-character, providing a second front as a coarse and unlikeable fellow. I think this last course of action has, somewhat ironically, grown out of one of the traits I like the most about my only-child status: a deep appreciation of all things beautiful. I often feel compelled to celebrate the beauty of women, the beauty of life, with my friends and in the work I do. Equally I grow frustrated with not having the words, the glib tongue, the confidence to share these wonders with others. This often leads to bouts of depression and introspection, where I rather mercilessly flail myself with my own character flaws, my doubts and my anxieties.

Finally, out of the three points raised earlier, I think that my introspective nature has exacerbated the problems I face. In a social situation it's like there are always two 'me's coexisting, the actor and the critic: when I'm out of a comfortable situation, I simply observe those around me, watching them and studying them, seeking traits to emulate and others to avoid. However, when I do anything myself, the same process applies and on occasions when I do something I hold in contempt in others, however minor, the critic is still working, still criticising those actions. When everything goes 'according to script' it's okay, but the first misstep usually results in embarrassment, discomfort and loss of equilibrium, which generally tends to snowball into a bad mood and occasionally outright anger or bad temper.

I just hope that as I mature and confront my failings; I can grow back into society, and overcome these social handicaps. As it is, there are episodes like this one, where, despite all my efforts and work, things seem to spiral out of control, where the feeling of being an outsider is so strong that it is difficult to function, to step out of a cycle of self-loathing.

Most importantly perhaps, I need to find another anchor point in my life besides my parents; the stories of loss and pain that other correspondents have provided are very similar to my own waking nightmares of losing my parents, fears that have kept me awake long into the night before now.

Reading the posts on your website has been a gentle boost for the time being, which may help me to stop from turning into the monster I occasionally portray myself as. To dishonour my family's values and limit my own potential by doing so, is a thought which I simply can't bear any longer.

Matt: staying attached to his parents

Matt is only twenty-seven but he has already found that his lack of social interaction as a child has left him without the confidence to relate easily to others. He has a close relationship with his parents and finds it difficult to leave home. Matt acknowledges that he has received a great deal of attention, particularly from his mother, and that other people may regard him as spoilt. Perhaps more significantly, he lacks the motivation to step outside of his parent's world and become independent of them. He fears that when they die he will be alone in the world. He has suicidal thoughts which are a result of a lack of knowing where he belongs, but recognises that at least while his parents are alive there is enough meaning for him to carry on living.

I am an only-child. It was not until I was about 21 and away at University that I really started having problems. At first when the problems started I was not aware of the significance of being an only-child and how that was related to them. At first I thought I was gay, but after having minor panic attacks for a period of 15 months I realised that it wasn't because I was gay, I just wasn't sociable enough and lacked the confidence and commitment to be in a relationship or find a girlfriend.

For a while I blamed my only-child situation on my parents, but knew this was something that they could not do anything about, nor could I blame them. They made a decision some 26 years ago that, because at birth there was a slight defect in my feet (clubbed); they did not want to take any other risks.

I am jealous of people with brothers and sisters. I often talk to my friends about it and they say how lucky I am, although they and I both realise, the grass is always greener on the other side. It's only in the last two years, that I have realised how ungrateful and lucky I have been. However, when you get use to a comfort zone, it is very difficult to break free from it, if you are never forced or need to. I thank my parents for my life and try to appreciate everything they do. Although I have also tried to break free and get my Mum to do less for me.

I am still very dependent on my parents. The panic attacks have returned, but now it is a fear of being lonely in the future. I still am living at home with them, although in the last 10 months since returning from Canada, I have been living in London, and attempting to move out again. However, knowing my parents are there, is a comfort which I have got used to. I know it is something that I need to get out of my system to prepare for when they will not be around for me. Whilst I know something will happen one day I need to force myself or be forced into a situation where I need to survive. I am considering a boot camp or some kind of survival weekend. I think joining the army is a bit extreme and I really don't believe I could survive it!

I think as an only-child, you can become selfish and spoilt, and although my parents said they didn't spoil me, my Mum definitely spoilt me emotionally with all the attention. My Canadian cousin perceived me to be a young spoilt person, although having explained some of the above, she understands. But that doesn't change others' perceptions of me in my teenage years. My Mum had to give up a child when she was 17 and I think this may have affected how much she mothered me and maybe to make up for the child that she gave up. My Dad is a very strong person and his upbringing made him that way. I think he suppresses my Mum and I feel I have to be around to give her support. I feel dependent on my parents' support and I think my Mum is dependent on me in many ways. I have considered moving to Canada, for the last few years, but after living there for a year, I realised it was selfish of me to leave my Mum here. My Mum has a brother and sister in Canada and I think it would be good for Mum and me that when Dad dies (assuming he is first), we spend more time or even move closer to them.

I am independent in many ways and I can do many things for myself. However, my motivation is lacking, hence I am lazy. I think I am used to be being told what to do, so unless somebody tells me what to do I don't do it. I think the comfort and the lack of competition in my life, combined with a lack of confidence (self-pity) has meant I procrastinate over a lot of things which just don't get done! In terms of the working environment, I guess I need to be interacting with people or my attention wavers! My motivation and lack of interaction means I sometimes get distracted and it takes longer for me to get tasks done. It is partly due to a lack of confidence, but also to a lack of independence.

I think the lack of a sibling makes you uncompetitive because you are not fighting or having to share anything. Even though I do play sports, I am not as competitive as I should be. I can give in easily and lose interest if things are not going right for me. This is the worst part: I do at times feel suicidal. Although at the moment and while my parents are alive, I don't think I will do anything stupid, which I know it is. I worry that when my parents are not around, I will not have the reason or the will to carry on. My parents are quite old (69 and 61), so when they get ill, even a cold, I do worry. They are currently away for the moment and so I do get scared of me not seeing them again.

Daisy: a little adult

Daisy was born in 1967. Her story illustrates how being at home taking the role of a 'little adult' did not prepare her for peer relationships, exemplified when Daisy began to attend school. Like many only-children, she was able to relate better to the teachers than to the other children. Friendships she found both suffocating and challenging, experiencing jealousy when she had to share the friendship. As an only-child, she wanted for nothing, but she also missed out on important learning experiences.

> Growing up as an only-child, I really did not think about what it was like to live in a large family. I was very much cocooned in my own little world that was, my mum, dad and me. I had a lovely childhood, we had a 'nice' home, a 'nice' car and I always had 'nice' clothes. My mum would have dinner parties, (this was in the 1970s) and we would all dress up in long dresses, and sit up at tables and eat nicely. Afterwards, I would be left to sit in a corner and read, or have to amuse myself, whilst my parents had a delightful evening.

> I was used to being on my own, not having to share my bedroom, or fight to get into the bathroom. I went to a little first school where everything was just so unblemished. Happy memories! I was always picked to do the 'dinner numbers' or to do errands. It was as if I was always the good girl. I never really talked about my day at school; I would just come home from school, do my homework, and play outside with friends. There was no older sister to style my hair, or practice make-up, no talk of boys or sharing music, I just learnt it on my own.

> I did however find it hard to make friends. I did not have a brother or sister who brought their own friends home for me to know. Going to school, as I got older, became a nightmare, and standing in the playground on the first day, not knowing anyone was awful. I was the 'new girl', no-one to run to, or show me where to go.

> Friendships were suffocating. If I made a friend, then I would stick with them, I never had a 'group'. I was very much a loner, and today I am happy to be alone all day if need be. My best friend I have known for 30 years, and over the years we have become very close, but only now have I finally learnt to let her go and not be jealous that she has so many other friends, including me, and I have to share her.

> I never had to share my sweets, although I was brought up to share them anyway. I never had second hand clothes and if I wanted something special for Christmas like a Xylophone, then I got it. My parents did not have to share their money between other children. I never played board games – there was nobody to play with, so I had fuzzy felts, sequins and pin pictures. My outlet was reading, something you could do on your own, and not have to talk.

Being an only-child taught me that one day when I got married I never wanted just one child, because I did not want them to go through what I went through, even though it sounds lovely, it was a very lonely and solitary existence at times. I was lucky in many ways, but I do feel that in other ways you miss out so much. I never learnt from brothers or sisters who had children, the experiences of looking after babies, I never changed a nappy until I had my own children. I had never looked after a baby and did not have a clue, until I had my own. I never had cousins to play with or aunties or uncles popping in or baby sitting.

In a way it was harder being an only-child who wanted for nothing, than being in a larger family, learning about life, and how to deal with the many hurdles that came along and having people to talk to.

Paul: socially disabled

Paul's story, in particular, shows the challenges of having no siblings and parents who diverge in the way they interact with their child. Paul's mother, also an only-child, has a very close relationship with her son. Paul's father felt ignored as a middle-child and appears to have experienced Paul's extremely close relationship with his mother as some kind of enactment from his past and has become extremely hostile to him as a result. Paul, highly intelligent and highly sensitive with no siblings or friends to interact with, feels socially disabled. He admits to being naïve about women and finding relationships difficult to negotiate. He has an only-child himself but would much prefer she had a sibling.

I am a 36 year old male, clinical depressed, clinically obese, unemployed for most of adulthood (previously University Lecturer, professional Musician, IBM salesman, Oxford University student – Physics – dropped out, Bath University student – Pure Mathematics degree, Kingston University – MA Music – dropped out). I am a high achiever (sort of, intermittently), well educated, with very low self-esteem, and poor at making and maintaining relationships.

My mother was also an only-child. My father was the middle one of three. His older brother and younger sister were idolised by his parents. He was always relatively ignored. I was a bit of a child prodigy in Durham where I began to grow up. I was taught by my mother and I was reading and writing by age three, also picking out nursery rhyme tunes on the piano unaided, with no lessons. I recently learned my father decided, when I was three, that I seemed to prefer my mother and my grandparents to him and basically decided he didn't like me then, and he has never changed his mind. I grew up with my mother telling me that I'm wonderful, clever, handsome, talented and great company, and my father telling me I'm a useless piece of crap. I crave that approval and those compliments still, but fear rejection more than I fear death. I think having siblings might have given me a more balanced view of myself.

I was the most popular and highest achieving pupil in school and totally naïve that life could be anything but wonderful, until age six. Then I moved south and suddenly I was constantly mocked for having a northern accent. A couple of bad teachers bullied me, probably because of my overachieving and overconfidence. At the same time my Dad started bullying me verbally and constantly putting me down. At 11, I was sent to an all-male school just as I was discovering girls. The school was 13 miles from home; most of my friends were 20 miles away, so I basically spent almost all of my evenings and weekends alone. A sibling was just what I needed. What I got was the affordability of home computers, so I became a computer addict. There was no internet back then and it was a hobby for the isolated.

I was a fat kid, ridiculed at school, with no friends at home or school for a couple of years, and I didn't know any girls. At 14, I became serially obsessed with a number of girls but didn't know how to talk to them. Also, having no close friends, no SIBLINGS and rather staid parents, I had no-one to discuss my feelings with. With no alternate influence, I somehow concluded that sexual desire was something to be ashamed of and that sex before marriage was wrong. I even believed that 'nice' girls didn't really like or want sex. I was incredibly naïve, not sexist. These factors affected my ability to make relationships with girls/women for a long time. I would only be interested in them if I thought I wanted to marry them which made me very intense and creepy and, of course, put them right off. In my late teenage years, I turned down advances of a few lovely and compatible girls because I couldn't see myself still with them in 50 years time, or because I suspected they'd kissed too many boys already (I didn't even imagine anyone might have lost their virginity by age 18).

Having said all that, my emotions were very contradictory. From adolescence through to age 31, I was absolutely desperate for a girlfriend to fill the void in my life, but pushed away anyone who was interested in me. I had a couple of brief sexual relationships in my 20s (the first aged 23) but hit 30 having never gone out with someone for more than a week. Aged 31, I met my future wife. We got very serious very quickly and were married five months after we started going out. Ironically, having desperately wanted the company, the self-esteem of being loved, and of course the sex, I was so used to spending the majority of my time alone that I felt totally suffocated in a serious relationship. I could never get enough time to myself. I think that was a fairly major factor in my marriage break-up. We had a child when I was 32, and split up when I was 33. I'm 36 now and desperate to be the good father I never had. I would love my daughter to have a sibling. My ex-wife says she doesn't want another child and I feel it's unlikely I'll meet anyone with whom I could have another child.

Kay: parenting her parents

In the next story, Kay is struggling with the responsibility and care of elderly parents. She says she did not have a lonely childhood but her story shows that her parents were young and emotionally immature when they conceived her. Kay's dad wanted her as a buddy and her mom has made her feel responsible for her emotional needs and as a result Kay got married at 20 to escape.

Kay, at 46, has always had a feeling that something was missing and has always wanted a sibling. She has had a number of relationships, the first lasted five years, the second thirteen. She knew the latter was over much earlier but felt unable to end it. Her latest husband has a five-year-old and she struggles not to be envious of that relationship. She struggles with the independence/dependence dilemma of wanting to be on her own and feeling intensely lonely. She is aware of the contradiction in the way she feels: sensitive, thin skinned and needy; and the way others see her as independent and strong. Her friends have been a lasting support but she finds it difficult to engage with the conflict inherent in all relationships and recognises she avoids arguments and instead becomes passive/aggressive. She believes this is because she had no siblings to interact with as a child. As a result, she has not learned to express herself but instead has learned to hold her feelings in.

I remember a relatively happy, uneventful childhood, although my parents divorced when I was approximately 18, but as a kid I don't remember feeling any kind of resentment towards them. My Dad, as an adult, is relatively benign but when I was young he was neglectful and selfish. He knew he was leaving me at the mercy of my Mom and he never did anything about it, never even talked with me about it. The one thing I feel about my Dad is that, for my whole life, he wanted to be my buddy; he didn't really want to act like a Dad. If I ever had a crisis, or really needed someone, he would not be the person that I called. Now that he has had some health issues, he wants me to be the devoted daughter and I resent this. When he was recovering from surgery, he talked about what a good daughter I am, becoming teary eyed etc. This really fell onto cold territory. I so wish I could say the same; that I thought he was such a good Dad, but I really can't. While being an only-child is quite difficult for me, in their defence, I also feel a lot of the issues with my parents were to do with getting married when they were 19 and 16.

My teenage years were not the easiest. My parents divorced after my Dad had an affair with a woman two years my senior. Unfortunately for me, I was the one who discovered the affair. This solidly embedded me in the middle of their divorce. My mother treated me, not like a daughter, but as a sounding board, a confidant. As I became older I was called disloyal and ungrateful if I wanted to have contact with my Dad.

I don't think I was lonely as a child. I had friends I could always bring along and a cousin close to my age. It was when I became an adult and I needed to talk to someone who could understand that I felt a sense of something missing. It really hit me when my Mother had surgery and I was sitting alone in the waiting room, waiting to hear how she was. I don't think I have been the same since. I would give anything to have a sibling.

I was married at age 20. I honestly think it was to get away from my Mother. I remember at 19 I wanted to get my own apartment and when I told her, she responded: 'You are just like your Father; you're going to leave me too'. I remember feeling pressure from other family members to take care of my Mom since my Dad left her. The marriage lasted 5 years, long enough to have two children. I raised my children on my own. My Mother helped with the kids, but always on her terms. I had another relationship with a man that lasted 12–13 years. It was over, way before it was over, but I was paralyzed, I couldn't seem to end it.

I am now remarried to a man seven years younger than me. My children live in other states and are 24 and 21. I am ruining this marriage with my overwhelming pity for myself. I have a five year old stepdaughter. There are times when I feel like I am competing with her for my husband's attention. This behaviour causes me to feel so ashamed. I have been so passive or passive-aggressive my whole life, always trying to make everyone happy. But what happens is that I reach a breaking point, and then all that I have repressed comes out. I don't think I ever learned how to argue effectively because I didn't have anyone to argue with. Arguments feel like the end of the world to me. I flee from conflict if only in my mind. I have been trying to be healthier, speak my mind before I get to bursting. This seems to have driven so many people away and I am more alone than ever.

I am a nurse and as my parents age, I am torn between responsibility and resentment. I believe my Mom is angry with my recent marriage. I recently had major back surgery and she never came to the hospital, never brought a meal to my home, in fact never came to see me and neither did my Dad.

Sometimes I am so lonely I feel like I can hardly stand it. But then sometimes I love being alone and enjoying my own company. I feel that sometimes I build up what being with another person means and feel that's what I want, but in reality I am, more often than not, fine by myself. I think people perceive me as this strong, independent woman. They are shocked to find that I am sensitive (overly so quite often), have a very thin skin at times, and can be really quite needy.

I have always had a lot of friends. After being alive for 46 years and having many friendships some lasting, some not, this is how I feel about friends and family: You can't pick your family and sometimes having family is not as good as it seems – You can pick your friends and they don't have to last your whole life. I have had really good friends that for a brief time in our lives we were really good for each other. We still feel fondly for each other, but the time of mutual need has passed. I have one 'best' friend. I will admit we are still friends because of her persistence. We've had a few really bad arguments, when we were away on vacation and one of us walked away in the middle of the night and stayed elsewhere, not speaking for months (her once, me once). When this has happened, I missed her so much I thought I wanted to die, I truly thought the relationship was over; I tried to delete her from my cell phone, but couldn't figure out how.

When she did call, I wasn't mad or receptive, I just really thought it was over and wouldn't have dreamed of calling her first.

I've tried so hard not to make the same mistakes as my Mom. I have tried to make my children feel that they can be themselves with me, not to feel responsible for me. I want to be with them or talk to them because it's what they want, not what they feel that they should do. I also now feel like I'm winning the inside battle over my step-daughter. I am able to dig deep and think; well of course my husband loves her that much and realize it's not a reflection of how much he loves me. He is very understanding of how I feel.

Again, thank you, thank you, thank you. Finding out about your work came to me at a very difficult time in my life and knowing what you were doing and reading other's stories helped me in a profound way.

Sylvia: overprotected

Sylvia's story is a good illustration of an only-child struggling to cope with going to school and her first real encounter with other children. Having worked for many years in secondary schools, I became aware of the difficulties many only-children have in mixing with other children. They often present for counselling, as a one-to-one situation with a rational adult is more familiar to them than the unpredictability of the school playground (Sorensen, 2006b). Like Sylvia, some children can become quite obsessive as a way to control the unpredictable world they find themselves in. Others may even become school phobic.

Sylvia was able to overcome her initial anxiety at school, but at home she had to keep her dad happy and the whole experience she describes as claustrophobic. She thinks she married comparatively young to escape her home situation, despite this her mother has rung every day since she left. Now at fifty-three, she still has to contend with her mother on a daily basis, taking her on family holidays and being her constant emotional support. From a life-stage perspective, she is moving towards the latter years but has managed to negotiate her childhood difficulties, sustained an intimate relationship, had her own children, all whilst having to be a continued emotional support to both her parents and specifically her mother since her father died.

My parents both worked but not in well paid jobs. My father was a salesman and my mother a school secretary. My mother had me when she was 29. My parents married six years before. It was implied that the delay was due to the common circumstances at that time of living with in-laws. As a child and young adult I asked my father why I didn't have any brothers or sisters and was told that my mother had a bad time having me. At that time I felt I could not ask my mother. Later, I asked my mother in adulthood and she said that it was because my father did not want any more children.

For as long as I can remember I hated been an only-child. I had what would be considered a happy childhood but always found it claustrophobic. I remember being about 10, walking around Richmond, and hoping that a twin would return from the past! We had 'quiet' Christmases because my parents said that was the way they liked them. My father was always very anxious about his health. Initially this was physical ailments and then psychological and he was on Librium for a number of years. A lot of time was spent keeping him happy.

I vividly remember starting school. I found the experience very difficult and was particularly frightened of the playground. I remember staying with a person called a welfare assistant but would be called a teaching assistant today. I was gradually 'weaned' from her but stayed by the wall. Academically, I did not have a problem at school but I did not relate to children on a social level. I was invited to birthday parties and can even remember the names of the children whose parties I went to and dreaded. Such social occasions caused me great anxiety. I simply had no idea how to play with children. My mother put this down to being shy. There was also little opportunity to play with children near to where I lived. They were older than me and went to a different primary school. My cousins were also older than me so there was no opportunity to play with family members.

Whilst at primary school I became quite obsessive about things – the parting in my hair had to be exact, my pillows in a certain position. This concerned my mother and she decided I needed an interest and bought a dog, supposedly for me. Although I liked the dog it became very much my mother's dog and really a substitute second child.

My social awkwardness affected me most when I moved to secondary school. My mother was encouraged by a teacher to apply for a scholarship for an independent school. As the school had to be written as first choice on the application forms for secondary school, I missed the opportunity to go to a local school. I passed the 11 plus but my mother was not happy about sending me to the local comprehensive school as this was seen negatively even though it had a 'grammar stream'. My peers from primary school who had passed for a grammar place went to the local schools and I went to a grammar school involving a long journey and changes of buses. I found the journey and the new school too overwhelming and became very distressed. Eventually after visiting the doctor and applying to more local grammar schools, I changed school after a term. Of course this was not easy, as friendships groups had already been formed. However the journey was much easier and I settled eventually and formed some lasting friendships.

I would not judge myself today as shy and think that I probably take after my father rather than my mother in social situations. I think my problem in the past was that I did not have opportunities to relate to other children as most of my time was with adults. Although it was not as easy then as it is today, to join after school clubs etc., I don't think my mother saw the need to give me opportunities to play with other children when I was younger. She thought that being an only-child was a privileged position.

My mother was very keen for me to become a teacher as this was what she said she wanted to do. I was happy with this and they supported me in qualifying. I married at 23 and remain married now. I think my relatively early marriage was to do with finding a legitimate way of leaving home after returning having qualified. I made attempts to look for flats but my mother was very discouraging.

Since marrying my mother has telephoned me every day. I tried to stop her but she just cried and became distressed and I was blamed for upsetting her so I just gave in. When I had children both my parents were good with my children and my father particularly enjoyed the role. My mother loved looking after them but tended to coddle them but I suppose that is natural. However, as they became older the focus came back on me. This escalated when my father died ten years ago.

My mother moved from her house (my parents had moved near me a few years previously) to sheltered housing. Since my father died, I have taken my mother on holiday. We went to both Australia and the States where she had always wanted to go and where my father refused to go. She was generous in contributing more than her own expenses but it was at a cost. She would do nothing on her own and travelling made her so anxious that it caused rows between us. Last year my husband said that it was becoming absurd, so we went to Morocco without her. She did not understand why we wanted to go there as it was not somewhere she would have chosen. She was upset and as compensation I took her to Ireland to see relatives for a few days.

In recent years she has had a fall and heart problems. Although I understand she gets anxious, her demands on me are excessive with early morning calls, calls while I am at work saying she is feeling low, can't tolerate her pain, the heat etc. I am now at a stage where I feel I love her but I don't like her. She has always tried to make me feel guilty if I don't do what she wants. This works less with me now but I know she is old and genuinely needs a level of support from me. I am relatively happy with the practical support but it is the extent of emotional support that she has always wanted that drains me and makes me feel resentful. I also know that I don't want to end up feeling guilty when she does die.

Maria: entangled yet neglected

Maria is fifty-three, unemployed, unmarried and with no children. As a child, she has only memories of loneliness and isolation and being in the middle of her parents' relationship. As an adult, she still has had a problematic relationship with her mother. She married at twenty to escape her situation at home, but as this did not work she returned. Maria has never felt heard or valued and feels ashamed of even having her own concerns. She wonders if she is normal to worry so much about so many things. She is now in a position where she is trying her best to look after her elderly parents but she has no one to look after her in her old age. This, not surprisingly, she finds frightening. She longs for the sort of close family she has never had and someone who is a witness to her life, as she has been to her parents.

My father's family came to the UK from Europe during world war two, to escape the war and the killing of Jews. After the war my Jewish Dad married Mum a very attractive English girl. His family threw him out when he announced he was marrying a non-Jew. I was born in 1954 and the Jewish family reconciled with mum and dad. I was the second child – the first died from a combination of forceps crushing the skull and rhesus negative blood. I was born premature and had a complete blood transfusion – which saved my life – as the rhesus negative factor is stronger in the second and subsequent children.

In 1956 we emigrated to Australia following my dad's parents, sister and husband. Several years later my parents built a house in an isolated outer suburb and we moved in. She was always upset about how far away she was from her family and used to cry a lot in front of me. She always seemed to dump her feelings onto me. Mum was bitter that she had to work and was always criticising dad – he was just never good enough. I couldn't have a bond with dad – he wouldn't risk mum's displeasure. The entire household revolved around mum and her needs and moods. Mum had another 2 miscarriages and I think she had a nervous breakdown – or at least a huge sulk – I am not sure what happened – it was never discussed with me.

I was always lonely as a child. I always felt it was me against them – as my dad always sided with mum even when she was wrong. I could never be right – or at least have my needs and opinions considered in an equitable way when there was a conflict with mum's needs and opinions. There were not many children where we lived and my parent's friends did not have kids in my age bracket. Visiting was also very lonely and boring for me. I always seemed to be alone and lonely. I married at 20, while I was still at university, to a man 13 yrs older – just to get out of the house. The marriage lasted 18 months and I had to return home as I had nothing – no job, no money, and no place to live. My parents always did the right thing but I never felt welcomed, supported and loved. I never even considered having children – I think my mum's experience – which was never spoken of – scarred me. Later in life, around 35 years, I started to realise that I would really like to have kids but had no partner at the time which made this an impossible wish. I grieved for a long time and would cry when I saw babies in the street or on TV.

It is really terrifying to be a small only-child where your survival and acceptance in the family unit depends on ensuring that your mother, the person who is meant to nurture and protect you, always has her needs placed before anyone else's. And when your father colludes in this situation it's terrifying. It still happens, even at this age. My mother (82 years) now has multiple health problems (blindness through macular degeneration, emphysema through smoking, heart and blood pressure issues). My dad (80 years) is basically her carer, something mum still belittles: *'he doesn't do much at all'.* I gently said to mum that dad *'looked a bit tired ... he often fell asleep just sitting down ... and perhaps with her eyesight she may not see this'*. Mum went nuts. I was accused of trying to destroy their marriage, of putting her down and all this really weird stuff. She wouldn't talk to me for about five months after this very gentle observation that dad looked tired. But what really hurt was that dad never made an effort to call me and reassure me that, despite mum's behaviour, he loved me and was thankful that I acknowledged his tiredness. He knew I was upset and that being thrown out of the family unit like this was very painful and I was really upset. As I am unemployed and worried about my future I really need a safe haven and somewhere I feel safe and accepted. The 'Family' is the only place I have.

In the year 2000 mum and dad returned to UK for a holiday. I gave them a large photo album and asked that when they visited family, to write a short story about their lives and submit some photos. I desperately wanted to learn where I came from and who my 'tribe' were. My parents didn't get the album photos and memories for me. In 2004, for my mother's 80th birthday, my dad flew out my mum's sister from UK as a surprise She and mum spent the week talking about 'old times' and I found this upsetting – not because I was jealous but because I realised I would never have someone in my life who was a testimony and witness to my life. No husband, brother, sister or child to do this. No one seems to even consider what life may be like for me when I am my parent's age. My mum's sister never really seemed interested in getting to know me or hearing my story – it was all about mum. I wonder if I am capable of close relationships even though I desperately want to be 'part' of something and someone's life.

Is any of this 'normal'? The myth is that onlies are spoilt etc. I feel almost emotionally abused, or at least neglected. I don't think that the 'outside' world has any comprehension of an onlies' life and how it can be a really painful, isolated experience like mine. My parents, the family and often my friends have constantly refused to acknowledge my life and my experiences – I feel ashamed.

Somehow, rather than being a valid and true summary of how my life's been, I feel as if I shouldn't say this as it will make me look as if I am maladjusted and have deep seated physiological problems. Why is it so hard as an 'only' to have your voice and rights recognised, heard and, on occasions, supported?

I am losing respect and regard for both my parents, especially my dad. This is very frightening for me because I wonder how I can have a relationship with any real meaning when I have limited or no respect for them. I was hoping that, before they die, we can have some sort of deeper understanding of each other and develop a soul felt reconciliation. There is an expectation that at my age I should *'be over'* all the aspects of my childhood, including my relationship problems with my parents. The fact that my parent's behaviour towards me is still an issue worries me. Is it possible to move on and get over it or is that too big to ask for people in my situation? Without my parents I have no one – what can I do?

I realise that I will bury my parents and it does my head in worrying about who will bury me. I have no one. I am also terrified about old age – the vulnerability of the aged without someone to look after them. Will I be some lonely old lady without anyone to make sure they take care of me in the nursing home? Will I have enough to live on in this age of governments withdrawing from social security? Will I die in my house and no one will know for days or weeks? I am so, so frightened and so lonely.

James: carried shame

James is in his mid-sixties, born before the end of the war with only a faint memory of his father as his parents divorced after he was born. James was brought up by his grandparents until his mother remarried. Throughout his childhood he had to cope with the stigma of having no father and being an only-child. After many years of self-development, he feels he has made some sense of his early life, realising how detrimental the enmeshed relationship he had with his mother has been on his emotional development and his significant relationships. He has two children from a previous marriage and admits to having chosen women in the past who he felt he had to look after, like he did his mother. The double-shame of his mother's illegitimacy and divorce coupled with that of being an only-child and perceived to be spoilt has had an impact, in the past, on the way he relates to others, particularly women.

I hadn't really thought about being an only-child as something that had a major influence on my life until I started reading the stories on your website. Being an 'only' wasn't something that I offered to the rest of the world as information. It wasn't such a big idea, but it was something that I kept to myself. I had had fantasies about having brothers and sisters but on the whole it wasn't a problem. I think it was only when my mother died when I was thirty, that it became significant.

I was born just before the end of the Second World War and grew up in a small coastal town in the West Country. My mother and father never lived together and he was in Germany when I was born. By the time the War was over he had met someone else and I was the only-child of divorced parents that I knew of in my school. I only ever remember meeting him twice and his absence remains with me to this day. My older cousin told me that my mother had never taken me out in my pram or pushchair. She went to work in London when I was two and sent me occasional postcards and visited every few months. During that time I lived with my grandparents whom I adored. I found school very difficult and being with all those other children was at times quite terrifying. No one had given me the rule book and I didn't know how to join in and fit in. I hated every moment of school right up until I left at sixteen. I then did a number of different trades before going into teaching.

My mother re-married when I was eight and I was taken away from my grandparents.

My step-father was probably the last person in the world who I would have chosen for a father. The feeling was probably mutual because he disappeared out of my life when my mother died. He was an only-child too and resented me and the attention my mother gave to me. It was only after my mother's death that I came to realise how horribly enmeshed we had been with each other. In the thirty plus years since her death I have done a lot of personal development work and now realise how much we were both crippled with shame. I inherited both my grandparents' shame over my mother's illegitimacy, and my mother's shame over losing her husband and being divorced. It was never voiced; I simply absorbed it from my environment. I also felt shame over being an only-child and dreaded other people's responses which indicated that there must be something wrong with me and that I was obviously spoilt.

The big theme for me as an adult only-child is a sense of loss and aloneness throughout my life. Because I have no siblings I had no one else who witnessed my childhood or shared my bereavement. I resent the fact that my mother's life became so enmeshed with mine that the whole focus of my life was to try and get her approval which I never received. This has affected my relationships with women. I have been married four times and have often chosen women who needed looking after, like my mother. Now that I am 'out' as an only child, I have met other onlies and the level of identification is very reassuring. I think your website has the potential to heal a lot of only-child wounds. It has certainly given me a voice to speak about things that people with siblings can find hard to understand.

Gunnar: the family romance

Gunnar's story, like James', reflects the closeness of the mother–son relationship. Whilst mothers are often close to their sons, the relationship can become intrusive if the mother tries to interfere when a partner is on the scene. Many emails I have received talk about the difficulties adult only-children have making boundaries with their mother. This can become harder when the mother, who often outlives the father, lives alone and becomes very dependent. Whilst this is difficult for both adult only-child males and females, I have become increasingly aware that the mother–son relationship has a particularly strong and often negative dynamic on the adult only-child male. Gunnar reflects on how this overly close relationship his mother has had with him has impacted on all his relationships and he also tries to imagine what it will be like when she dies and he is alone.

> I am a 75 year old male from Sweden. My mother is alive but she is in her late 90's and we have a very close relationship. My dad died 18 years ago but I was always much closer to my mother than him. We had a special relationship and she often shared things with me that she didn't tell my father. She always did everything for me both as a child and even as an adult. For example, she would do my washing and ironing even when I was living with my partner. Often she cooked food and brought it round which really annoyed my girlfriend. Although I love my mother I feel she has been too close all my life and at times this has interfered in my relationships.
>
> I enjoyed my childhood very much. I had a great deal of freedom and I could come and go as I pleased. I was always out with friends and I think as a result I became very outgoing. I always had plenty of friends but only a few really close ones. However I have had problems in relationships with women as I easily feel suffocated when emotional

demands are made on me. On those occasions, I just want to get out and go somewhere social where I feel able to be my easy going self. I have often wondered whether the close relationship I have with my mother has in some way made me like this. Now she is old, I feel very responsible towards her and ring her everyday, do her shopping and generally ensure she is okay. The roles are reversed! My present partner does not get involved as she feels I spend more time with my mum than with her. This can bring a lot of tension and I feel drawn in opposite directions. In many ways my partner and I lead separate lives as she is some years younger than me and she still has a job and a career.

I think I have spent much of my life looking for substitute siblings. I have joined lots of clubs to get that sense of belonging but it never seems to really work. I have never had a child, which is a disappointment, but I would never have just had one, even though I enjoyed my childhood, in my advancing years I see being an only is a lonely place to be.

I do wonder what it will be like when my mum dies. In some ways it will be a relief but in others I think I will really miss her, as she has been there all my life, unlike anyone else. I suppose that is the hardest thing about being an only one – you don't have the possibility of sharing the memories with a sibling. Sometimes my mother talks about things that I don't remember and I think it would be really good if I had a sibling to ask. When she has gone it will be like a whole part of me will disappear too. I know that sounds quite dramatic but it feels like she is part of me and it will be very strange living without that part.

Reflections

Twelve stories have been presented in these last two chapters to illustrate the issues that are most common in the emails I have received from the United Kingdom and abroad. Some readers may feel the stories do reflect an indulged only-child, others may see some of the consequences of being brought up without siblings. Whether you are an only-child or not, I think the stories all contain aspects of adult only-child experience. Whilst not everyone has described the details of their childhood without siblings, for those who have, this has sometimes been a lonely experience. Many have commented that they have had difficulties in later life most specifically in significant, intimate relations. We have seen that for some the impact of growing up an only-child has affected issues over confidence, self-worth and the degree to which they have psychologically separated from parents or can maintain intimacy in friendships and partnerships.

Some people have chosen to have children whilst others have been unable to sustain a satisfactory relationship for this to happen. Many have become very involved in their parent's lives, and have found it difficult to leave home and become an independent person. Others left home at an early age to escape the claustrophobia of the family triangle. For those who have stayed at home, old age can seem very fearful as they realise that once their parents die they will be on their own. Although this fear is not true of everyone, the need to have someone to witness one's life is important and particularly for the adult only-child who already has a sense of separateness or something missing as a result of growing up without a sibling.

My initial research was concerned with female adult only-child experiences, so it has been important to include a male perspective. Although many of the issues are the same, one thing that is noticeable is that men are often particularly close to their mother and do take an actively caring role in their old age, perhaps more frequently than men who have female siblings. I will discuss this further in the next chapter. One of the consequences of a very close relation between a male only-child and his mother is that it appears to seriously inhibit their ability to have significant relationships with women.

In Part III, I will look in more depth at the implications for therapy when working with adult only-children. The themes that are raised here and in the co-researchers' stories from Part I will be looked at in more detail and I will offer an only-child matrix and archetype to understand more fully the psychological dilemmas facing the adult only-child.

Part III
Implications for Therapy

8
The Only-Child Archetype: A Folktale

In Part III, the therapeutic implications of only-child research is discussed. As a practicing psychotherapist, I am primarily motivated to do research that benefits other clinicians and people involved in the field of social science. Perhaps one of the most personally satisfying aspects of the research is that it has also been beneficial to many only-children who have had their experience witnessed. However, my work will, I hope, benefit a variety of professionals working with not only young only-children but adults as well. This chapter sets out to describe the idea of an only-child archetype to provide a way of understanding the complexity of only-child experience. The rest of Part III discusses the implications of a matrix of only-child experience and the themes which it encapsulates.

My original research attempted to disclose the lived experiences and affective lives of female adult only-children across their lifespan. The research revealed an identifiable set of adult only-child characteristics and phenomena that have also been confirmed and supported through my own website, Internet message boards and only-child workshops that all transcended the gender divide. By choosing to look at the only-child experience through the construct of voice, the complexity of the intra-, inter- and extra-personal factors that make up that experience were captured. The importance of holding the matrix of these phenomena together, in order to do justice to both the similarities and differences, was a significant issue and one which led me to introduce the idea of an only-child archetype.

There appears to be a number of re-occurring issues that adult only-children bring to therapy and workshops, about their sense of self and their difficulties in relating to others. What makes these uniquely only-child is when they are connected to a lack of siblings. This is why first-born children may have many only-child attributes as initially they had no siblings. These phenomena, taken together, revealed in the three worlds of private, personal and public form the basis of what could be regarded as the characteristics of an only-child archetype.

Archetype comes from the Greek word 'archetypos' meaning 'first of its kind' and is defined as the original model from which all other similar persons, objects or concepts are merely derivative. It has been argued, by Jung (1959) in particular, that in the personality, archetypes function as predispositions driving our motivations, beliefs, values, emotions and behaviour to give us a sense of meaning in our lives. Jung used the concept of archetypes as innate prototypes for ideas, which may subsequently become involved in the interpretation of observed phenomena. He theorised that humans have a collective unconscious or shared memory of experiences resulting in a resonance of concepts, such as hero and heroine that transcends time, place and culture. An archetype is an unlearned tendency to experience things in a certain way and has no form of its own, but acts as an organising principle on the things we see or do.

An archetype

The use of the word archetype is not without reservations. In many ways, the word 'syndrome' seems more applicable. Taken from the Greek word 'sundromos' meaning 'running together', it is used for a group of symptoms that collectively indicate or characterise a disease or psychological disorder, and can be attributed to a distinctive or characteristic pattern of behaviour. The strong medical connotations and the negative meaning usually attached to the word syndrome convinced me that the word archetype is less emotive. Archetype is therefore used here to signify an identifiable set of characteristics that are likely to be specific to the lived experiences of only-children. Archetypes, latent in the collective unconscious, are revealed through fairy tales, myths and legends. In order to understand the use of the word archetype to discuss only-child phenomena, a folktale of the *Handless Maiden* is used as an illustration.

The folktale is explored as an archetype in terms of resonance and identification with the life experiences of adult only-children. The story of the Handless Maiden, like all folktales, encapsulates motifs of particular archetypes. Thus the story gives a three-dimensional aspect to only-child lived experience and demonstrates some of the themes which will later be discussed in the only-child matrix. The following is a shortened version of the tale adapted from the version used by Robert Johnson (1995).

The handless maiden

A miller lived with his industrious wife and their beautiful daughter. The daughter's job was to care for the miller's mule, which walked in endless circles to turn the millstone to grind the corn. She would sit under the ancient pear tree at the back of the mill and talk to him as he trod his path, often decorating his leather harness with wild flowers that she had picked from the banks of the brook that ran through the garden of the mill house. Having no brothers or sisters, she would amuse herself when her parents were busy working, by walking through the fields and meadows around the mill. She knew all the animals and birds and wild flowers and where the foxes lived and the nightingales nested.

All was happy and content in this little world, and then one day the devil came to visit the miller asking him if he would like to be shown how to produce more flour, with less effort. The only payment the devil asks is 'That which stands at the back of the mill' and the miller, assuming that the devil means the ancient pear tree, readily agrees. The devil uses the brook to turn a water wheel that turns the millstone. The miller is now able to grind corn effortlessly and faster than before. He no longer has to rely on his mule and so the mule grazes behind the ancient pear tree, growing fat and content. One day the devil comes to collect his fee and the miller happily takes him to cut down that which stands at the back of the mill. But he finds his daughter standing with the mule and the devil claims her for his payment. He chops off both her hands and carries them away with him.

The miller's daughter has paid an awful price for her family's new found wealth. She cannot complain because her mother tells her she is lucky as there is now sufficient money for the household to have servants and so she does not need to do anything for herself that requires hands. But slowly, bit by bit, the handless maiden became more and more depressed until she started to weep and could not stop. One day she left the mill and walked into the dark quiet depths of the forest. Here she found some peace although hungry and without hands, helpless to serve herself. Finally, almost at the stage of exhaustion she blunders through briars into a garden with a beautiful pear tree and many ripe pears. Without hands she manages to eat one of the pears and she does this for many days and so manages to keep herself alive. She does not know that each pear is labelled and numbered and the pears all belong to the king.

Now the king is a kind and just man but wants to know what is happening to his beloved pears. He hides in wait to see if he can catch sight of the thief, and he sees the pathetic figure of the handless maiden. The king falls instantly in love with her but the handless maiden tells him that she cannot possibly be a queen without hands. He assures her that as a queen everything will be done for her but to make her feel better he has hands made of silver for her to wear.

Initially happy with her new silver hands, she has a baby boy and desperately wants to look after him with her own hands. Again the king tells her there is no need for her to do anything because the servants can take care of both her and the child. Saddened, she eventually takes her baby son in her arms and heads for the solitude of the forest. The handless maiden suffers hardship and discomfort but she feels happier surviving alone with her son in the woods.

But then disaster strikes as she is bending over the river to drink. She drops the child into the water and instinctively dips her useless silver hands into the water to save her baby and a miracle occurs: she draws the baby from the waters of the river and her hands are restored to flesh and blood and she is whole again.

We can see that this is a story about a young girl, made helpless by her parents' adult-focused ways. With no brothers or sisters, her main companion is a mule and although adored by her parents there are no child interactions; so she lives in her inner world and relates to nature. Their adult pursuits provide a comfortable life, but one in which she functions as a small adult rather than a child. She does not learn childish ways and is dependent on her parents. The metaphor for this is her lack of hands, everything is provided for the handless maiden, and whilst some would see this as lucky or privileged it does not give her the opportunities for social and emotional maturity. She longs for independence and eventually leaves to follow the archetypal heroine's journey. In Jungian terms the journey of the Self. However, her retreat into her intra-psychic world is not at first fruitful. She soon finds herself married with a child and again dependent on others. Although seemingly adult, symbolised by her artificial silver hands, in reality she is still helpless and unable to nurture her new 'baby' animus-self. Finally, she separates herself from this dependent situation and after a period alone in the forest achieves completeness.

The story of the Handless Maiden demonstrates the themes revealed in the adult only-child life-stories:

- The sense of being special, but alone and sometimes lonely.
- The feeling of disconnection from their own and others childishness.
- The enjoyment of times alone in their intra-psychic worlds, whilst experiencing alienation from the inter-personal or social world.

This is the helplessness of the Handless Maiden. Her relationships are placatory and compromise the development of a sense of self. Although special to her parents, her father's agreement with the devil demonstrates her lack of separateness from the world of her parents and then later her husband's. Her difficulties in maintaining a personal sense of who she is results in her retreating back into the safety of her psychic inner world, to recoup from the problematic nature of the social world. It is the silver hands of the maiden that make her acceptable to the social world but they do not enable her to feel connected to it. When she begins to develop her active animus/masculine side, she is able to move beyond the passive anima/female role. Her final retreat into the forest with her budding animus leads her to literally 'take hold' of her life. Her hands are made flesh, no longer a replica, they are genuinely hers. This, I believe, symbolises the integration of the dependent and independent dilemma, the tension between the intra-psychic and inter-psychic, which is at the heart of the only-child archetype. It also illustrates the shift from the passive to the active, normally attained with the birth of a sibling.

In this chapter, a model was offered which I have chosen to call an only-child archetype. To enrich this archetypal definition, the archetypal images in the folktale of the Handless Maiden were explored. By describing only-child phenomena as an only-child archetype originating primarily in a lack or absence of sibling encounters, I have managed to hold the inter-connectedness of only-child phenomena and have avoided making comparative evaluations or privileging only-children as a separate species. At the same time, I have acknowledged the multifaceted impact of the 'lack' of siblings and the various ways in which this lies at the heart of the only-child experience.

9
The Only-Child Matrix

In the previous chapter, the idea of an only-child archetype was introduced which is built on the idea of an only-child matrix of meaning that emerged from the life-stories found throughout this book. In Chapter 4, the construct of voice was used to identify an intra-, inter- and extra-dimension of only-child characteristics. Continuing this theme, a matrix of these three strands of intra-, inter- and extra-psychic offers a three-dimensional understanding of the way these three interact within the only-child personality (see Figure 1: The Only-Child Matrix).

Only-child matrix

At the centre of the only-child matrix is the intra-psychic, the private world of the only-child with two themes juxtaposed: that of the only-child's feeling of specialness coupled with a feeling of aloneness and lack of connection to others. This is a result of never having been dethroned by a sibling and at the same time missing out on the social and emotional learning a sibling provides. Without the 'rough and tumble' of sibling interaction, opportunities for dealing with jealousy, anger, envy and conflict in the relatively safe environment of the home are lost. This can leave the only-child longing to remain in the specialness of their youth, without the essential emotional and social development required to make good relationships. Having spent a great deal of time in their own company, only-children develop ways of being alone which can be difficult to integrate in later relationships, resulting in them feeling a greater tension between the human needs to have both space and intimacy.

The intra-psychic world is surrounded by the inter-personal, for we are always inter-connected with other people. However, for the only-child

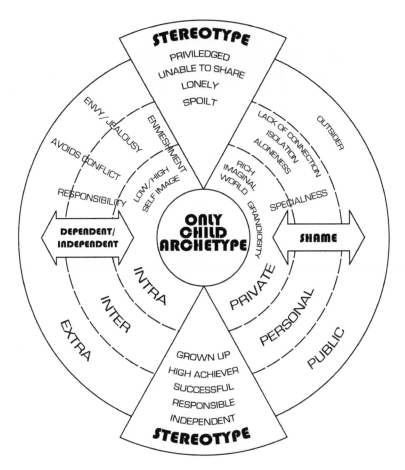

Figure 1 The Only-child matrix

the inter-personal world may bring particular problems originating in the family. Difficulties in separation and family enmeshment, although by no means inevitable, do challenge the only-child in a way people who have siblings may be more able to avoid. Feeling responsible for parents' happiness, whether real or imagined, can have a detrimental effect on a developing sense of self. Feeling responsible for fulfilling parental expectations means only-children carry a greater burden as the one living testimony of parental achievement. Letting go of this responsibility is a challenge often unmet until the death of the parents. Lack of separation and enmeshment and continually being the centre of attention also affects other relationships causing friction and tension, exacerbated by the only-child's attempts to avoid conflict by trying to placate and please or withdraw and isolate themselves.

Finally, the extra-psychic or public world impacts on the other two worlds. The negative only-child stereotype has a detrimental affect on the only-child's sense of self. In Chapter 1, the view that only-children are spoilt, privileged and have it all; are considered to be socially challenged; unable to share; and lonely is abundantly clear in the literature quoted. The stereotype exists whether or not it is valid or invalid and affects how only-children are perceived and how they perceive themselves. The matrix also shows the positive stereotype, promoted more commonly in the United States, that only-children are high achievers, successful, independent and mature.

All three circles are connected and give rise to what is described as the only-child matrix which holds these three worlds together, indicating where they overlap in the personal, private and public. The lines around each circle are broken to reveal the fluidity of the model as the intra-, inter- and extra-psychic worlds interlink and merge.

Let us now look in detail at the themes which go to make up the only-child matrix. Case material will be introduced to identify how the archetype can be used as a therapeutic model for understanding the only-child experience and some thoughts about the implications of my research on therapy and practice will be discussed. The contents of this only-child archetype will briefly be unpacked under the headings of:

- lack of connectedness;
- aloneness and space;
- commitment: dependence versus independence;
- specialness, grandiosity and responsibility;
- self-esteem;
- lack of sibling opportunities;
- triangular relationships;
- enmeshment;
- separation and individuation;
- the effect of the only-child stereotype; and
- shame

The significance of siblings on the psychological and emotional development of children has been the subject of much study by psychologists and social scientists (Chapter 1). It is clear from these studies that there is a great deal of evidence demonstrating the importance of sibling relationships for social and emotional learning. Opportunities to learn social skills in the relatively secure environment of the family are subsequently lost to the only-child, leading to difficulty with behaviours associated with competition and conflict and knowing the 'boundaries' or 'rules' of social and emotional relating.

Whilst I am not suggesting all only-children are socially and emotionally deficient, there is some research (Rosenberg & Hyde, 1993) linked in Chapter 1 to attachment theory that suggests there are three types of only-children, two of which can de described as insecurely attached and match the only-child archetype. There is a great deal of evidence in my research data that despite the fact onlies appear confident and mature, this is rarely the way they feel. Lack of siblings not only interferes with self-development but frequently leads to a triangular and enmeshed family unit where there can be difficulty in separating. This may be compounded by a sense of isolation, difference and shame engendered by the social stigma of being an only-child. Lack of siblings also means a lack of witness to one's life, not just in childhood but subsequently in adulthood. The popularity of the onlychild website illustrates the significance of witness for the adult only-child. The stories from the website demonstrate how essential witness is to the only-child's sense of self. Parents offer this witness, but so do siblings; and the fear many adult onlies feel concerning their parent's death (Chapter 7) is a result of the potential loss of a witness to their existence when their parent(s) die.

In the following overview of the only-child matrix, I am offering a way of looking at a set of phenomena that may speak to non-onlies who perhaps have step-siblings, or are first children or are an 'unplanned' youngest child. Whilst they have had the experience of dethronement the birth of a sibling provides, they can have elements of this archetypal only-child experience as a result of a large age gap between siblings, or being a minority gender in a large family and so on.

Lack of connectedness

For many only-children, the desire to relate is intense but the feeling of being able to connect, or having a sense of connectedness, is missing. Instead, there is a sense of lack, a lack of connectedness. This is described in different ways in the life-stories, for example, Magritte's story (Chapter 3) is a story of disconnectedness, Yukinori's story (Chapter 6) concerns his constant striving to connect with people, but ultimately all the stories reflect a striving to get, or experience, something that appears to be missing. There is little more than a simple acknowledgement of this lack in the literature on only-children. However, a complex description of the impact of this lack is to be found in the phenomeno-logical psychology of Merleau-Ponty. An essay based on a lecture given by Merleau-Ponty, when he was Professor of Child Psychology at the Sorbonne, gives an insight into the inter-subjective significance siblings play in the development of language, affect and perceptual world:

> In sum, the intellectual elaboration of our experience of the world is constantly supported by the affective elaboration of our inter-human relations. The use of certain linguistic tools is mastered in the play of forces that constitute the subject's relations to his human surround-ings. The linguistic usage achieved by the child depends strictly on the 'position' (in psychoanalytic terms) that is taken by the child at every moment in the play of forces in his family and human envir-onment.
>
> (Merleau-Ponty, 1947; trans. 1964, p. 112)

He describes how a girl of thirty-five months acquires language through the experience of the birth of her baby brother. Through de-centreing her place in the family (what I have termed elsewhere as dethroning), the child learns to accept a relative abandonment by her parents as she is no longer the focus of their attention with a younger child arriving. The girl therefore has to adopt what Merleau-Ponty describes as an 'active' attitude, letting go of her former 'passive' attitude. This is accompanied by the linguistic phenomena of a move from present to imperfect tense, as well as the adoption of four verbs in the future tense. Future tense indicates a time of 'aggressiveness' which he views as the process of actively moving towards a future, rather than passive acceptance of the present. Greater use of the terms 'me' and 'I' also indicate the adoption of a more personal attitude and separation. The acquisition of the imperfect tense at the birth of her brother, Merleau-Ponty says: 'indicated that the child was becoming capable of understanding that the present changes into the past' (ibid, p. 112).

The experience of a sibling birth gave this child an opportunity to re-structure her relations with her human environment. She has been able to overcome her jealousy of the de-centreing of her position, and the use of the imperfect tense reveals an acceptance of the movement from present to the former present (imperfect). She used the imperfect tense in connection with the birth of her brother, he *is* now what she *used to be*. As Merleau-Ponty concludes:

The child's experience of the constellation of his own family does more than impress on him certain relations between one human being and another. At the same time that the child is assuming and forming his family relations, an entire form of thinking arises in him. It is a whole usage of language as well as *a way of perceiving the world* [my italics].

(ibid, p. 113)

It is the perceptual shift in Merleau-Ponty's description that is particularly pertinent to the understanding of the only-child experience. The shift moves the child out of the present and allows her to separate and see herself as the object of her world, as well as the subject. The child's language indicates this separation from being central to the parents' world to one where she sees herself as a part of a sibling family. This requires overcoming jealousy and gives the opportunity to both re-structure relations with others she lives with and simultaneously acquiring new dimensions of existence of past, present and future (ibid: 110). In line with Feldman (1981), Mitchell (2000, 2003), Coles (2003) and Winnicott (1957), siblings clearly play an important role in separation and maturation.

If a child fails to have this opportunity through the birth of a sibling, there is not only a lack in his/her experience, but this lack is an embodied feeling that something is missing. What exactly is missing? I would suggest opportunities for inter-subjective relating with children as opposed to adults. Whilst play with other non-sibling children can alleviate this to an extent, the overcoming of jealousy; the beginning of separation from parents; and the movement from the passive to the active 'I' and 'me' all contribute to a developing sense of identity, one which is interconnected with others. The following is a case study that illustrates how I believe this same shift can occur in therapy.

Sophia, an only-child brought up in a middle-class family in Greece, contacted me for long-term therapy as a result of my website. In her thirties, she had seen a number of therapists over many years of suffering from depression. She believed that the root of her problem lay in the fact she was an only-child. However, she had found that previous therapists had tried to show her that perhaps there were other factors she had not considered, even suggesting sexual abuse.

Sophia spent most of the session speaking about the disadvantages of her plight as an only-child. I was aware of thinking I could understand that many people listening would think she was making much out of what appeared to be a very reasonable lifestyle, loving, though probably enmeshed parents. She had only been able to separate by moving countries and marrying a UK citizen.

I listened attentively, shared some of my own sense of what she was saying and she left feeling 'so much better'. We then had a six-week break. I felt the session had gone well and that she had experienced being heard at an only-child level that had not happened to her before in therapy. On her return, she said she had continued to feel much better about herself, had returned to Greece and found that neither her friends who had siblings nor her parents angered her as previously, not even when her friends spoke about their siblings. She told me she felt something very profound had shifted within her, particularly when I had said: 'Perhaps your mother was also very sad not to have had any more children'. She had never thought of it like that and I believe much of her subsequent shift was a result of letting go of her only-child world, one where she was the centre of all her thoughts and feelings. Through shifting her perception to another person, that of her mother, she had shifted from the passive to the active 'I'. This meant she literally dethroned or de-centred herself (in the words of Merleau-Ponty) thus changing her perceptual world. In so doing, she was able to move from being the centre of her world and was then able to stand outside herself to empathise with those around her in a way she was unable to do before. This ability to stand outside the self, I believe, is very difficult for only-children who are bound up in their intra-psychic worlds and also the centre of their parent's attention. I also think this is why they are perceived as spoilt. By not being dethroned by the birth of a sibling they not only lose out on valuable emotional and social development, but it also takes them longer to separate and build their own identity. As a result, they tend to stay within their intra-psychic world, which is safe, and not move from the passive position to the active inter-relational one. I would also argue that the public (social and cultural) messages influence an only-child's sense of being separate in a predominantly sibling society.

Aloneness and space

The only-child's internal world appears to be very important and is the basis for imaginary play that has to be internal rather than external because of the lack of children to play and compete with. A feeling of aloneness is a strong theme in all the life-stories and continually expressed in workshops and Internet message boards. I have encountered many times what is perceived as the *negative* aspects of my research which is about the sense of aloneness and loneliness that is expressed by adult onlies, although they themselves do not necessarily view it as negative. Parents of onlies tend to be very worried that their child will be lonely if they do not produce a sibling and it is the most frequent type of posting on parent message boards such as BabyCentre.com.

The sense of aloneness appears to begin in childhood when the only-child has no siblings and yet is aware other children do. This can be exacerbated if the child feels excluded from their parents' relationship or is kept away from other children and not given the opportunities this contact would bring. School is potentially a place to make friends, but it can also be a place where the realisation that you don't 'know the rules' begins. This knowledge can be isolating. Many only-children find themselves on the edge of groups and social occasions, feeling alone in a crowd. Some describe feeling an outsider or feeling on the edge of social events. A partner's family can be experienced as difficult to negotiate, all this is clearly evidenced on the Beinganonly message board (Chapter 5). But the greatest challenge nearly all adult only-children talk about is when parents die, an event many adult only-children fear. It was the death of my parents that propelled me to do this research. I felt my sense of aloneness intensify with the realisation no one was left to whom I could talk about my childhood, no one to share recollections, no one left as a witness to my early life.

Two of the consequences of a sense of apartness arising from the data are that adult onlies need space, which can be described as a need to be unengaged with another, and they have problems with commitment. Whilst many life-stories indicate this need for space, there is often a comparable longing for intimacy. Commitment requires giving up independence, something onlies prize because it is a familiar place to be, particularly for the resistant/avoidant, insecurely attached child/adult. Amy's story (Chapter 3) is a good example as she spent much of her childhood alone and as an adult has found it difficult to maintain her space which is precious to her, similarly Ivy's (Chapter 6). The tension between being with people and having enough space is particularly difficult to negotiate in relationships. It is also exacerbated by onlies' lack of sharing experience of both physical and emotional space. This dilemma can be difficult for partners who may be needed one moment and then not, this 'blowing hot and cold' is something I have been accused of, but to me it demonstrates my need for time out.

Despite the difficulties in relationships which many only-children experience, their time alone enables them to re-experience themselves and re-charge and go back into the world of people. This is why onlies though alone do not feel that they are lonely. During these times of withdrawal, creativity can be an important aspect of re-charging. Thus the challenges in the experience of being brought up an only-child can be compensated for in the joy many only-children experience in being alone and creative. The negative side is the sense of being apart, separate and disconnected from others. Even if you despise your sibling, a sense of connection is present, a sense of shared history and of belonging to a family after your parents die. At best, this can be compensated for with partners and friends. At worst, a sense of deep aloneness and even loneliness can be experienced, particularly after the death of parents.

Commitment: dependency versus independence

As mentioned above, the dependence/independence continuum is a fundamental dilemma for the only-child and the heart of the only-child archetype. The following case study illustrates one configuration of the dilemma.

Eve, a thirty-year-old mother of a young baby presented agitated and despairing because of difficulties in her marital relationship. Before the birth of the child, she had been a career woman and had continued to work long hours. She felt her husband was not pulling his weight on the domestic front, and she felt very critical about everything he did: he was too slow and not thorough, not seeing housework as a priority. She resented this because his easy-going attitude meant she had lost 'her time' which she spent going for runs to keep fit. After the initial session, I was left with two thoughts – one that she had great difficulty in accepting help or acknowledging she needed it, unless it was done in exactly the way she did it; the second, concerning her resentment towards her husband due to the loss of 'her time', was that she needed to re-charge to cope with being a mother and full-time worker. I intuitively guessed she was an only-child, partly from these two behaviours but also because I had difficulty in following her line of thought. She rarely contextualised what she spoke about, assuming I followed, instead giving me a monologue of her inadequacies juxtaposed with wanting and not wanting her husband's involvement.

Only-children are often so immersed in their own worlds they forget that an outsider cannot intuit what is going on for them. I believe this is partly a result of inner dialogues and competing voices, coupled to always having someone's full intellectual and emotional attention. Not ever having had to compete for attention, onlies live with an expectation that the other person will be attuned to them and they will not have to work hard to communicate successfully.

Having ascertained her only-childness, I tentatively shared a few of my observations, and although we only had a short contract of five sessions we were able to explore the commitment: dependence/independence continuum very fruitfully. By the last session, she had realised she did need to allow her husband into her world and this was indicated in her ability to begin communicating more clearly with him and thankfully with me. By the end, we laughed at the way I had struggled to enter her world and she left saying she realised she could not retain her independence as a mother, so she no longer 'blamed' her husband for not being an extension of her. She said she felt more able to commit to him rather than just their baby and to tell him how important it was for her to have 'her time', whilst accepting the way he did the washing-up!

This case study highlights the paradox for many only-children of wanting to be in a relationship but also wanting to retain their independence. Eve hated conflict so she avoided being clear about her needs. Her view of her self as strong and independent had been lost through having a child and left her even more desperate to retain her control of everything around her. However, although she appeared 'superwoman' to her husband and colleagues, inside she said she felt she 'had no idea who she was and what she wanted'. Therapy enabled her to realise she needed to make changes and that she could still get what she needed through communication and compromise.

Specialness, grandiosity and responsibility

Whilst my research showed that not every only-child had felt special to their parents, all had experienced the expectations from others that they were special and by definition spoilt. Being the one child, to receive all the focus of parental attention is not without problems and this is illustrated in all the stories. To be special often means you carry the happiness of another and thereby you become responsible for that happiness. Being special can be problematic even if you have siblings, but for the only-child it goes hand in hand with a loss of opportunity to be dethroned or de-centred to provide that important shift of perceptual field. By failing to experience dethronement, only-children find that when they do lose their specialness it can come as a shock, but it can also cause problems relating to others if they continue to maintain their sense of specialness which can lead to grandiosity.

I use the term 'grandiosity' to explain the problems that arise for the only-child who is seen as 'special' by their parents primarily because they are the only one. We saw in the stories from China and Taiwan, where one child is the norm or the only choice, this specialness is particularly common. Although it is important for every child to feel special, when specialness is combined with a lack of sibling comparison and parental enmeshment, the child is unable to develop a sense of who they are in relation to others. When a sibling is born, the process of dethronement takes place as parents re-focus their attention on the new child. The child learns to accept a relative abandonment by her parents because she is no longer the focus of their attention. Therefore, this experience of a sibling birth gives the child an opportunity to re-structure her relations with her human environment, overcome jealousy and grandiosity and *gain a sense of belonging*. This is what the only-child misses.

From the life-stories, it became clear that one way only-children aim to please their parents and maintain their sense of specialness is to be responsible. Rather than acting as a child, they behave in an adult way. This is often both rewarded and expected. Childishness is seen as inappropriate behaviour. Expectations to behave in an adult way, as described in Chapter 1, are seen to be a positive trait in the US literature on parenting an only-child and one to be encouraged. This gives rise to the phenomenon of the 'little adult' who is well behaved and continually feels responsible, particularly for other people's feelings. The following quote came from a young contributor to my website commenting about her own experience of the dilemma of being a child and expectations of being an adult.

> I was a child in an adult world expected to act like an adult but constantly told 'remember you are a child'. I felt like screaming that 'I AM a child! I AM a baby!' It's like a contradiction in itself.

The problem of the 'little adult' will be discussed further in the section on separation and individuation. The public view of the special only-child has an enormous impact, clearly seen in all the life-stories and, I believe, underpins the opinion onlies are spoilt and will be returned to in the discussion on shame.

Self-esteem

The research richly illustrated that onlies often feel they have missed out on the 'rough and tumble' of sibling relationships, with a subsequent loss of opportunities to learn social skills in the relatively secure environment of the family. Whilst I am not suggesting that all only-children have problems, especially those with good parental attachment patterns, I do feel that those who have not had the benefit of secure attachment will find it even more difficult to deal with the lack of dethronement. Similarly, the lack of emotional and social learning, provided by siblings, will affect their sense of self-esteem. Attachment theory stresses the need for human beings to be social. The *securely* attached only-child will have been given enough security to cope with peer and adult relationships. However, not all only-children are so fortunate. Stereotypes are damaging but usually contain a grain of truth, or from a postmodernist perspective, one view of reality. The *insecurely* attached child would be prone to many of the characteristics often associated with only-children: demanding and needing attention or cut-off and aloof. A case study of an only-child called Nina is offered by Gerhardt (2004) to illustrate a child's emotional regulatory difficulties. It is also an illustration of another configuration of the only-child archetype, yet interestingly the fact she was an only-child did not enter Gerhardt's discussion at all.

> *Nina*, an only child, grew up as the focus of her parent's devotion, they adored her and hoped for great things from her, but did not have a happy relationship with each other. She (Nina) was under pressure to meet their needs – and in particular it seemed to me to meet her mother's psychological needs. Nina tried to be a good girl, and tried to succeed in the sports her mother enjoyed. She was scared of causing her mother any hurt, disappointment or feeling of abandonment....
>
> In the process, Nina lost touch with her own wishes and her own feelings...The family atmosphere was affectionate and even intense, yet the individuals within it did not clearly speak for themselves.
>
> (Gerhardt, 2004, p. 107)

Nina did not like to stay with friends in case her mother felt left out, and she is described as having a merged personality with her mother. The family is enmeshed and Nina found it difficult to separate and grow up, as she was terrified of the world and had little ability to regulate herself emotionally. Through therapy, it became apparent Nina's mother could not manage her own feelings and so was unable to regulate Nina's emotional states. Nina could not tell her mother anything without her over-reacting. Her mother was unable to contain any of her daughter's negative feelings: when Nina's best friends moved away, her mother told her 'You're not lonely, you have your family.' If the room was hot, her mother would assume Nina, like her, was also hot.

Gerhardt explains that when people cannot handle difficult feelings, they avoid them. Lack of emotional confidence, she believes, leads to ambition and perfectionism in an attempt to find self-esteem elsewhere (seen in the previous section: 'commitment' case study on Eve). She describes perfectionism as a means to avoid conflict, offending or upsetting people, initially those on whom you depend, but later it is taken into adult relationships.

Gerhardt's story of Nina offers an illustration of insecure attachment leading to anorexia. Gerhardt focuses on the client's relationship with her parents who see her as an extension of themselves. However, the story is also the one about an only-child with insecure and enmeshed parenting, having many echoes with the life-stories and experiences sent to me via the website. Low self-esteem, avoidance of conflict and the need to please make up Gerhardt's 'perfectionism', and are very common only-child traits. The fact that Gerhardt does not discuss her being an only-child is important. Instead, she is totally focused on the parent–child triad as the primary influence on development and does not consider overtly the impact a lack of siblings might have.

Many years of working with young people in youth counselling centres, colleges and universities has given me numerous opportunities to notice both similarities and differences in the only-child experience. I will offer a very typical case of Jo, a twelve-year-old only-child encouraged by her parents to come to therapy because of her difficulties with bullying and maintaining friends.

Jo looked more mature than her twelve years and was easily able to engage in conversation, but it belied a deeper very young Jo who revealed herself later. She spoke about being bullied at school and how various girls kept turning against her despite the fact they were apparently 'good friends'. She was attractive and articulate and did not appear to me to be a prime candidate for bullying. She seemed over-generous, which the friends had linked with her being an only-child and they considered her 'privileged'. Jo did not particularly like this label but her generosity seemed to be tied with her need to 'earn' friends similar to Lyn's story in which she bought chocolate in order to gain friends. A strong need for perfectionism and to be in control of her surroundings also emerged during the sessions. Routines were very important to Jo and she behaved like a little adult waking herself up, bathing, tidying her room, making her sandwiches, feeding her animals and on return from school completing similar activities which if she missed, caused her enormous anxiety. I became aware of how much she restricted her life in order to maintain these routines. The only exception she made was if she was going to meet a friend but often they let her down and she felt devastated.

I worked with Jo for several months and realised one of her major difficulties was dealing with any sort of emotional upset. I had briefly met her mother who appeared caring and concerned, but also at her wits end over what she considered to be her daughter's oversensitivity to others. She had been off school with various anxiety-related attacks, and I began to get a sense of enmeshed parenting similar to Gerhardt's case study of Nina. Jo enjoyed coming to talk and particularly liked the fact that I disclosed I was also an only-child which appeared to give her permission to talk more openly about her experience. She dealt with the sale of her horse, by denying its impact and then focused on acquiring a number of other pets, mostly rabbits. They were her 'true' friends and did not let her down. As time went on, her anxiety appeared to be getting worse and eventually she was able to confide about the difficulties that were emerging in her parents' relationship. We ended soon after as they felt unable to fund the sessions further. She had, however, learned to better negotiate friendships and the bullying had stopped. I believe her control and perfectionism were ways of dealing with her anxiety, induced more strongly because of the triangular relationship with her parents.

Triangular relationships

Not all only-children have two parents and this in itself is an important aspect of diversity in the only-child experience. This section, however, deals with triangular relationships which are inevitable when there are two parents and one child. Feldman (1981) calls this the 'family romance' and sees it as unhelpful to healthy psychological development.

The only-child–parent triangle means that only three interactions are possible, child-mother, child-father and mother-father. The interactions the child can take part in will all have an adult element and the only interactions that can be observed are adult ones. In contrast, where there are two siblings the number of possible interactions doubles and includes child–child interactions and adult–child observation. An increase in siblings leads to more child–child interactions, which then become the dominant mode, whereas for the only-child adult–child interaction is always the dominant mode and creates greater intensity. This is why it is so difficult for only-children to gain a perception of themselves because they never have the opportunity in the family to step outside and observe themselves as their siblings see them.

However, it is the intensity of the triangular relationship that is primarily remarked upon by co-researchers and website mailings. It is also a theme that frequently emerges in the only-child workshops. In the workshops, drawings and body sculpting are used to reflect the family dynamic of each participant. The drawings and sculpts powerfully depict where the power lies in the family. Sculpts and drawings usually consist of two dominant parents with a small child. The child is often drawn at only a tenth of the size of the adults, either ensconced in the middle or on the periphery looking in. Often the child has arms outstretched to the parents in the gesture that asks to be picked up; this is a primary attachment behaviour and one that requires the mother to respond physically. Do these drawings indicate an unfulfilled need for secure attachment?

Another indicator of the power of the triangular relationship from a life-stage perspective is demonstrated by body sculpting. Using three volunteers to represent each member of the family in *childhood, adolescence, adulthood* and *present* dramatically captures the family dynamic. It demonstrates that for many only-children, *adolescent* rebellion is often an internal rather than external process; very few felt they could be overtly rebellious. By *adulthood*, a greater distance has usually been negotiated, although some participants appear still enmeshed, others had literally 'left the country' to discover who they were. In the *present*, the sculpt poignantly depicts the death of one or both parents and the gap this had left in their lives. Those with parents alive, on seeing their family sculpt, spoke of the guilt and concern they had for not being more available to their elderly parents. Each exercise is extremely powerful and facilitated a great deal of emotion and served to confirm the importance of the life-stage significance of only-children, particularly over the death of parents.

Two important issues emerged from only-child workshops; these are family enmeshment and power. It was not uncommon for an alliance of two against one. This was evident in many of the original interviews with co-researchers, but was revealed particularly strongly with body sculpting. My own experience had been an alliance with my mother against my father, or an alliance between my mother and father against me. As a result, I did not establish a separate relationship with my father until my mother died. This scenario, of a bond with one parent to the exclusion of the other, is common with only-children. This often leaves only-children feeling manipulated and torn. Many felt that they had been given 'too much information' about their parents' relationship, becoming a confidante to one or other and told inappropriate information for a child. All these feeds into the enmeshment process, described by Love and Robinson:

> Parents who are enmeshed with their children often negate the child's thoughts and feelings. They reward their children for thinking and feeling the same way they do, or for conforming to an ideal. Through these daily lessons, the child learns to equate intimacy with invasion; they learn that being close to someone invites repression and manipulation.
>
> (Love & Robinson, 1990, p. 106)

Whilst triangular relationships require two parents, enmeshment can also occur in the case of the single parent and only-child.

Enmeshment

Gerhardt (2004), Love and Robinson (1990) and Winnicott (1957) see enmeshment occurring when a mother's wounded-ness contaminates her ability to parent her child because her own unmet needs get confused with the child's. The healthy psychological distance necessary for conscious parenting is difficult to achieve when the child is experienced as an extension of the parent. If you are enmeshed with someone or the idea of someone, it is impossible to know who you are. If you don't know who you are, you feel as though you do not exist without the other person. It is as if they are defining you. Enmeshment is literally giving yourself away to another, living outside of yourself. It leaves you without a sense of self and makes it difficult to have relationships with other people because you are trying so hard to be what you think they want you to be. It can be a very self-defeating pattern to get locked into and one that appears prevalent in adult only-children.

As the single most important predictor of how a person will parent (Stern & Bruschweiler-Stern, 1998) is how one was parented, that means the pattern of attachment established with a baby is determined largely by the pattern of attachment received from the mother. This is unconscious parenting and it is an inheritance. It is hidden from our awareness, but we rely on accumulated wisdom of past experiences to shape the present moment for us. Unconscious parenting is also reactive. Parents know they have touched a sore spot in themselves when they find themselves under or over-reacting to something their child says or does, even though they may remain unaware of why.

Enmeshment is clearly not something unique to only-children and is a result of parents' own experience of insecure attachment. However, the possibility of parental enmeshment is more detrimental when there is only one child available to meet the need of the parent. The power and intensity of that relationship can be overwhelming to the only-child. As we saw in the case of Nina, it can lead to a total loss of a sense of self. This view concerning only-children is shared by Love and Robinson who talk about enmeshment as 'emotional incest':

> One-child families have a higher than normal incidence of emotional incest. With no other child to dilute the intensity of the parent-child bond, the only child stands out in bold relief.... everything about the only child is watched closely, including his health, physical development, school performance, talents, weaknesses, and achievements. This can turn parenting into an obsession.
>
> (Love & Robinson, 1990, p. 90)

In my opinion, books like Newman's (2001), although supposedly dispelling the myths surrounding only-children, do in fact show obsessive aspects in their parenting advice. The significance of why an only-child is an only-one is also important (Chapter 4). There are many reasons. Some of the common ones are: lack of fertility, death of a baby, separation and divorce, late parenthood and parental illness. However, a question I was also curious to know, and related to those reasons, are the *messages* only-children carry about being an only-child. The mailings from the website indicated two types of stories: *'one is enough'* and *'you are my world'*.

One is enough

Many people had this story, which included messages like: 'My mum said she found it difficult to cope with me, so she couldn't face having any more children' or 'I was a difficult baby so they decided to stop after me'. My own story has similarities and I will briefly tell it to illustrate why I think my relationship with my mother was one of enmeshment.

> My mother was the youngest of four and an opposite sex twin. Her mother became ill after the birth and was not available because of frequent hospitalisations. My mother's eldest sister took a great deal of responsibility for the twins' care although she was only six years

old. My mother's story is that the sister favoured her twin brother, fed him and not her! Having spoken to my aunt, there appears to be some reality, in that my mother got little early mothering, and her mother like her, favoured the boy-twin. My mother had a difficult relationship with her own mother. When she found herself pregnant, and as yet un-married, a hasty wedding to my father took place which her parents did not attend. It must have been an immensely difficult time, as she was in the process of completing her teaching certificate; there was little money, and just a one room flat for the three of us. I was born seven months after the wedding. (I had been brought up believing I was two months premature). My mother returned to work when I was six weeks old, and I was looked after by 'Eve' from 7.00am to 7.00pm. My mother had given up her teacher training and now worked in the City as a comptometer operator. My early years were difficult, I was ill with bronchial asthma, pneumonia, pleurisy, whooping cough and diphtheria, and I often refused to eat. My memories are of my parents continually arguing. When I asked for a sibling the answer was 'You are enough work' and 'You wouldn't like to share your things'. Later on, my mother admitted she hated the dependency I had on her as a baby. I was taught to be very independent from an early age, not to show emotion: 'Crying is just feeling sorry for yourself', and not to have any emotional needs myself.

I think my relationship with my mother was one of 'dismissing attachment' (Stern & Bruschweiler-Stern, 1998). We were very close, but I never felt I could have an opinion that was different from either hers or my father's. Training to be a therapist at the age of twenty-five facilitated my separation, but I felt she never forgave me for it and was dismissive of the field of work I had entered. I also felt she was envious of my achievement, which in itself is not uncommon, but this was never spoken. My own therapy has helped me to understand my earlier life; that my mother's inability to nurture me as a baby was the consequence of her own lack of nurture. The legacy for me has been continual issues concerning confidence, self-worth and enmeshed relationships.

You are my world

This is a story of 'enmeshed attachment' (Stern & Bruschweiler-Stern, 1998), but one where the child becomes the centre of the universe for the parent and in popular folklore probably leads to the stereotype of the spoilt only-child. Poppy's story (Chapter 3) is a good example; it is a story of overprotection, to the point of suffocation. Her mother involved herself with every aspect of Poppy's life, even to the point of watching her in the school playground at break times. She played endlessly with Poppy but always on her mother's terms. Her mother always knew what was best for Poppy, limited her freedom and made the world outside into a frightening place against which she cautioned her daughter. Poppy, as an adult, is convinced her mother was living her life through her. Her mother never worked and wanted continual input into Poppy's life. My interviews with Poppy were characterised by immense anger towards her suffocating upbringing, and although now in her fifties, she still finds it difficult to come to terms with the damage she feels her mother inflicted on her psychic and emotional development. Poppy's marriage and career were all ways she tried to please her mother. It was not until her late forties she finally felt in charge of her own life, finding a woman with whom she wanted to spend her life and re-training as a counsellor. Like other adult only-children, Poppy appears confident and high achieving, but underneath is full of doubts and incongruities.

These two stories: *'one is enough'* and *'you are my world'* are very common stories of enmeshment. Most only-children could place themselves in one or other of these categories. More importantly, although enmeshment is not unique to only-children, lack of siblings and the social and emotional regulation they can offer means that it is much more detrimental to the only-child.

The literature on only-children (Chapter 1) suggests that there are two basic reasons why parents might 'choose' to have only one (bearing in mind that many only-children, especially in the past, are not by parental choice):

- To be able to combine a career and a child.
- To avoid the perceived negatives of more than one child, such as sibling rivalry, and sharing time and attention with more than one.

First, is it any more difficult to combine a career and two children than a career and one child? Personally I think not. The second reason is far more debatable. Chapter 1 demonstrates more beneficial reasons for children to have siblings than the alternative and this research bears this out further. Having one child means it is easier for parents to slip into meeting parental needs, rather than those of the child. Research on insecurely attached children, in a variety of different cultures, found that 'consistently 35% are insecure' (Goldberg et al., 1995, p. 11). This statistic could mean that the rising popularity, particularly in the United

States, of having only one child may also be an indication of the levels of insecure attachment. Only-children need to mix with other children at an early age, which day-care can provide. In China, we saw how important that has been to counteract some of the excesses of parent/grandparent influence. However, children *also* need a well-attuned parent who is not exhausted from combining a career and a child. At least, if a child has a sibling there is another person to relate to and reflect back their experience of the parenting they are both experiencing. This is not an argument against career versus parenting; I believe both can be combined, but I make a plea that only-children may be more in need of opportunities to play with other children and have an attuned parent who is available to them.

Separation and individuation

The following is a poem written in a *'Parenting the Parents'* workshop, by a participant who has been unable to sustain an intimate relationship, although she functions well in the world, has a career and is friendly and sociable. I was very touched when she gave me this poem to use as part of my research. She was able to identify with others in the workshop who felt the same way and to realise she is not alone in her feelings of isolation and lack of connection.

> Daddy I needed you to help me grow up
> become more balanced,
> less worried,
> less temperamental,
> less emotionally needy
> I know you are pleased
> with what I am
> more than my mother
> but you still expect me
> to watch over you

> > Mummy, I needed you
> > to be less possessive
> > less doting
> > you wanted me to be
> > your shadow
> > your re-incarnation
> > your chance to have another life
> > to compensate for your failed one

Now I am so messed up
I don't know how to move on
I want to have what most people have emotionally
let me go
let me be free
I will still love you much,
too much

      If only I had not been
      a good girl
      If only I had not been
      so obedient
      Some day I'll understand
      why it has been so difficult
      to keep afloat

One of the strongest images that emerged from interviews and work-shops is a term I have taken from transactional analysis: the 'adapted' child (Berne, 1961; Stewart & Joines, 1987). Although I use the term, which has similarities to Winnicott's (1958) 'false-self' and Rogers' (1961) 'self-concept', I am not advocating that the structure of the self is either unitary or primarily the result of the Oedipal triangle. It is necessary for all children to adapt and be socialised but when this goes too far, the 'natural' or 'free' child becomes more and more excluded. Being 'the little adult' was a common experience for both my co-researchers and myself. However, the real problem comes when the child needs to individuate and separate from their parents, having lost touch with their 'organismic' or 'ideal self' (Rogers, 1961).

A typical scenario of an enmeshed only-child is *Jack*. In his mid-twenties, married with a successful career, he came to me for brief therapy. He was having difficulties in his relationship with his wife who appeared to be spending a great deal of time drinking. It rapidly emerged Jack spent long hours at work, because it was there he felt most alive. It also became apparent that his mother, living in the north, rang him every day and more often if his mother was feeling particularly down. The mother had an uncanny knack of knowing when Jack walked through his front door, ringing within minutes and the conversation lasting up to half an hour.

I was curious to know if he was an only-child as this is a very typical scenario for only-children. Having established he was an only one, I asked him how his partner felt about the calls and he said they did not bother her. We set about discussing making boundaries with his mother, which he found extremely difficult at first, particularly when the inevitable backlash of emotional blackmail was released. However, within six sessions, he had maintained the new boundaries and his partner shared that she did resent his mother's intrusion. The relationship between them improved and she decided to enter counselling to address her drinking.

Nearly all adult onlies I see in therapy, both men and women, have similar problems of separation, usually with their mother. Another typical scenario would be *Peter*, who works in the family business; he has an extremely difficult relationship with both parents. He dislikes his father whom he perceives as too controlling, and although he loves his mother, she appears to expect him to treat her like the husband she wishes she had. Peter has found it impossible to have a relationship with a woman of whom his mother approves and although he is now in his forties, he has concluded it is better to give up trying than go through the emotional upheaval of upsetting her. Peter is an intelligent, personable man, who has found it impossible to separate and leave home. His fear of leaving the safety of the enmeshed world of his parents is too daunting. Equally to find out who he is, and what he wants, is too challenging. In my experience, it is often harder for only-child men to separate from their mother than only-child women, particularly if the mother has been left through divorce or death or is a single parent. The male only-child becomes a replacement partner, a difficult place from which to extricate oneself and one that has a detrimental effect on relationships in adult life:

> People who grow up in enmeshed families are likely to have boundary problems later in life. Some will perpetuate the loose boundaries they had as children, never being sure where they begin and others leave off...Others have the opposite reaction: they build a wall around themselves to protect themselves from further injury. These are the people you feel you never get to know. They don't ask you about your problems, they have few if any intimate friends.
>
> (Love & Robinson, 1990, p. 50)

Jack is an example of someone with loose boundaries and Peter someone who has increasingly built a wall around him. When attachment to a parent remains in adulthood, intimate relationships automatically become a triangle and a similar dynamic to the childhood triangle is set up. Neither Jack nor Peter has many close friends and they have found relationships difficult to navigate. This is a common theme on the Internet message boards. Here Randolph shares his experience with others:

> I've read all the messages about making/keeping/losing friendships and suffer all the same sort of issues. I have also come to recognize something in myself I named: 'The Spotlight of Attention'. When I have found a new friend or someone I found interesting, I turn my attention towards them. I am the world's best friend, do way too much to please them, would walk through burning coals to help them ... ... and then they freak and vanish.
>
> My ex-wife came from a large family. They all went round and round with all sorts of games and tricks to garner attention in the family herd. When she met me, I turned on my Spotlight of Attention, and gave her more attention than she ever had. Her response, of course, was to go into another room and lock the door. It seems that ALL THAT ATTENTION SCARED THE HELL OUT OF HER!
>
> Being an only, I know how to get into a subject and dig into it deeper than anyone else. I can spout off more completely useless trivia than anyone else I know. Details ... details .... the rest of the world isn't used to this, and frankly, it intimidates them! We SCARE them by just doing what we find normal. I have learned to at least TRY and not smother people I meet with my expectations. I might not get it right all the time, but I think I am getting better. I mean, sometimes I don't return e-mails for days – instead of my instinct, which is mere seconds after receiving it! Sometimes I wait a number of hours before returning a friendly phone call- instead of blasting right back as if the fate of the world depends on it. (Randolph)

The intensity described here is the adult onlies' legacy from a childhood of parental attention which affects all other relationships and compounds the attempts made by onlies to separate and individuate. As Randolph describes: '*I do way too much to please them*', and this sets up a powerful dynamic that is hard for others to reciprocate. One of the many answers he received from other onlies elaborates further the dilemma:

> – Friendships (for onlies) come with WAY more expectations. Because (a) no siblings to learn about being close to someone you don't necessarily have everything in common with; (b) being so close to adults, many children's games/past-times seem, well, childish.

– The 'why did they leave me?' 'why don't they like me?' theme that I've read in the previous postings seems to be a residue from the total attention only children get from their parents. The world revolves around us! We expect similar treatment and attention from friends. Therefore confusion/feelings of inadequacy when it clearly doesn't...causes us to withdraw.

– We have a crazy need to be special, as we were to our parents, leads to not saying things in large groups, leads to severe relationship intensity/expectations, leads to choosing only friends to whom we will be Very Special, therefore greater potential for hurt if the friendship doesn't last, or it turns out we're not special to that person – Then we withdraw.

A too close alliance with a child by a parent interferes with the development of a sense of a separate identity. The child is eager to please the parent and be the person, the 'little adult', they want them to be. The parent is looking for an ally and the only-child is likely to comply to ensure the parent's love. Ensuring love becomes more important to the only-child than developing a sense of identity. This behaviour was common in many of the life-stories, at an age when most adults would be expected to have a stronger sense of identity (Chapter 7). Quite often only-child adults find it difficult to know where they fit on the dependent–independent continuum. Some onlies repeat the pattern of being dependent which they had as a child, others become very controlling, similar to their parents. Onlies' lack of emotional maturity clashes with their social maturity thus creating problems in friendships and with partners. The only-child adult may appear confident and coping, but emotionally they are frequently unsure and in need of reassurance. Both the above postings reflect this social and emotional dilemma. The need to be special, with the message 'please like me, please don't leave me' of dependency, is rarely a good starting point for relationship.

The effect of the only-child stereotype on parent and child

As a child, I was aware of a negative only-child stereotype, and my work with young people who are only-children has convinced me that stereotypes remain. This theme of a culturally and socially induced stereotype is an important aspect in the only-child experience and affects the child and parents alike. The following email, received via the website, indicates that parents are also challenged by stereotypical attitudes. The message shows how circumstances such as secondary infertility are an important dynamic in the situation of only being able to have one-child.

> I have enjoyed your website very much, I am the parent of an only child and a counsellor. My partner and I have spent many years attempting to come to terms with our secondary infertility and are regularly set back, and hurt at the prejudice we, and especially our young son, experiences in being an only child. Having read some of the experiences of only children getting together on your site, I am deeply touched, and can only imagine that we as parents could gain a lot from meeting others in the same situation, who want to parent their onlies 'positively'. I look forward to hearing from you.

This is but one of many similar emails and I became increasingly sensitised to the concern parents expressed about having an only-child, and the negative, often rude, comments they received from others. A fellow therapist confided that she continually received comments at the school gate, perhaps some were intended to be positive but she was aware that behind remarks such as 'Oh Jenny seems so independent for an only-child' or 'I would have expected her to be too clingy being the only one' lurked the negative only-child stereotype. Whilst I have argued that parental concern over the possibility that their child may be regarded as spoilt is detrimental to their parenting, trying too hard not to spoil may mean parents are in danger of being harsher than parents with more than one child. Parenting message boards in the United States reflect less concern over the fear of spoiling, but this is in contrast to the United Kingdom. Many parents I have spoken to are acutely aware of the so-called 'privileges' only-children are perceived to have over those with siblings. Parents face a dilemma between giving their child everything and fear of overindulgence. This can have negative repercussions as this email from Australia illustrates:

> I was assured by my parents when I was growing up that I was spoilt and luckier than other children because I had no siblings I had to share with. I believed this for some time, but as I grew older I realised it was a fallacy! (Evelyn)

As China has the largest numbers of only-children, it is interesting to note that their research centres on the dilemma of *social* development of Chinese only-children. We saw in Chapter 1 that findings in Chinese research though important are inconsistent. For example, some investigators (Jiao et al., 1986) suggest that negative social behaviour patterns are found in Chinese only-children. They are spoilt by their parents, show disrespect to elders, resist discipline and are more egocentric. Other scholars (Chen & Goldsmith, 1991) say only-child behaviours are problematic and are the result of limited experience with other children in the home, combined with inappropriate parenting styles. US researchers' conclusions deny these undesirable social behaviours in China (Falbo et al., 1997; Poston and Falbo, 1990;). In the Chinese popular press, it appears prejudice *is* still rife towards onlies as this article illustrates:

> The Chinese have a special name for those tots: xiao huangdi, or 'little emperors'. They are regularly deplored in the state-run press. China's children are growing up 'self-centred, narrow-minded, and incapable of accepting criticism,' declared Yang Xiaosheng, editor of a prominent literary journal, in a recent interview in the Beijing Star Daily. Wang Ying, the director of Qiyi's kindergarten, concurs: 'Kids these days are spoiled rotten. They have no social skills. They expect instant gratification. They're attended to hand and foot by adults so protective that if the child as much as stumbles, the whole family will curse the ground.'
>
> (Chandler, 2004, para. 3)

China has such a different culture from the West that it is difficult to either gather a full picture or make any valid comparisons. Certainly the urban population, who are strictly curbed by the one-child policy, do tend to put all their attention and energies into their one child, especially to make up for the deprivation in their own childhoods. The new generation is different, having come of age in an era of unprecedented prosperity. Their parents and grandparents endured years of famine under Mao's communal agriculture policies and the chaos of the Cultural Revolution. They remember the trauma of the crackdown in Tiananmen Square, whilst this is history for the Chinese born since 1980. Whatever the case in China, prejudice appears rife and may be the result of the previous generations' conscious and unconscious envy of a new generation who does not have to endure harshness or 'eat bitterness'.

In the United Kigdom, I would argue that the only-child stereotype impacts on an individual and on a social level. Parents may be consciously aware of the negative stereotypes but they will still bring them consciously and unconsciously into their parenting. The child may not be aware of this negativity but it will affect them, nonetheless, as a sense of shame. The question of shame arose only in the longer series of interviews with some of my original co-researchers (Carol and Kate who are incidentally both therapists). I do not think this is surprising. Shame is something which people defend against either feeling or talking about. This was certainly true of my own experience and has been a useful personal insight resulting from my research. A sense of shame can be experienced at being seen to be privileged for not having to share with siblings and being overprotected and spoilt. The shaming stereotype impacts on both parents and child. Let us look more closely at the concept of shame.

Shame

> Are you an only child?
> Haven't you got any brothers or sisters?
> my heart sinks
> my stomach turns
> I fear the next remarks –
> I expect your mum and dad spoil you –
> don't they?
> I smile wanly
> what can I say?
> If I say yes –
> heads nod knowingly
> If I say no –
> eyebrows raise
> ever so slightly in disbelief
> I can't win
> I say nothing
> I look down
> shuffle my shoes
> feel ashamed.

When I wrote these stanzas, reflecting on my experience of growing up an only-child in the 1950s, I was unaware how significant they would be. My subsequent doctoral research into the experiences of adult only-children exposed issues that revealed a covert level of shame as a central issue which for many only-children led to a shame-based personality persisting into adulthood. I will briefly set out some ideas, mainly from analytic and psychoanalytic writers, concerned with the manifestation of shame before I offer my own interpretations. Parental empathy and attunement set up the foundations that lead to a healthy sense of self-worth (Fordham, 1986; Kohut, 1977; Neumann, 1988; Stern, 1985; Stern

& Bruschweiler-Stern, 1998; Winnicott, 1958). Shame occurs when the care-giver is unable, for what ever reason, to continue giving enough parental attention and care. The disruption can lead the infant to begin to mistrust the interactional patterns of the care-giver. Some fluctuation is both inevitable and unavoidable, but constant fluctuations can lead to insecure attachment patterns. When an infant, despite all its efforts, cannot elicit a good enough continuity of attention from the care-giver, basic trust and self-confidence is lost and shame is experienced. As Kaufman states:

> Shame originates interpersonally, primarily in significant relationships, but later can become internalised so that the self is able to activate shame without an inducing interpersonal event. Interpersonally induced shame develops into internally induced shame. Through this internalising process, shame can spread throughout the self, ultimately shaping our identity.
>
> (1985, p. 7)

Infants and children need to feel that the parent truly wants a relationship with them as a *separate human being,* loved in their own right. This separateness or private space gives the child a sense of his own personal life – of being alone in the presence of another (Winnicott, 1958). However, if this is not provided, the infant loses its spontaneity and seeks to fulfil the parent's need rather than its own. This is because either the parents need the infant's affirmation of love too much, or parental anxiety does not allow any relaxation in their constant controlling care (Jacoby, 1991). The loss of spontaneity and loss of a sense of being in touch with his own needs leads the infant to mistrust the outside world. It also inhibits the growth of confidence and self-esteem. As Jacoby states: 'The less self-confidence and self-esteem one has, the greater the likelihood that one will fall victim to intense shame and fear of shame' (1991, p. 23). Internal identification with the type of parental care received will either be love-based, fear-based or shame-based. This is because identity emerges as a result of the process of identification followed by internalisation of the following three aspects:

- affect-beliefs we have about ourselves;
- the way we are treated by significant others; and
- the images of those interactions we have received from those significant others.

These three become internal representations which function as an intra-psychic guiding capacity in our internal lives (Kaufman, 1985). Both Wurmser (1981) and Wharton (1990) suggest that shame arises in early infancy when the infant's striving for recognition is ignored. Shame manifests as an inner conflict between the need to establish a relation-ship with the outside world and the need to preserve the integrity of the self. Hultberg (1988) and Jacoby (1991) speak of two forms of shame that have opposing functions. One is about a person's personal integrity, the private part of ourselves which is guarded by thoughts of shame if exposed. Here the potential for shame works to protect the individual from society. The other form of shame is connected to social adaptation and is the process by which people are socialised into acceptable ways of behaving.

Whilst shame resides 'on the borderline between self and other' (Jacoby, 1991, p. 22), shame also plays an important role in negotiating interpersonal closeness and distance which we have seen is an important issue for onlies. Shame helps in the decision of how close I can allow someone into both my personal psychic and physical space. This is also based on a person's ability to trust and that in turn is connected to a person's childhood experience. When self-esteem, confidence and trust are lacking, shame is more prevalent and instead of protecting the individual it gets in the way of satisfying relationships. Having briefly reviewed both the origins of shame and how they are kept alive in the personality, I now want to offer my own interpretations about the impact of shame on only-child development in the United Kingdom. These ideas are based on both my findings and my personal and profes-sional experience and are central to the only-child archetypal matrix.

As we have seen, the intra-personal experience of shame is based on the infant's early experience of care-giving and the infant's striving for recognition, love and communication. Interlinked is the inter-personal relationship with the care-giver which needs to be one of attune-ment (Jacoby, 1991; Kaufman, 1985; Stern, 1985; Wharton, 1990). Attunement leads to the development of confidence and self-esteem, but without it shame is engendered because the inter-personal bridge between care-giver and child is broken. This continues to occur if the care-giver finds it difficult to emotionally separate and allow the child space to develop a separate personality. 'Excessive parental control combined with a particular climate in which a child feels powerless as well as trapped, together are a seedbed for shame' (Kaufman, 1985, p. 57).

We saw in the section on enmeshment and separation that some only-children experience the type of parenting Kaufman describes as leading to a shame-based personality:

> Shame can also be rooted in a parent looking to a child to make up for the parent's deficiencies or to live out the parent's dreams as though the child were but an extension of the self of the parent. Or again, the parent may directly look to the child literally to be parent to the parent; in this case, the natural flow of the parent being there primarily for the child is reversed such that the child must now tend to the parent's needs instead. Still again, the parent may repeatedly convey to the child that he or she is never to need anything emotional from the parent; this communicates in no uncertain terms that the child should have been born an adult and so must relinquish childhood without ever having had it.
>
> (Kaufman, 1985, pp.46–7)

This, I believe, results in the 'little adult' so common in my interviews and website postings. The other aspects of parental behaviour, Kaufman describes, is also reminiscent of parenting revealed in many of the life-stories (Chapter 3). Lyn remembered when one of her parent's friends described her as 'never having been a child'. Poppy was the 'teacher's little helper', despising childhood games. Georgina thought her peers silly in their play, she preferred adult pursuits. Amy and Anna felt unable to ask for help or support because they believed they would be 'smothered' by their mother. Poppy, Kate and Amy believed their mothers were attempting to live their lives through them. Magritte describes being unheard and unloved.

Whilst I believe parents do the best they are able in the circum-stances, I also think that the oldest/only-child will often experience simultaneously less confident and overly concerned parents, simply because the parents are new to parenting. As later siblings arrive, parents usually grow in confidence and modify their attention and behaviour, and siblings themselves offer other opportunities for inter-relating and alternative perspectives on the family not available to the only-child. As the only-child does not incur either of these benefits, they remain both the eldest and the youngest child and continue to carry both these positions in the family. They are caught in a conflict between being the 'responsible' eldest child whilst simultaneously being the 'dependent' youngest. Only-children, therefore, hold the attributes of the eldest and youngest. They are regarded as responsible yet privileged as the eldest, indulged and spoilt as the youngest. However, most importantly, what they lack is a sibling comparison to monitor and compare their experience in the family.

Finally, we have the extra-personal experience, provided by education and work which carry the cultural and social norms. Even though the phenomenon of the only-child is becoming more common we still live in a predominantly sibling society, and as I have discussed earlier, prejudice and stereotypes abound. These engender shame, and in particular what is often termed 'carried-shame'. Carried-shame is assimilated not necessarily through conscious awareness but in Jungian terms resides in the shadow and collective unconscious. This shame is carried, but does not belong to the carrier, and they in turn may not be aware on a conscious level of the burden they carry.

Social and cultural carried-shame (extra-personal) can become linked to inter-personal and intra-personal carried-shame. In addition to this, 'circumstantial shame' which may be the reasons why a person is an only-child, that is, an unplanned pregnancy, divorce, infertility, fear of childbirth, ill health and so on may also become linked. Circumstantial shame can cause an unspoken atmosphere in the parent's and only-child's life because it is held as a 'secret' in the family. This contributes to a shame-based personality which experiences appropriate shame (shame that helps us to realise we have done someone or something wrong) as crippling, whilst at other times engendering shameful feelings even though they are not linked to the person's behaviour. This can be evidenced in the life-story of James (Chapter 7), who bore circumstantial shame both from his mother's illegitimacy and divorce as well as carried shame from being an only-child.

As I mentioned above, I was not conscious of the shame I carried as an only-child until I began only-child research. It was at the edge of my awareness and I became aware of its influence as I prepared to submit my doctoral agreement. On the day, I found some of the audience relatively hostile to the idea of only-child research. In hindsight, I do not think this was the case, but I was experiencing my *own* shame in choosing a topic that focused on what, I think, most people regard as a privileged set of people. This may be conscious or unconscious and gives rise to envy of the only-child status. Whilst I recognise my shame was self-induced, I am also aware that there is a reality to my concern. For example, I watched another only-child researcher being given a rough ride presenting her research at a conference and this manifested as an envious attack on what she had presented. It was seen as too 'negative' and by implication did not reflect the 'privileges' that go with being an only-child. Similar accusations of negativity have been levelled at the findings of Pitkeathley and Emerson (1994) by Laybourn (1994), discussed in Chapter 1.

Carried-shame is an integral part of the only-child experience even if it is only experienced on the extra-personal level. However, as I have discussed, I think a proportion of only-children also suffer inter-personal and intra-personal shame, a consequence of their family dynamic and family secrets. This circumstantial-shame becomes linked to the cultural and social shame surrounding only-child perceptions. This is not inevitable, but there is reasonable evidence in my co-researchers' stories that it is quite common. I experience deep shame when I have attention focused on me and yet I know at another level I long for it. This is part of my shadow, those aspects of myself I find difficult to accept.

Having discussed the elements that make up the only-child matrix, it is hoped that readers have gained a clearer view of what it might mean to be brought up an only-child and the consequences for adult life. The final chapter summarises the themes discussed in the book and highlights areas which need more research.

10
Gathering the Threads

This book offers a variety of stories concerning the life-stages of adult only-children which are particular to their experience. The stories are collected from many parts of the world and, I believe, speak for themselves in offering an understanding of some of the challenges and differences onlies encounter. Growing up without siblings means missing out on a valuable transition, a shift in perceptual worlds. Without this shift, problems, particularly in relating, are likely to occur. Typical only-child ways of being may be manifested as a result of this deprivation and are something therapists might usefully consider. The experience of growing up without siblings is different and not one that has received much recognition in psychotherapeutic literature. With the increase in the numbers of only-children, it becomes even more vital to bring the specific life issues that onlies experience to the attention of clinicians. It could be said that being an only-child has similarities with the condition of colour blindness. No one can either see that you are colour blind or that you perceive the world in a different way to those who are not. In other words, your perceptual world is different and in many ways inaccessible to the other. It is impossible for someone who is not colour blind to fully understand this experience; at best they can accept the difference in perception. The same is true of the only-child experience. A realisation and appreciation that there is a difference is what I hope this book has achieved.

In Chapter 1, we noted that research on birth order and its effect on the developmental aspects of personality is often viewed as problematic. Sulloway's (1996) meta-analysis on birth order studies showed birth order as significant. He viewed only-children as more free to develop aspects of their personality than sibling children. However, he also noted that the lack of siblings makes only-children more susceptible to influences such as parents' social values and that they are less extra-verted than firstborns, because lack of siblings inhibits social practice. My research revealed that some only-children rather than being freer to develop aspects of their personality are, more often than not, less free because of the burden of parental expectation and this can led to compliance and a need to please. The 'little adult' is more likely to be a 'mini me' reflection of a parent than an emotionally mature authentic young adult. Lack of siblings removes the possibility of having someone of your own age group reflecting back childlike ways of behaving. The only-child's experience of having mainly adult role models gives them a superficial maturity and leads to them feeling less confident and even inadequate inside, compared to what they convey to the outside world. However, none of this is inevitable and one positive view arising from my research is that female onlies often feel less socially compelled into stereotypical female roles, evidenced by Magritte's story and particularly true of securely attached only-children.

One of the greatest impacts on only-children is living with the know-ledge that when their parents die they will be alone in the world. In Matt's story (Chapter 7), we saw how this impacts on his life, causing him to stay at home and remain dependent. Although Matt's suicidal thoughts concerning the idea of his survival after his parents' death may appear extreme, they are echoed in many of the life-stories, for example Kate, (Chapter 3), who felt she could not exist separate from her mother. Evelyn, a nurse in Australia, shared some interesting observations:

In my capacity as a nurse, I have had to pull aside frazzled adult only-children of dying patients in my care, who are trying to represent several siblings at a death bed by themselves, with responsibilities also to their children and partners as well. I have firmly but kindly reminded them that they cannot make up for children their parent didn't have at a time like this. The disadvantage of having only one child must be shared by the parent; their own family needs them too and they can't do it all. I have been thanked for my 'insight' and 'experience', but have to admit my insight was from professional observation *and* personal experience! (Evelyn)

I think it is particularly important for therapists to grasp what I would describe as an only-child's fear of the loss of existential validation. Evelyn noted in Australia, where she has practiced as a nurse for thirty years, that she *'had been surprised for some time that only children have issues that are overlooked, and counsellors appear fixated with stereotypes'*. I will return to the issue of existential validation in my final reflections. First I will explore Evelyn's issue concerning counsellor assumptions.

Therapists and birth order assumptions

An interesting piece of research from the Journal of Counselling and Development by Stewart (2004) looked at therapist assumptions on birth order. All participants received a vignette describing a hypothetical male client named Paul. A career counselling dilemma, rather than an exclusively personal problem or crisis, was used in the vignette to lessen the probability that participants would guess the study's hypotheses concerning the effects of birth order. In all other respects, except for Paul's birth order as either being the first, middle, youngest or only-child, the vignettes were identical. Stewart's (2004) research showed that birth order did affect the way clinicians viewed Paul and it made a difference to their perceptions of Paul as a first, middle, youngest or only-child. He particularly noted that 'the participating clinicians viewed the only-child as particularly likely to experience problems'.

Birth order assumptions with UK therapists

Stewart's (2004) research made me curious to know whether clinicians in the United Kingdom might have similar prejudices concerning birth order. I undertook a small piece of research to see how therapists viewed the status of only-child. I sent four statements, based on my research findings, asking therapists to consider and respond personally and/or as a therapist to them. I was not interested in doing a statistical analysis; rather I wanted to see what assumptions people might make on a personal and professional level. I also hoped to have a sense of people's level of awareness over the issues only-children face and to have a dialogue with any one who wanted more information. Thirty therapists were invited to answer the statements; some of whom were only-children (five), others had an only-child (two) or were living with one (two). All were supervisors and varied in therapeutic experience from three to twenty-five years. Overall, I was impressed with the awareness of only-child issues by the twenty-four who responded. Some of their responses were very insightful and I have given a flavour of the types of responses for each statement.

Only-children are generally regarded as privileged, overachievers, who have been given it all

Most people felt the first statement was a common view but not necessarily true and some knew of onlies who fitted the description. They also thought other things were often true:

- 'materially provided but not necessarily emotionally';
- 'huge pressures to achieve';
- 'seen as extension of parents';
- 'isolated and lonely'; and
- 'missing out on social skills'.

Only-children are likely to be spoilt by overindulgent parents

The second statement showed that people who were an only or had an only were very aware of the negative effects of fear of spoiling:

- 'As an only child I have grown up and lived with people's constant projection of this view on me';
- 'one of my clients felt straightjacketed by parents, as a child, life was rigid, highly routinised';
- 'my parents went to great lengths not to spoil me – my clients have also said their parents went too far'; and
- 'Much more likely to be brought up very strictly yet also given all the opportunities'.

Others felt they were no less likely to be spoilt than sibling children, but some therapists said they worked with parents of onlies to *'step back'* and helping them to say *'No'*.

People growing up without siblings have more difficulties with relationships

Most therapists felt this was not the case and gave examples of clients who had grown up with cousins or had grandparents around. Others agreed because: *'they have not learned to tolerate compromise or negotiate with other to accommodate the needs of others'*. However, the only-child therapists said:

- 'I am not sure about this. I and my son (an only) feel diffident about making friends but we both have a small circle of very deep friendships';

- 'I take longer to get over disagreements and conflicts...and feel responsible for my partners happiness'; and
- 'my experience of having no siblings has resulted in difficult relationships with peers and sexual partners'.

It seems that only-children themselves are more aware of difficulties, although, of course, it does not make them inevitable.

The special relationship in the triangle of only-child and two adults creates separation difficulties in adulthood

Two therapists said it would depend on attachment patterns; others said separations tended to be difficult '*irrespective of sibling group size*'; elderly parents were also given as a reason for difficulties in separation for only-child clients.

Onlies said:

- 'To separate to me feels liberating. I never felt close to my parents and I have attachment difficulties in adulthood. I wonder when and if I can attach plus commit on a long term basis';
- 'Not true in my case – we were never a triangle'; and
- 'The responsibility of being a single child means that separation will mean abandoning the parents. Living out parental hopes and expectations makes it difficult to find a separate life of one's own'.

One interesting response focused on clients who could not separate from the demands of parents and partner and this was echoed by a number of other therapists. '*Only children have not had a blueprint to deal with the parents – they are on their own*'.

Although only a brief survey, there is some evidence that whilst therapists did not necessarily accept the only-child stereotypes, they were more likely to speak from a position of no real difference between only-children and sibling children. However, since completing the questionnaire some re-contacted me to say that having raised their awareness they had become much more sensitised to the issues concerning onlies and in particular the negativity the only-child stereotype promotes. Therapists who were also only-children, or had only-children, appeared to be more cognisant of difference. They all felt on a personal level that growing up an only-child was and had been challenging. They wrote about the intensity of being the only-one and carrying all the hopes and expectations of parents and the aloneness and isolation it had caused.

Therapists *with* an only-child were particularly aware of the issues of spoiling and the affect of the 'public' view of having just one child.

Do non-only-children fit the only-child archetype?

One criticism I have received concerning this research is that many features of the only-child archetype can be attributed to non-onlies. I would agree. Non-onlies who have siblings but for whatever reason grew up with minimal contact are likely to experience aspects such as aloneness, isolation and lack of emotional and social opportunities. The two client case studies which follow are included because they demonstrate much of the only-child constellation pattern, yet one is the eldest of four and the other has a younger brother.

Patti was brought up in the same family as her three younger brothers but had little contact with them, because first there was a six to ten-year age gap and secondly as a girl of devout evangelical parents, she was expected to keep herself separate, work hard at school, do the house-work before her parents returned and lead a life that contained no peer socialising or even the possibility of friendships with other children. Her only socialising was church on Sundays. Patti, now in her thirties, had a history of depression. She was finding it extremely difficult to make or maintain relationships and felt very responsible for her widowed mother. Academically, she had done well at university and now held a management job, but her prospects of promotion were low because of her social difficulties. Her relationship with her mother dominated her life as she was still expected to spend weekends with her and provide for her financially and emotionally, despite the fact she had three brothers who did not contribute in a similar way. In other words, she felt very responsible for her mother's happiness and well-being but also felt isolated and alone.

We only had five sessions and Patti did not attend the last. I found it easy to engage with her, but I was not successful in helping with her sense of loneliness, isolation, responsibility towards her mother and feelings of ineptitude in social situations. I think this was primarily because she would not allow me into her private world; she disliked this neediness in herself and wanted to remain separate and independent from me.

Similarly, *Dina* had a younger brother born twelve years after her. Like Patti, she was having difficulties at work, particularly knowing the rules of communicating effectively. Her relationship had broken down because of her fear of commitment and needing her own space. She was able to explore these issues and by the end of therapy had worked through this and was back in the relationship. During this time, she also challenged her mother's continual need to ring her, at least everyday, and set boundaries between the two of them. Again, like Patti, many of her issues fit the only-child archetype which is characterised by a lack of sibling relationships, leading to difficulties in emotional and social learning, coupled with parental enmeshment and difficulties in separating, individuating and balancing independence and intimacy.

Only-children of single parents and adopted only-children

In the original only-child research, I chose not to include these two groups of only-children as the impact of being from a one-parent family or adopted were issues that were difficult to disentangle from those of being an only-child. However, the website gave opportunities for more of an exploration of this dynamic.

Whilst enmeshment was clearly an issue for both these type of only-children, more often than not the only-child brought up by a single parent felt very much on a par with the parent, seeing the mother more of a sister than a parent. Overall, the only-children from single parents, who wrote to me, were often from the United States and they focused mainly on the problems of separating and being responsible for an ageing parent.

Adopted only-children are very aware of the issues of adoption colouring their experience of being an only-child. The main issues raised are the sense they were 'chosen' by their parents; the feeling that high expectations were placed on them to be the child the parents expected; and the sense of not really 'belonging' was particularly strong. Clearly, there is room for research into both these groups of only-children.

Final reflections

This concluding chapter marks the culmination of my research findings and I will briefly summarise my ideas. They focus on an only-children experience of 'lack', 'difference' and 'seperateness' through not having siblings. The importance of both finding a voice and witnessing had been a major factor for the hundreds of adult only-children who have shared their life-stories with me through interviews, message boards and personal correspondence. Finding a voice is both an internal process and an inter-personal one. Voices need to be heard, not just voiced, and this is the importance of witnessing. Through this research, I have come to realise that witnessing is important not just in the therapy room but in everyday life. Groth (2001) writing about existential validation and the inter-dependence we have on one another states:

> Just as I accept my dependence on others for the ongoing valida-
> tion of my existence, I recognise my responsibility for their exist-
> ence...With the exception of that extraordinary event of maternal
> existence-bestowing, existential witnessing is always bilateral and
> mutual. I cannot validate the existence of another person unless he
> validates my existence.
>
> (2001, p. 89)

Groth is acknowledging both the importance of the maternal relationship and all subsequent interactions with others. He talks about
validating the other person through existential witness and receiving
validation back from them. Like Groth (2001), I believe this need
for mutuality is fundamental to the development of a sense of who
a person is. Exceptional circumstances mentioned by Groth, (2001),
such as feral children, for example, the wild boy, Victor of Averyon,
who experienced only animal interaction and was never able to master
language or social interaction, can be understood in terms of a lack
of mutuality or 'complementarity' (Laing, 1990). Similarly, people
who withdraw from the world, having less and less interaction with
others, have nothing to offer for validation and receive nothing from
others. Such people, like schizophrenics, the very elderly and infirm,
are vulnerable to daily existence because they lack on-going validation.

Only-children also suffer from a lack in their *development* by not
having siblings to interact or to have a witness of their life events. This
can also have the affect of making them potentially vulnerable to existence, affecting their sense of being-in-the-world.

In Chapter 1, we saw that there is much evidence for the importance of siblings for social interaction and emotional development. I am
taking this further by stating that the only-child growing up without
siblings will miss out on a large part of existential witnessing that siblings
provide. I believe this lack is tacitly known by onlies, as illustrated in my
workshops, only-child life-stories and the 'beinganonly' message board.
It is *experienced* as 'something missing' or a 'lack of connection' because
that is exactly what it is. This may sound simple, even obvious, but I
think it is also quite profound and the major reason why people with
siblings find it so hard to grasp onlies' sense of difference (and conversely
why some onlies deny the difference), as to acknowledge it would bring

the anguish of that difference to the forefront of their experience. Laing wrote:

> All 'identities' require an other: some other in and through a relationship with whom self-identity is actualised. The other by his or her actions may impose on self an unwanted identity.
>
> (1990, p. 82)

Bearing this in mind, I have described that one of the difficulties for only-children who miss out on sibling interaction is that they are more likely to be enmeshed with one or both parents. I have argued that we know ourselves through inter-subjectivity and inter-relations with others. Self-identity is actualised in the young child not *just* by parental interaction but also by sibling interaction and later by interaction with others. If parental interaction is 'good-enough', having no siblings may not be so important. However, where insecure attachment and enmeshment occur, there is little to dilute that experience, as siblings are not available to contribute to the development of a self-identity. This leaves the only-child vulnerable to existence, as described by Groth (2001), and illustrated powerfully in my co-researchers' stories. Only-children need their experience to be validated, the experience of both lack and difference. This is what I offer as a therapist and researcher: the importance of existential validation of the onliness in the lives of only-children.

References

Adler, A. (1928) 'Characteristics of the first, second, and third child'. *Children*, 3, pp. 14–52.

Adler, A. (1962) *What Life Should Mean to you*. London: Unwin.

Adler, A. (1964) *Problems of Neurosis*. New York: Harper & Rowe.

Adler, A. (1992) *Understanding Human Nature*. Oxford: Oneworld Publications Ltd (First published 1927).

Atkinson, R. (1998) *The Life Story Interview: Qualitative Research Methods*. London: Sage.

Bank, S. P. & Kahn, M. D. (1975) 'Sister-hood brother-hood is powerful: sibling subsystems and family therapy'. *Family Process*, 14, pp. 317–19.

Bannister, P., Burman, E., Parker, I., Taylor, M. & Tindall, C. (1994) *Qualitative Methods in Psychology*. Buckingham: OUP.

Barrett, L., Dunbar, R. & Lycett, J. (2002) *Human Evolutionary Psychology*. Hampshire: Palgrave Macmillan.

BBC, Radio 4, Woman's Hour (2004) Retrieved January 2004 from: *www.bbc.co.uk/radio4/womanshour/13-01-03/friday/info3.shtml*.

Belmont, L. & Marolla, F. A. (1997) 'Birth order, family size, and intelligence'. *Science*, 182, pp. 1096–101.

Berne, E. (1961) *Transactional Analysis in Psychotherapy* (2001 edition). London: Souvenir Press.

Birch, M. (1998) 'Reconstructing research narratives: self and sociological identity in alternative settings', in J. Ribbens & R. Edwards (2000) *Feminist Dilemmas in Qualitative Research*. London: Sage, pp. 171–86.

Blake, J. (1974) 'Can we believe recent data on birth expectations in the United States?' *Demography*, 11, pp. 25–44, in T. Falbo (1984) *The Single Child Family*. York: Guilford Press, p. 176.

Boer, F. & Dunn, J. (eds) (1992) *Children's Sibling Relationships: Developmental and Clinical Issues*. Hillsdale, NJ: Erlbaum Bradbury TN.

Bohannon, E. W. (1998) 'The only child in a family'. *Pedagogical Seminary*, 4, pp. 475–96.

Braud, W. & Anderson, R. (1998) *Transpersonal Research Methods for the Social Sciences, Honouring Human Experience*. London: Sage.

Brody, G. H. (1998) 'Sibling relationship quality: its causes and consequences'. *Annual Review of Psychology*, 1 January.

Bryant, B. (1992) 'Sibling caretaking: providing emotional support during middle childhood', in F. Boer & J. Dunn *Children's Sibling Relationships: Developmental and Clinical Issues*. Hillsdale, NJ: Erlbaum Bradbury TN, pp. 55–70.

Burkitt, I. (1991) *Social Selves: Theories of the Social Formation of Personality*. London: Sage.

Byrd, B., De Rosa, A. & Craig, S. (1993) 'The adult who is an only child'. *Psychological Reports*, 73, pp. 171–7.

Byrne, A. et al. (2004) *Researching our Lives*. Working Paper 2004.

Chandler, C. (2004) *Little Emperors: China's Only Children* (4 October). Retrieved May 2004 from: www.Asianfortune.com/Features/CoverStories/Inside the New China.

Chen & Goldsmith (1991) in Zhao, W. (1995) 'Parenting styles and children's satisfaction with parenting in China and the United States'. *Journal of Comparative Family Studies*, 22 June.

Ching, C. C. (1982) 'The one child family in China: The need for psychosocial research'. *Studies in Family Planning*, 13, pp. 208–14.

Chua Chin Hon (2003) *Little Emperors come of Age – China's One Child Policy*, Straits Times (28 November) Retrieved February 2003 from: *209.157.64.200/focus/fnews/1030556/posts*.

Clandinin, D. J. & Connelly, F. M. (2000) *Narrative Enquiry: Experience and Story in Qualitative Research*. San Francisco: John Wiley and Sons.

Claudy, J. G. (1984) 'The only chid as a young adult: results from project talent', in T. Falbo *The Single Child Family*. York: Guilford Press, pp. 211–52.

Coles, P. (2003) *The Importance of Sibling Relationships in Psychoanalysis*. London: Karnac.

Conle, C. (1996) 'Resonance in preservice teacher inquiry'. *American Educational Research Journal*, 33(2), pp. 297–325.

Crick, N. R. & Dodge, K. A. (1994) 'A review and reformulation of social information-processing mechanisms in children's social adjustment'. *Psychology Bulletin*, 115, pp. 74–101.

Das, S. and Babu, N. (2004) 'Children's acquisition of a theory of mind: the role of presence vs. absence of sibling'. *National Academy of Psychology, India*, 49(1), pp. 36–44.

Denzin, N. K. & Lincoln, Y. S. (1998) *Collecting and Interpreting Qualitative Materials*. London: Sage.

Dubow, E. F. & Tisak, J. (1989) 'The relation between stressful life events and adjustment in elementary school children: the role of social support and problem-solving skills'. *Child Development*, 60, pp. 1412–20.

Dunn, J. (1996) 'Brothers and sisters in middle childhood and early adolescence: continuity and change in individual differences', in G. Brody (1998) 'Sibling relationship quality: its causes and consequences'. *Annual Review of Psychology*, 1 January, pp. 31–46.

Dunn, J. & Munn, P. (1986) 'Sibling quarrels and maternal intervention: individual differences in understanding and aggression'. *Journal of Child Psychology and Psychiatry*, 27, pp. 583–95.

Dunn, J. & Slomkoski, C. (1992) 'Conflict and the development of social understanding', in C. U. Shantz & W. W. Hartup (eds) *Conflict in Child and Adolescent Development*. Cambridge: Cambridge University Press, pp. 70–92.

Eliot, L. (1999) *Early Intelligence*. London: Penguin.

Epston, D. (1992) *Experiencing Contradiction, Narrative and Imagination*. Adelaide, South Australia: Dulwich Centre.

Epston, D. & White, M. (1998) *Catching up with David Epston: A Collection of Narrative Practice Based Papers 1991–1996*. Adelaide, South Australia: Dulwich Centre.

Etherington, K. (2001) 'Writing qualitative research – a gathering of selves'. *Counselling and Psychotherapy Research*, 1(2), pp. 119–25.

Etherington, K. (2002) 'Working together: editing a book on narrative research methodology'. *Counselling and Psychotherapy Research*, 2(3), pp. 167–76.

Etherington, K. (2003) *Trauma, the Body and Transformation*. London: Jessica Kingsley.

Etherington, K. (2004) *Becoming a Reflexive Researcher Using Our Selves in Research*. London: Jessica Kingsley.

Fabes, R. A. & Eisenberg, N. (1992) 'Young children's coping with interpersonal anger'. *Child Development*, 63, pp. 116–28.

Falbo, T. (1984) *The Single Child Family*. York: Guilford Press.

Falbo, T. (1994) *Positive Evaluations of the Self and Others Among Chinese School Children*. Austin University of Texas, Papers 94-95-09 and 94-95-10.

Falbo, T. & Polit, D. (1986) 'Quantitative review of the only child literature: research evidence and theory development'. *Psychological Bulletin*, 100(2), pp. 176–89.

Falbo, T., Poston, D. L. & Jr Xie (eds) (1997) *Zhongguo Dusheng Zin Yanjiu (Research on Single Children in China)* Shanghai: East China Normal University Press.

Feldman, G. (1981) 'Three's Company: Family Therapy with Only-Child Families'. *Journal of Marital and Family Therapy*, 7, pp. 43–6.

Fordham, M. (1986) *Exploration into the Self*. London: Karnac.

Forer, L. K. (1977) 'Use of birth order information in psychotherapy'. *Journal of Individual Psychology*, 33, pp. 105–18.

Frank, A. (1995) *The Wounded Story Teller: Body Illness and Ethics*. London/Chicago: University of Chicago Press.

Freud, S. (1912–13) 'Totem and Taboo'. *The Standard Edition of the Complete Works of Sigmund Freud*. London: Hogarth Press.

Freud, S. (1923) 'The dissolution of the oedipal complex', in J. Strachey (ed.) *The Standard Edition of the Complete Works of Sigmund Freud*. London: Hogarth Press.

Gee, J. P. (1999) *An Introduction to Discourse Analysis – Theory and Method*. London: Routledge.

Gergen, K. J. (1988) 'If persons are texts', in S. B. Messer, L. A. Sass & R. L. Woolfolk (eds) *Hermeneutics and Psychological Theory*. New Brunswick, NJ: Rutgers University Press.

Gerhardt, S. (2004) *Why Love Matters: How Affection Shapes a Baby's Brain*. Hove: Bruner Routledge.

Gilligan, C., Brown, L. M. & Rogers, A. (1990) 'Psyche embedded: a place for body, relationships and culture in personality theory' in A. J. Rabin, R. Zucker, R. Emmons and S. Frank (eds) *Studying Persons and Lines*. New York: Springer.

Goldberg, S., Gotoweic, A. & Simmons, R. J. (1995) 'Infant-mother attachment and behaviour problems in healthy and chronically ill pre-schoolers'. *Development and Psychopathology*, 7, pp. 267–82.

Gould, R. L. (1978) *Transformations: Growth and Change in Adult Life*. New York: Simon and Schuster.

Graham-Bermann, S. & Gest, S. (1991) 'Sibling and peer relations in socially rejected, average, and popular children', in J. S. Hyde (1993) 'The only child: is there only one kind?' *Journal of Genetic Psychology*, 154, pp. 269–82.

Groth, M. (2001) 'The body I am: lived body and existential change', in E. Spinelli & S. Marshall (eds) *Embodied Theories*. London: Continuum, pp. 81–97

Guardian (2004) *Only the Lonely*. Ebner, S. (8 February) Retrieved February 2004 from: *www.guardian.co.uk*.

Guardian (2002) *Sole Survivors*. Freeman, H. (5 June) Retrieved February 2004 from: *www.guardian.co.uk*.

Guastello, D. & Guastello, S. (2002) 'Birth category affect on the Gordon personal profile variables'. *JASNH*, 1(1), pp. 1–7.

Guba, E. G. & Lincoln, Y. S. (1989). *Fourth Generation Evaluation*. Newbury Park, CA: Sage.

Hawke, S. & Knox, D. (1977) *One Child by Choice*. New Jersey: Prentice Hall.

Hong Guo (2000) *The Little Emperors Grow Up – Psychology of Children-Brief Article*. *Psychology Today* (January 2000) Retrieved Feb 2004 from: *www.findarticles.com/p/articles/mi_m1175/is_1_33/ai_58616817*.

Howe, M. G. & Madgett, M. E. (1975) 'Mental health problems associated with the only child'. *Canadian Psychiatric Association Journal*, 20, pp. 189–94.

Howe, N. & Ross, H. (1990) 'Socialization, perspective-taking, and the sibling relationship'. *Developmental Psychology*, 26(1), pp. 160–5.

Hughs, C. (2002) *Feminist Theory and Research*. London: Sage.

Hultberg, P. (1988) 'Shame: a hidden emotion'. *Journal of Analytical Psychology*, 33(2), London: Academic Press, pp. 109–26.

Hyde, J. & Rosenberg, J. S. (1993) 'The only child: is there only one kind?' *Journal of Genetic Psychology*, 154, pp. 269–82.

Jacoby, M. (1991) *Shame and the Origins of Self-Esteem*. London: Bruner Routledge.

Jenkins, J. (1992) 'Sibling relationships in disharmonious homes: potential difficulties and protective effects', in F. Boer & J. Dunn *Children's Sibling Relationships: Developmental and Clinical Issues*. Hillsdale, NJ: Erlbaum Bradbury TN, pp. 125–38.

Jiao, J., Ji, G. & Jing, Q. (1986) 'Comparative study of behavioural qualities of only-children and sibling children'. *Child Development*, 57, pp. 357–61.

Johnson, R. A. (1995) *The Fisher King and the Handless Maiden: Understanding the Wounded Feeling Function in Masculine and Feminine Psychology*. San Francisco: Harper.

Jordan, J. (1993) 'The relational self: a model of women's development', in J. van Mens-Verhulst, K. Schreurs & L. Woertman (eds) *Daughtering and Mothering: Female Subjectivity Reanalysed*. London: Routledge.

Josselson, R. (ed.) (1996) *Ethics and Process in the Narrative Study of Lives. Vol. 4*. London: Sage.

Jung, C. G. (1959) *The Archetypes of the Collective Unconscious*, trans. R. F. C. Hull. Vol. 9, Part 1 of *The Collected Works of C. G. Jung*. London: Routledge & Kegan Paul.

Kappelman, M. (1975) *Raising the Only Child*. New York: Dutton and Co.

Kaufman, G. (1985) *Shame: The Power of Caring*. Vermont: Schenkman Books Inc.

Kaufman, G. (1991) *Shame: The Power of Caring*. Vermont: Schenkman Books Inc.

Klein, M. (1932) *The Psychoanalysis of Children*. London: Hogarth.

Kleining, G. & Witt, H. (2001) *Discovery as Basic Methodology of Quantitative and Qualitative Research*. Forum Qualitative Social Research. Retrieved June 2003 from: www.qualitative-research.net.

Kluger, J. (2006) *The New Science of Siblings* (2 July). Retrieved July 2006 from: www.time.com.

Kohlberg, L. (1963) 'Moral development and identification', in H. Stevenson, J. Kagen & C. Spiker (eds) *Child Psychology*. Chicago: University of Chicago Press.

Kohut, H. (1977) *The Restoration of the Self*. New York: International Universities Press.

Laing, R. D. (1990) *The Self and Others*. London: Penguin.

Laybourn, A. (1994) *Only Child: Myths and Reality*. London: TSO.

Ledouux, J. (1999) *The Emotional Brain*. London: Penguin Press.

Leman, K. (1985). *The Birth Order Book: Why You Are the Way You Are*. Grand Rapids, MI: Spire books.

Levinson, D. (1978) *The Season's of Man's Life*. New York: Aronson Inc.

Love, P. & Robinson, R. (1990) *The Chosen Child Syndrome: What to Do When a Parent's Love Rules Your Life*. London: Piatkus.

Mabey, J. & Sorensen, B. (1995) *Counselling for Young People*. Buckingham: OUP.

MacIntyre, A. (1981) *After Virtue: A Study in Moral Theory*. London: Ducksworth.

Mair, M. (1977) 'The community of self', in D. Bannister (ed.) *New Perspectives in Personal Construct theory*. London: Academic Press.

Mair, M. (1989) *Beyond Psychology and Psychotherapy: A Poetics of Experience*. London: Routledge.

Makihara, H., Nagoya, M. & Nakajima, M. (1998) 'An investigation of neurotic school refusal in one parent families'. *Japanese Journal of Child and Adolescent Psychiatry*, 26, pp. 303–15.

Mauthner, N. & Doucet, A. (1998) 'Reflections on a voice centred relational model: analysing maternal and domestic voices', in J. Ribbens & R. Edwards (2000) *Feminist Dilemmas in Qualitative Research*. London: Sage, pp. 119–47.

McLeod, J. (1997) *Narrative and Psychotherapy*. London: Sage.

McLeod, J. (1999) *Practitioner Research in Counselling*. London: Sage.

McLeod, J. (2001) *Qualitative Research in Counselling and Psychotherapy*. London: Sage.

Meredith W. H., Abbott, D. & Lu, T. Z. (1989) 'A comparative study of only children and sibling children in the People's Republic of China'. *School Psychology International*, 10, pp. 251–6.

Merleau-Ponty, M. (1947) *The Primacy of Perception*. Edited by J. M. Edie (1964) 'The child's relationship with others'. Evanston, IL: Northwestern University Press, pp. 96–155.

Merleau-Ponty, M. (1962) *The Phenomenology of Perception*, trans. C. Smith. London: Routledge & Kegan Paul.

Miller, T. (1998) 'Shifting layers of professional, lay and personal narratives: longtitudnal childbirth research', in J. Ribbens & R. Edwards (2000) *Feminist Dilemmas in Qualitative Research*. London: Sage, pp. 75–81.

Miller, N. & Maruyama G. (1976) 'Ordinal position and peer popularity'. *Journal of Personality and Social Psychology*, 33, pp. 123–31.

Minuchin, S. (1974) *Families and Family Therapy*. Cambridge, MA: Harvard University Press.

Mishler, E. G. (1990) 'Validation in enquiry-guided research: The role of exemplars in narrative studies'. *Harvard Educational Review*, 60, pp. 415–42.

Mitchell, J. (2000) *Mad Men and Medusas: Reclaiming Hysteria and the Effects of Sibling Relationships on the Human Condition*. London: Penguin.

Mitchell, J. (2003) *Siblings*. Cambridge: Polity Press.

Moustakas, C. (1990) *Heuristic Research*. London: Sage.

Mueller, E. C. & Vandell, D. L. (1995). 'Peer play and friendships during the first two years', in H. C. Foot, A. J. Chapman & J. R. Smith (eds) *Friendship and Social Relations in Children*. New Brunswick, NJ: Transaction, pp. 181–208.

Nachman, P. & Thompson, A. (1997) *You and Your Only Child: The Joys, Myths and Challenges of Raising an Only Child*. New York: Harper Collins.

Neaubauer, P. B. (1982) 'Rivalry, envy and jealousy', in A. J. Solnit (ed.) *Psycho-anlytic Study of the Child*. Vol. 37. New Haven, CT: Yale University Press, pp. 121–42.

Neaubauer, P. B. (1983) 'The importance of the sibling experience', in A. J. Solnit (ed.) *Psychoanalytic Study of the Child*. Vol 38. New Haven, CT: Yale University Press, pp. 325–6.

Nelson, K., Plesa, D. & Henseler, S. (1998) 'Children's theory of mind: an experiential interpretation'. *Human Development*, 41, pp. 7–29.

Neumann, E. (1988) *The Child*. London. Karnac.

Newman, S. (2001) *Parenting an Only Child: The Joys and Challenges of Raising Your Only One*. 2nd edition. New York: Broadway Books.

Nielsen, J. M. (1990) *Feminist Research Methods: Exemplary readings in the Social Sciences*. Boulder, CO: Westview.

Nyman, L. (1995) *The identification of birth order personality attributes*. Journal of Psychology, 129, PP. 51–9.

Observer (2001a) *The One and Only*. Lorna, V. 28 September. Retrieved February 2004 from: *www.guardian.co.uk*.

Observer (2001b) *Lone Stars*. Deeble, S. 10 June. Retrieved June 2004 from: www.observer.guardian.co.uk.

ONS (Office of National Statistics) www.statistics.co.uk.

Peck, E. (1977) *The Joy of the Only Child*. New York: Delacorte Press.

Pepper, F. C. (1971) 'Birth Order', in A. G. Nikelly (ed.) *Applications of Adlerian theory: Techniques for Behaviour Change*. Springfield, IL: Thomas, pp. 49–54.

Perner, J., Ruffman, T. & Leekam, S. R. (1994) 'Theory of mind is contagious: you catch it from your sibs'. *Child Development*, 65, pp. 1228–38.

Petzold, M. (1998) 'Only children in the People's Republic of China: behavioural disorders as a result of the one-child-family'. *Pscyhologie in Erziehung & Unterricht*, 35, pp. 81–9.

Pickhardt, C. E. (1997) *Keys to Parenting the Only Child*. New York: Barrons.

Pitkeathley, J. & Emerson, D. (1994). *Only Child: How to Survive Being One*. London: Souvenir Press.

Polanyi, M. (1969) *Knowing and Being*. Chicago: University of Chicago Press.

Polit, D. & Falbo, T. (1987) 'Only Children and Personality Development: A Quantitative Review'. *Journal of Marriage and the Family*, 49, pp. 309–25.

Polkinghorne, D. E. (1995) 'Narrative configuration in qualitative analysis', in J. A. Hatch & R. Wisniewski (eds) *Life History and Narrative*. London: Falmer Press.

Poston, D. L. & Falbo, T. (1990) 'Scholastic and personality characteristics of only-children and children with siblings in China'. *International Family Planning Perspectives*, 16, pp. 45–8.

Reese, L. (1999) *A Generation of Little Emperors. TIME, Asiaweek*, 154(12) (27 September) Retrieved November 2005 from: www.time.com/time/asia/magazine/99/0927/children_palace.html.

Ribbens, J. & Edwards, R. (2000) *Feminist Dilemmas in Qualitative Research*. London: Sage.

Riessman, C. K. (1993) *Narrative Analysis – Qualitative Research Methods*. Vol. 30. London: Sage.

Roberts, L. & White-Blanton, P. (2001) ' "I always knew mom and dad loved me best": experiences of only children'. *Journal of Individual Psychology*, 57(2), University of Texas Press, pp. 125–40.

Robson, C. (2002) *New World Research. A Resource for Social Scientists and Practitioner-Researchers*. 2nd edition, Oxford, UK: Blackwell.

Rogers, C. (1961) *A Therapist's View of Psychotherapy*. London: Constable & Constable.

Rosenberg, B. G. & Falk, F. (1987) 'First-born and intelligence: sibling presence-absence or single parent affect?', in J. S. Hyde 'The only child: Is there only one kind?' *Journal of Genetic Psychology*, 154, pp. 269–82.

Rosenberg, B. G. & Hyde, J. (1993). 'The only child: is there only one kind of only?' *Journal of Genetic Psychology*, 154, pp. 269–82.

Rosenberg, B. G. & Leino, V. (1987) 'The impact of sibling present-absence over the life-span', in J. S. Hyde 'The only child: is there only one kind?' *Journal of Genetic Psychology*, 154, pp. 269–82.

Ross, H. S., Filyer, R. E., Lollis, S. P., Perlman, M. & Martin, J. L. (1994) 'Administering justice in the family'. *Journal of Family Psychology*, 8, pp. 254–73.

Ruddick, S. (1989) *Maternal Thinking: Towards a Politics of Peace*. Boston, MA: Beacon.

Sarbin, T. R. (1986) 'The narrative as a root metaphor for psychology', in T. R. Sarbin (ed.). *Narrative Psychology: The Storied Nature of Human Conduct*. New York: Praeger, pp. 1–37

Sidhu, R. (2000) 'Differential family climate of children with and without siblings'. *Indian Journal of Psychometry and Education*, 31(2), pp. 117–21.

Sifford, D. (1989) *The Only Child: Being One, Loving One, Understanding One, Raising One*. New York: G.P. Putnam's Sons.

Silverman, D. (2000) *Doing Qualitative Research*. London: Sage.

Sorensen, B. (2006a) 'Spoilt or spoiled: the shame of being an only'. *Therapy Today*, 17(3), pp. 41–6.

Sorensen, B. (2006b) 'Not special but different: the only-child experience'. *Self & Society*, 33(6), pp. 41–6.

Sorensen, B. (2006c) 'Only child challenges and how counsellors can help'. *The Journal of Counselling Children and Young People*, October 2006, pp. 9–13.

Spence, D. P. (1982) 'Narrative Persuasion'. *Psychoanalysis and Contemporary Thought*, 6, pp. 457–81.

Standing, K. (1998*)* 'Writing the voices of the less powerful: research on lone mothers', in J. Ribbens & R. Edwards (2000) *Feminist Dilemmas in Qualitative Research*. London: Sage, pp. 186–203.

Stern, D. N. (1985) *The Interpersonal World of the Infant*. New York: Basic Books.

Stern, D. & Bruschweiler-Stern, N. (1998) *The Birth of a Mother: How Motherhood Changes You Forever*. London: Bloomsbury.

Stewart, Allan E. (2004) 'Can knowledge of client birth order bias clinical judgment?' *Journal of Counselling and Development*, 22 March.

Stewart, I. & Joines, V. (1987) *TA Today: A New Introduction to Transactional Analysis*. Nottingham: Lifespace Publishing.

Stocker, C. & Dunn, J. (1990) 'Sibling relationships in childhood: links with friendships and peer relationships'. *Applied Developmental Psychology*, 8, pp. 227–44.

Sullivan, H. S. (1953) *The Interpersonal Theory of Psychiatry*. New York: Norton and Co.

Sulloway, F. J. (1996) *Birth Order: Born to Rebel*. London: Abacus.

Sunday Times (2004) *Only the Lonely*. Sorensen, B. 22 February. Retrieved February 2004 from: www.timesonline.co.uk.

Telegraph (2004) *A Lonely Existence*. Sorensen, B. 7 February. Retrieved February 2004 from: *www.telegraph.co.uk*.

Thompson, V. V. (1974) 'Family size: implicit policies and assumed psychological outcomes'. *Journal of Social Issues*, 30, pp. 93–124.

Toman, W. (1969) *Family Constellation*. New York: Springer Publishing.

Westoff, C. F. (1978) 'Some speculations on the future of marriage and the family'. *Family Planning Perspectives*, 10, pp. 79–83.

Wharton, B. (1990) 'The hidden face of shame: the shadow, shame and separation'. *Journal of Analytical Psychology*, 35(3), London: Routledge, pp. 279–99.

White, M. (1989) *Selected Papers*. Adelaide, South Australia: Dulwich Centre.

White, M. & Epston, D. (1990) *Narrative Means to Therapeutic Ends*. New York: Norton.

Wiley, R. (1995) *The Semiotic Self*. Chicago: University Press of Chicago.

Winnicott, D. W. (1957) *The Child and the Family: First Relationships* (Broadcast talks). London: Tavistock.

Winnicott, D. W. (1958) *The Capacity to be Alone in the Maturational Processes and the Facilitating Environment*. London: Hogarth Press, reprinted London: Karnac Books, 1990.

Winnicott, D. W. (1978) *The Piggle: An Account of the Psychoanalytic Treatment of a Little Girl*. London: Hogarth Press and the Institute of Psychoanalysis.

Wolcott, H. F. (2001) *Writing up Qualitative Research*. Sage Qualitative Research Methods Series, 20. Newbury park, CA: Sage.

Wurmser, L. (1981) *The Mask of Shame*. Baltimore & London: The John Hopkins University Press.

Zhang Hua (2003) *The One Child-Family, Celebrity, Cause for Social Concern*. *China Today*. Retrieved June 2003 from: *www.chinatoday.com.cn/English/e20036/p18htm*.

Further Reading

Ahern, K. J. (1999) 'Ten tips for reflexive bracketing'. *Qualitative Health Research*, 9, pp. 407–11.

Beiser, H. R. (1993) 'Meeting at the crossroads: women's psychology and girl's development'. *Journal of the American Medical Association*, 11(4), pp. 1446–7.

Belmont, L., Wittes, J. & Stein, Z. (1976) 'The only child syndrome myth or reality?' in T. Falbo & D. Polit (1986) 'Quantitative review of the Only Child Literature: Research Evidence and Theory Development'. *Psychological Bulletin*, 100(2), pp. 176–89.

Bond, T. (2004) *Ethical Guidelines for Researching Counselling and Psychotherapy*. Rugby: BACP publications.

Bowlby, J. (1980) *Loss, Sadness, and Depression: Attachment and Loss*. Vol 3. London: Penguin.

Bowlby, J. (1988) *A Secure Base: Clinical Applications of Attachment Theory*. London: Routledge.

Brown, L. M. & Gilligan, C. (1992) *Meeting at the Crossroads: Women's Psychology and Girls' Development*. Cambridge, MA: Harvard University Press.

Bruner, J. (2002) *Making Stories: Law, Literature, Life*. New York: Farrar, Straus and Giroux.

Butler, J. (1994) 'For a careful reading', in *Feminist Dilemmas in Qualitative Research*. London: Sage, p. 136.

Charmaz, K. (1993) 'Meeting at the crossroads: women's psychology and girl's development'. *Gender and Society*, 7(4), pp. 614–16.

Crosseley, M. L. (2000) *Introducing Narrative Psychology: Self Trauma and the Construction of Meaning*. Buckingham: OUP.

Crotty, M. (1998) *The Foundations of Social Research: Meaning and Perspective in the Research Process*. London: Sage.

Code, L. (1993) 'Taking subjectivity into account', in J. Ribbens, & R. Edwards (2000) *Feminist Dilemmas in Qualitative Research*. London: Sage, p.137.

Davies, B. (1989) *Frogs and Snails and Feminist Tales*. Sydney: Allen and Unwin.

Erikson, E. H. (1950) *Childhood and Society*. New York: Norton.

Erikson, E. H. (1959) 'Identity and the life cycle'. *Psychological Issues*, 1, pp. 1–172.

Etherington, K. (2000) *Narrative Approaches to Working with Male Adult Survivors of Sexual Abuse: The Clients, the Counsellors, the Researchers Story*. London: Jessica Kingsley.

Fenton, N. (1928) 'The only child'. *Journal of Genetic Psychology*, 35, pp. 546–56.

Fonagy, P. (2001) *Attachment Theory and Psychoanalysis*. New York: Other Press.

Gilligan, C. (1982) *In a Different Voice: Psychological Theory in Women's Development*. Cambridge, MA: Harvard University of California Press.

Hammersley, M. (1987) 'Some notes on the terms "validity" and "reliability"'. *British Educational Research Journal*, 13(1), pp. 73–81.

Hammersley, M. (1992) *What's Wrong with Ethnography? Methodological Explorations*. London: Routledge.

Hollway, W. & Jefferson, T. (2000) *Doing Qualitative Research Differently*. London: Sage.

Holmes, J. (2001) *The Search for the Secure Base: Attachment Theory in Psychotherapy*. Hove: Bruner Routledge.

Howe, D., Brandon, M., Hinings, D. & Schofield, G. (1999) *Attachment Theory, Child Maltreatment and Family Support: A Practice and Assessment Model*. London: Palgrave/Macmillan Press.

Isaacson, C. (1988) *Understanding Yourself Through Birth Order*. US: Adams Media Corporation.

Isaacson, C. & Radish, K. (2002) *The Birth Order Effect: How to Better Understand Yourself and Others*. US: Adams Media Corporation.

Josselson, R. & Leiblich, A. (1999) *Making Meaning of Narratives: in the Narrative Study of Lives*. Vol. 6. London: Sage.

Kaufman, G. (1993) *The Psychology of Shame*. London: Routledge.

Koontz, K. (February 1989). 'Just me'. *Health*, 21, pp. 38–9.

Lerner, R. M. & Spanier, G. B. (1978) *Child Influences on Marital and Family Interactions: A Life-Span Perspective*. New York: Academic.

McLeod, J. (1994) *Doing Counselling Research*. London: Sage.

Moustakas, C. (1990) *Loneliness*. UK: Jason Aronson.

Moustakas, C. (1994) *Phenomenological Research Methods*. London: Sage.

Munn, P. & Dunn, J. (1989) 'Temperament and the developing relationship between siblings'. *International Journal Behaviour Development*, 12, pp. 433–51.

Pistrang, E. (1995). *Research Methods in Clinical and Counselling Psychology*. Chichester: Wiley and Sons.

Polanyi, M. (1964) *Science Faith and Society*. Chicago: University of Chicago Press.

Polanyi, M. (1983) *The Tacit Dimension*. MA, New York: Doubleday.

Rutter, M. (1972) *Maternal Deprivation Reassessed*. London: Penguin.

Schore, A. (1994) *Affect Regulation and the Origin of the Self: The Neurobiology of Emotional Development*. New York: Laurence Erlbaum Associates.

Schore, A. (2003) *Affect Dysregulation and Disorders of the Self*. New York: Norton.

Solomon, E. S., Clare, J. E. & Westoff, C. F. (1956) 'Social and psychological factors affecting fertility'. *Milbank Memorial Fund Quarterly*, 34, pp. 160–77.

Stewart, A. E. & Campbell, L. E. (1998) 'Validity and reliability of the White-Campbell psychological birth order inventory'. *Journal of Individual Psychology*, 54, pp. 41–60.

Strauss, A. & Corbin, J. (1998) *Basics of Qualitative Research*. London: Sage.

Sulloway, F. J. (1997) 'Birth order and personality'. *Harvard Mental Health Letter*, 14, pp. 5–7.

Weedon, C. (1987) *Feminist Practice and Poststructuralist Theory*. Oxford: Basil Blackwell.

Wilkinson, S. (1994) 'Editors introduction'. *Feminism and Psychology*, 4(3), pp. 353–4.

Index

adapted child, 31, 184
aloneness, xi, 31, 67, 86, 97, 101, 107, 115, 122, 153, 164, 166, 170–2, 200
Amy, *see* life-stories
analysis, *see* research
Anna, *see* life-stories
archetype, 160
   only-child, 20, 156, 159–63, 166, 167, 172, 175, 201–2
attachment, xi, 5, 6, 23, 24, 26, 33, 175–6, 178, 179, 180, 181, 183, 185, 191, 200

BBC radio, 33, 96, 106
Beanpole families, 3
Beinganonly, 110–2, 171, 203
   posts, 112
birth order studies, 4, 9–11, 35, 196
body sculpting, 178

Carol, *see* life-stories
case studies
   Dina, 149–52
   Eve, 172–3, 176
   Jack, 184–5
   Jo, 176–7
   Maria, 149–51
   Nina, 175–7, 180
   Patti, 201–2
   Peter, 185
China, 3, 15, 16–19, 20, 36, 174, 183, 188–9
co-researcher, *see* research
collaboration, 49
commitment, 81, 100, 138, 166, 171, 172–3, 176, 201
confidence, 191–3
confidentiality, 48
counselling
   adult onlies, 15, 33, 146, 185, 198
   young people, 178

creative, 48, 67, 85
cultural scripts, 20, 31

Daisy, *see* life-stories
dependence, 53, 88, 130, 143, 166, 172–3, 203
dethronement, 25, 77, 167, 173–5
Dina, *see* case studies

emails, 108, 110, 132, 188
   and articles, 13–14
   dying parents, 197
   not such a good thing, 108–10
   only-child pensioner, 106–7
enmeshment, 22, 32, 100, 114, 165–6, 174, 178, 179–82, 193, 202, 204
Ethics, *see* research
Eve, *see* case studies
evolutionary theory, 9–11
existential validation, 197–8, 203, 204

family
   romance, 23, 154, 177
   systems, 23–5, 35, 36
   therapy, 4, 23–5
feminist research, 38, 40
flexible design, 37, 46, 48

Georgina, *see* life-stories
grandiosity, 114, 128, 130, 166, 173–4
Gunnar, *see* life-stories

handless maiden, 160, 161–3
heuristic, 40–1, 44

imaginary friends, 76, 87, 100, 113
independence, 172–3
   China, 18, 19
   handless maiden, 163
   and intimacy, 202
   and oedipal, 24
   and separation, 25

216   *Index*

individuation, 25, 166, 174, 183–4
interviews, *see* research
isolation, 28, 63–7, 80, 88, 100–1, 107,
    132, 167, 200, 201
Ivy, *see* life-stories

Jack, *see* case studies
James, *see* life-stories
JO, *see* case studies
John, *see* life-stories

Kate, *see* life-stories
Kay, *see* life-stories
Kim, *see* life-stories

life-stages, 97–102, 131
  adolescence, 100
  childhood, 98
  late adulthood, 102
  middle adulthood, 101
  school age, 99
  young adulthood, 100
life-stories
  Amy, 64–72, 88, 89, 90, 91, 92, 98,
      101, 193
  Anna, 57–60, 86, 87, 88, 89, 90, 91,
      93, 95, 98, 101, 193
  Carol, 75–8, 85–6, 90–3, 95–6,
      99–101, 190
  Daisy, 139–40
  Georgina, 52–6, 87–8, 90, 91, 92,
      93, 94, 99, 100, 193
  Gunnar, 154–5
  Ivy, 116–29
  James, 152–4
  John, 135–7
  Kate, 72–5, 77, 78, 85–92, 94, 98,
      101, 197, 190, 193
  Kay, 143–6
  Kim, 133–5
  Lyn, 60–4, 85, 86, 87, 88, 89, 90, 91,
      92, 93, 96, 101, 193
  Magritte, 79–82, 85, 86, 87, 88, 90,
      91, 92, 93, 98, 100–1, 193
  Maria, 149–52
  Matt, 137–9
  Paul, 141–3
  Poppy, 67–72, 85, 86, 87, 88, 89, 90,
      92, 93–5

Sylvia, 146–9
Yukinori, 122–30
life-story research, 42
little adult, 21, 22, 31, 73, 100, 139,
    174, 176, 184, 187, 193, 197
little emperors, 97, 189
loneliness, 16, 34, 64, 86, 107, 111,
    149, 171, 172
Lyn, *see* life-stories

Magritte, *see* life-stories
Maria, *see* case studies
matrix, xiii, 164–7
Matt, *see* life-stories
media, 3, 4, 20, 34–5, 36, 113
message boards, 34, 83, 92, 93, 96,
    159, 170–1, 186, 188, 202
meta-analysis, 20–1, 30, 35, 196
mother complex, 6

narrative research, xi, 37, 41–4, 47
neuroscience, 14
newspaper coverage, 18, 34
Nina, *see* case studies

oedipal
  complex, 6
  triangle, xi, 23–5
'one is enough', 180–2
  reasons for being, 182
only-child
  .com, 29, 105
  .org, xi, xiii, 49, 106
  archetype, *see* archetype
  matrix, 165
  myths, 6, 31–3, 34, 36, 180
oversensitivity, 91, 177

parenting books, 29–34, 38, 94
Patti, *see* case studies
Paul, *see* case studies
Peter, *see* case studies
Poppy, *see* life-stories
power
  family, 178, 180
  personal, 58, 68
  stereotype, 94, 96
  researcher, 35, 40, 41, 43, 46, 49
psychoanalytic literature, 5–9, 36

qualitative research, 5, 35, 38–9, 50
quantitative research, 5, 14–15, 46

reciprocity, xi, 46, 50, 108, 113
reflexivity, ix, 37, 40, 46, 48, 49
research
  analysis, 48
  co-researchers, 49–50, 52
  ethics, 49–50
  interviews, 38, 40, 47–8, 49
  reliability, 50–1
  validity, 8, 10, 41, 50

self-esteem, 10, 16, 20, 30, 98, 102,
  174–6
selfish, 4, 16, 29, 32, 97
separation, 89, 98, 102, 109, 165, 168,
  169, 174, 180–1, 183–7, 200
shame, 20, 75, 93, 95–6, 99, 190–5
siblings
  comparison, 194, 196, 197
  experience, 102, 203
  opportunities, 8, 11, 166
  relationships, 5, 7–8, 12–14, 22, 24,
    28, 48, 91, 167, 174
smothered, 66, 68, 88, 193
specialness, 54, 58, 75, 87, 164, 173–4
spoiled, 15, 29, 72, 189
stanzas, 94, 190
  use of, 52
stereotype

in China, 97, 189
  negative, 32, 39, 88, 93, 94, 166,
    181, 187–9, 200
  positive, 166
success ethic, 20, 21
Sylvia, *see* life-stories
syndrome, 160

therapist's assumptions, 198–201
triangular relationships, 166, 177–9
types of only-child, 25

validity, *see* research
voice, xii, xiiii, 37, 39, 40, 43, 45–8,
  48–9, 83, 164, 202
  centred model, 44–45, 48–9
  extra, 93–6
  inter, 89–93
  intra, 85–9
  three voices, 83–4

website, 106–9, 131, 132, 137, 152,
  180, 187–8
  emails, 135, 167, 174
witness, xiii, 39–40, 107–8, 111–2,
  113, 114
workshops, 8, 106, 113–14, 159, 170,
  178, 184, 203

'you are my world', 181, 182
Yukinori, *see* life-stories

CPSIA information can be obtained
at www.ICGtesting.com
Printed in the USA
LVHW111612120519
617553LV00008B/300/P